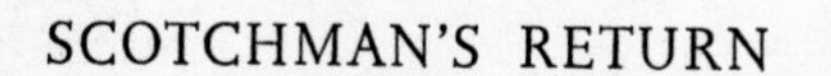

SCOTCHMAN'S RETURN

Hugh MacLennan

SCOTCHMAN'S RETURN

and other Essays

1960

EAST CHICAGO PUBLIC LIBRARY
3601 GRAND BOULEVARD
EAST CHICAGO, INDIANA

CHARLES SCRIBNER'S SONS

NEW YORK

136
1692

COPYRIGHT UNDER THE BERNE CONVENTION

ALL RIGHTS RESERVED

No part of this book may be reproduced
in any form without the permission of
Charles Scribner's Sons

A-1

Library of Congress Catalog Card Number 60-14018

DESIGNED BY LESLIE SMART FTDC FRSA FSIA

PRINTED IN CANADA BY

T. H. BEST PRINTING COMPANY LIMITED

814
M164s

AUTHOR'S NOTE

All the essays in this volume were written between 1954 and 1960, and all but three appeared originally in *The Montrealer*. Of the three which did not, the one called *The Classical Tradition and Education* was originally a public address; the one called *The Future Of The Novel as an Art Form* was an address offered in Saskatoon on the occasion of the Golden Jubilee of the University of Saskatchewan; the one called *Came the Revolution* has been so thoroughly re-worked that it can almost be called a new piece.

I wish to thank the editors of *The Montrealer* and also the authorities of the University of Saskatchewan, for their kind permission to reprint these pieces between covers.

Not all of the pieces included here are in the precise form of their original appearance. In some cases cutting was necessary; in others I had to do a certain amount of re-writing in order to replace the tie-ins with the current events which had evoked the central ideas of the pieces.

Not many novelists, I am told, enjoy the essay form, but for years I have become increasingly devoted to it. A personal essay is a little fragment of yourself: a mood or a cluster of ideas which somehow have emerged from yourself. It is the friendliest form of writing I know, and truly I don't think it egotism so much as a desire for friendship which has made this particular novelist an addict of the form in which Lamb excelled all others in England, and Thoreau all others in the United States.

CONTENTS

To my Mother

I SCOTCHMAN'S RETURN

Whenever I stop to think about it, the knowledge that I am three-quarters Scotch, and Highland at that, seems like a kind of doom from which I am too Scotch even to think of praying for deliverance. I can thank my father for this last-ditch neurosis. He was entirely Scotch; he was a living specimen of a most curious heritage. In spite of his medical knowledge, which was large; in spite of his quick nervous vitality and tireless energy, he was never able to lay to rest the beasties which went bump in his mind at three o'clock in the morning. It mattered nothing that he was a third-generation Canadian who had never seen the Highlands before he visited them on leave in the First World War. He never needed to go there to understand whence he came or what he was. He was neither a Scot nor yet was he Scottish; he never used those genteel appellations which now are supposed to be *de rigueur*. He was simply Scotch. All the perplexity and doggedness of the race was in him, its loneliness, tenderness and affection, its deceptive vitality, its quick flashes of violence, its dog-whistle sensitivity to sounds to which Anglo-Saxons are stone-deaf, its incapacity to tell its heart to foreigners save in terms foreigners do not comprehend, its resigned indifference to whether they comprehend or not. "It's not easy being Scotch," he told me more than once. To which I suppose another Scotchman might say: "It wasn't meant to be."

So far as I could tell, my father found it almost impossible to believe that anyone not Scotch is entirely real. Yet at the same time, buried in the fastnesses of his complex mind, was the contradictory notion that if a Scotchman ever amounts to anything important, he will not be any too real, either, for some beastie will come along and spoil him. As engineers keeping the ships going, as captains serving the owners of the lines, as surgeons, teachers, clergymen and the like, as loyal seconds-in-command—in these niches the Scotch might expect to fare well. But you seldom found them on the summit, and if by reason of an accident one of them got there, something bad was pretty sure to happen. When Ramsay Macdonald became the first man with a Mac in his name to become a British Prime Minister, my father shook his head gloomily over Macdonald's picture on the front page of the paper, and when I asked him why, he said: "He won't do." He had an overweening admiration for the English so long as they stayed in England, and for the Royal Navy above all other English institutions. Indeed, one of his motives for becoming a doctor was an idea in the back of his youthful mind that as a surgeon he might become an R.N. officer. But he was no light Anglophile. I well remember a summer afternoon in the mid-twenties when a British squadron paid Halifax a courtesy call, and better still do I remember that the two leading ships were *H.M.S. Hood* and *H.M.S. Repulse*. As my father at that time was doing some work in the military hospital, he was called to perform an emergency operation on an officer of the *Repulse*, and the Commander of the ship later invited him to tea in the wardroom. He took me along, and as I also was brought up to love the Royal Navy, this was a great thrill to me. It turned out to be an experience almost traumatic.

No sooner had we taken our seats in the wardroom than the officer-of-the-watch entered resplendent in the dress of the day and carrying his cocked hat under his arm. He laid the hat beside him on the table, nodded to a steward for his tea, glanced at us, and when he saw we were civilians and natives, his lips parted in an expression of disdain in which, to quote a famous English author who has noted such expressions as carefully as Shelley the lips of Ozymandias, delicacy had no part. Ignoring my father, this officer inclined his eyes vaguely in my direction and said: "D'you live here?" "Yes, sir," I replied. "Beastly place," was his comment and then he fell silent. So did everyone else.

After several minutes the silence was broken by the racket of an R.C.A.F. training biplane stunting over the harbour and the arrogant disdain on the face of the former officer-of-the-watch was replaced by something very like a flush of anger. "So you have those wretched things over here, too?" he asked my father accusingly. I noted with some pride that my father did not reply to this officer, but instead turned to another man who had been embarrassed by his colleague's behaviour, and asked mildly if the development of aircraft had made it necessary for the Navy to alter its battle tactics. This officer was beginning to reply in some detail when the officer-of-the-watch interrupted: "Do you," he asked my father, "seriously believe that a wretched little gnat like that aircraft could possibly threaten a ship like this?"

No, it was not a successful tea party, nor did it last much longer. My father rose as soon as he felt it courteous to do so, we were escorted to the ladder and handed down into the launch, and as the launch drove through the fog my father was informatively silent. After a while he said, as though excusing the officer's rudeness: "Of course, the weather has been depressing here and they've come up from New York." But before the launch touched the jetty he added: "All the same, he shouldn't have said that." I understood then that my father had not felt himself snubbed, but that the Scotch in him had been gravely concerned by the officer's *hubris* concerning the air force. A beastie had been alerted to keep a special eye on that slim, powerful but extremely vulnerable battlecruiser which was the last brain-child of the ferocious Admiral Jackie Fisher, the ship which Winston Churchill later described as having the brilliance and the fragility one is apt to associate with the children of very old men. Years later in the terrible December of 1941, when the news came from Malaya, I recalled that afternoon aboard *Repulse* with a thrill of sheer horror.

My father was also the reason why I never visited the Highlands when I was a student in the Old Country. Nor did he think I should have done so. "You'll see them one of these days," he said. And he added as an afterthought: "If you're spared and well." And he added as another afterthought: "When you do see them you'll understand." Naturally he did not tell me what I would understand, assuming I would know, but this comment did nothing to foment a desire in me to travel north of the Highland Line.

But we can't escape ourselves forever, and more of ourselves than we choose to admit is the accumulated weight of our ancestors. As I grew older the thought of the Highlands began to haunt me, and in the summer of 1958, after having lived for a long time under a great strain, I decided to get a change and sail to England on a freight ship. I landed in Manchester and of course went south, but after spending a week in London, I went north on the train to Edinburgh and on a Monday morning I found myself in a car-rental agency in the Haymarket making a deal for a Vauxhall.

Ahead of me was the only American I saw in the Old Country that year who behaved as Europeans desire Americans to behave abroad. After complaining about the tastelessness of British food, the harshness and skiddiness of British toilet paper and the absurdity of driving on the left-hand side of the road, he finally came to the topic of the Edinburgh Sabbath which he had just survived.

"Do you realize," he said to the car dealer, "that in the United States there's not even a village as quiet as this town was yesterday?"

The Scotchman looked up at him, inwardly gratified but outwardly glum.

"Ay!" he said, and assumed incorrectly that the American understood that both himself and his country had been rebuked.

When he turned to me after the American had departed, and had identified my nationality by my driving licence, he allowed himself the luxury of an irrelevant comment.

"Ye appear to have deeficult neighbours," he said.

"Perhaps you have difficult neighbours, too?"

"Ay!" he said, and seemed pleased, for an instant later he said "Ay" again.

More or less secure in the Vauxhall I headed north for Stirling and the Highland Line, and after a night by Loch Katrine struck north by Balquhidder, mistook my road to Glencoe and went too far west, and soon found myself beside Loch Awe. I also found myself, with some surprise and mortification, unwilling to perceive any beauty in this region because Loch Awe is in Campbell country, and in the near past of several centuries ago, the Campbell chiefs had been an anathema to the less successful clans they pillaged.

The roads in the Highlands, as those will know who have travelled them, are not only so narrow that in most sections two baby Austins are unable to pass, they are also infested with livestock. Sheep fall asleep on their narrow shoulders and cars must stop again and again while bullocks make up their minds whether or not to move out of the way. The roads were built by some English general, I think his name was Wade, who had the eighteenth-century English notion that if he built roads the communications between the clans would improve. Only lately have General Wade's roads been hard-topped, and never have they been widened except at regular intervals where cars may turn out to allow approaching cars to pass. They are adequately marked if you are familiar with them, but I was not familiar with them and again I lost my way. I went into the pub of a hamlet to ask where I was and discovered behind the bar an elderly gentleman with white hair and the demeanour of a Presbyterian elder, and beside the bar three workmen silently sipping ale.

"What's the name of this place?" I asked the publican.

"The Heather and Bull," he said.

"I meant, what's this community?"

"Mostly Protestant," he said, "but in recent years wi' a small smattering of Roman Catholics." He turned to one of the workmen: "John, how many Catholics now?"

"About eighteen percent. Going on for twenty."

"They're risin' fast," said a third man.

"Ay!" said the publican. And turning to me he asked when I had left Canada.

"How on earth did you guess I'm a Canadian?"

"You are not English, that is certain, and you are not American. You still have some of the voice." He put out his hand: "God bless you!"

We talked of Scotland, Canada and theology and I forgot what I had intended to ask him. An hour later, when I shook his hand and received my directions, his noble face was as solemn as a memory from childhood.

"You will be disappointed," he warned me. "Scotland is full of nothing but Irish now. Och, we have no dignity left."

An Anglo-Saxon or an American might assume a racial situation from this remark, but it was the sort of thing I grew up with, the sort of remark I have made myself, in different connotations, all my life. Its meaning was clear to me if to nobody else. The old gentleman was unburdening himself of a beastie which had nothing whatever to do with the Catholics, the Irish or with anything, possibly, that he himself could put into words.

The next day I was in the true north of Scotland among the sheep, the heather, the whin, the mists and the homes of the vanished races. Such sweeps of emptiness I never saw in Canada before I went to the Mackenzie River later in that same summer. But this Highland emptiness, only a few hundred miles above the massed population of England, is a far different thing from the emptiness of our own Northwest Territories. Above the sixtieth parallel in Canada you feel that nobody but God has ever been there before you, but in a deserted Highland glen you feel that everyone who ever mattered is dead and gone. Those glens are the most hauntingly lovely sights I have ever seen: they are vaster, more moving, more truly vacated than the southern abbeys ruined by Henry VIII. They are haunted by the lost loves and passions of a thousand years. Later that summer on the lower reaches of the Mackenzie, after talking to an Athabascan Indian with Celtic eyes and the name of McPherson, I remembered the wild loneliness of Lochaber and it occurred to me that only a man from a country as lonely and ghost-ridden as the Highlands could have had the insane determination to paddle a canoe through the Rocky Mountains and down La Grande Rivière-en-bas to the Beaufort Sea, and that nothing was more in the life-style of the Highlander than Alexander Mackenzie's feat in searching for the Northwest Passage in a canoe. After an achievement of incredible boldness and endurance, what, after all, did this Highlander find but nothing?

Yet, as a by-product, he and others like him surely found much of Canada, even though one of them, solitary on the Qu'Appelle or the Saskatchewan, admitting the grandeur of the woods and prairies of the New World, sang from a broken heart that he was an exile from his native land, and while making possible the existence of a country so vast that Scotland would be lost in it, regretted his inability to wield a claymore in defence of a barren glen presided over by an imbecile chief. The exiled Irish never forgave their landlords, but the exiled Highlanders pined for the scoundrel Pretender, and even regretted the proprietors who preferred sheep to humanity, enclosed their own people and drove them starving across the western ocean with such an uncomprehended yearning in their souls that some of them ended up in log cabins along the Athabasca and on the shores of James Bay.

In the parish of Kintail, whence some of my own people were driven a century and a half ago, I was told there are now barely four hundred inhabitants. In my ancestors' days there were more than twelve thousand.

"Where are they?" the minister said when I asked him. "Where indeed but in Canada? And some in Australia and New Zealand of course, but most of them in Canada."

With them they brought—no doubt of this—that nameless haunting guilt they never understood, and the feeling of failure, and the loneliness of all the warm-hearted, not very intelligent folk so outmoded by the Anglo-Saxon success that they knew they were helpless unless they lived as the Anglo-Saxons did, failures unless they learned to feel (or not to feel at all) as the Anglo-Saxons ordained. Had my father been clairvoyant when he told me I would understand when I went to the Highlands?

I'm not sure that I do understand or ever will understand what he wanted me to know. But one evening watching a rainbow form over Loch Leven, the mists drop down the hills into rain, then watching the sky rent open and such a tumult of golden light pour forth that the mountains themselves moved and were transfigured, still moved and then were lifted up until they ceased to be mountains and turned themselves into an abstraction of sheer glory and gold—watching this I realized, or thought I did, why these desperate people had endured so long against the civilization of the south. Unlike Ulysses, they had failed to stop their ears when the sirens sang, and the sirens that sing in the Highlands, suddenly and when you least expect to hear them, have voices more dangerously beguiling than any in the Aegæan Isles. Beauty is nearly the most dangerous thing on earth, and those who love her too much, or look too deeply into her eyes, they pay the price for her, which often is an empty stomach and a life of misunderstanding.

So it was here, though an economist would point out that the land is barren and that in the early days the people lacked education and civilized techniques. But this practical attitude merely begs the question of why the people stayed so long: stayed, in fact, until they were driven out. These mountains are almost as useless to the cultivator as the upper reaches of the Laurentian Shield. The Gaelic tongue sounds soft and lovely, but compared with English and French it is a primitive means of communication. The ancestors of almost a quarter of modern Canada never did, and in their native glens they never could, develop even the rudiments of an urban culture. When they made the acquaintance of the English this must have sorely troubled their conscience, for they were religious, they were Christianized after a fashion, and the parable that meant most to them was the Parable of the Talents. Only a few of their chiefs could possibly be called intelligent, and the conduct of the chiefs of their only really successful clan (it shall be nameless here, though every Highlander knows the one I have in mind) was of the crafty peasant sort, the more base because it exploited the loyalty of a people who were already enslaved by their own conception of honour. But though these chiefs did well for themselves, they only became rich and famous after they had conspired with the English enemy. No leader, not even a genius, could have raised in the terrain of the Highlands a civilization capable of competing with England's. Yet the Highlanders held on to the glens; incredibly they held on to them until the end of the eighteenth century. Often I have said to myself that my grandfathers three times removed lived in a culture as primitive as Homer's, and last summer in the Highlands I knew that they really had.

Driving south through Glencoe where the Campbells massacred the Macdonalds, I remembered the first time I met Angus L. Macdonald, who then was Premier of Nova Scotia and previously had been Canada's Minister for the Navy. With a suddenness that would have been startling to anyone but another clansman, Mr. Macdonald turned to me in a company of people and from the depths of a mutual empathy he said: "To be a Celt is never to be far from tears."

But we Celts are withal a mercurial people also; our sorrowful moods pass like the mists on the braes and the sunlight strikes through when we least expect it. A week later I was in the most fatally civilized country in the world, Sweden, waiting for a Pan-American Clipper to take me home.

Just as I belong to the last Canadian generation raised

with a Highland nostalgia, so also do I belong to the last which regards a trans-Atlantic flight as a miracle. When I was a boy I saw the first tiny plane to fly the ocean, the American seaplane N.C.4, which took a very long time moving by stages from Halifax to Sydney, to Bonavista Bay, to the Azores and finally to Lisbon. Eight years later plane after plane set out on non-stop ventures and disappeared into the sea.

Now, eating a filet mignon and sipping champagne in the supreme luxury of this Pan-American aircraft, I looked down on the waste of seas which, together with the mountains of British Columbia, had divided the clansmen from their homes over a century ago. Sitting there idle I felt an unwarranted lift of joy and omnipotent power. The plane nuzzled into the stratospheric wind, she rolled as slowly and surely as a shark speeding through the water in which it was born, she went so fast that though she left Stockholm as late as 4.30 in the afternoon it was still bright daylight when she put down in a rainstorm in Keflavik. She took on fuel and set out again, I slept for an hour or two, wakened to a change in the propeller pitch and learned we were circling Gander, which as usual was buried in fog. After an hour the pilot said over the intercom:

"The weather in Gander has deteriorated to zero-zero. We are now proceeding to New York. We will arrive in Idlewild at 7.40 Eastern Daylight Time. We will arrive on schedule."

Here, of course, was the supreme triumph of the civilization which, in wrecking the clansmen, had made it possible for me to think of Canada as home. The plane tore through the fog, the stewardess brought a delicious breakfast, and just as I was sipping my coffee the sun broke dazzlingly through the window into the cabin. I looked out and there, in a semi-circle of sunshine, the only sunshine apparently in the whole northern hemisphere at that particular moment, lay Cape Breton Island. The plane sloped down to eight thousand feet and I saw beside the Bras d'Or lake the tiny speck which was the house where my mother and sister at that very moment lay asleep. We did reach New York on schedule and that same day I ate my lunch in the Medical Arts restaurant on the corner of Sherbrooke Street and Guy. The man next to me at the counter asked where I had been and I told him I had been in the Scottish Highlands.

"It must have been nice," he said.

"It was. But it's also nice to be home."

Am I wrong, or is it true that it is only now, after so many years of not knowing who we were or wanted to be, that we Canadians of Scotch descent are truly at home in the northern half of North America?

2 BY THEIR FOODS...

During my life I have twice been asked by letter to tell what I like best to eat and why, my answers to be included in two separate publications. The requests were flattering, so I tried to narrow down my choices to some *pièce de résistance* by which, gastronomically speaking, I might become celebrated. In the end I welshed on my answers, for you might as well publish the results of your Rohrschach test as give a description of your favourite food. Favourite dishes can be as revealing as recurrent dreams; even the neophyte traveller learns as much about a nation's character by observing what its people eat as by talking for hours to its cab drivers.

Germans, for instance, have an obsession with caraway, and caraway lurks in every dish, a fatal undertone beneath the heavy, seemingly honest surface of German food, and you get into the habit of waiting for those black, curled little seeds to catch in your teeth, for the abrupt incongruousness of the caraway taste to shock your taste buds, just as you get into the habit of expecting a fatally recurrent behaviour-pattern to show up in German politics.

Austrians love pastries and whipped cream, succulent

torten and rich brioches, bread with little nutriment but baked with crunchy crusts delicious to tongue and teeth. Charming they indubitably are, these people who suffer the tragedy of living just below a nation of caraway-eaters, and wise (or infatuated) in their determination to disguise the bitterness of life wherever possible. The coffee drunk by Austrians is a dark and heavy brew, but as your taste dwells with the whipped cream floating on top, its bitterness is revealed only in the final drops.

Perfect in its ardour is the food of Italy. Not only the pizzas, spaghettis, macaronis and raviolis with their divine harmonies of parmesan, ground meats, onions, tomatoes and herbs, but the chianti, so honestly rough on the tongue it forms a bridge from the pastas to the fresh figs, oranges, tangerines and walnuts that cap a true Italian meal—such a diet breeds people of a fine but delicate vanity, opera singers and beautifully understanding women, but few successful lusters after power.

Most complicated, and complicated without being subtle, is the diet of that intricate people, the Swedes. Strong, contrasting textures, robust flavours implicitly critical of each other, an immense variety of carefully thought-out detail enclosed within a single central idea—that is *smorgasbord*. The smoked eels, fish and meats of Sweden are beyond compare, the pickles blunt but seldom sour, the vegetables fresh. Neither delicate nor rich, masculine but not uneasily so, neither one thing nor the other but everything simultaneously, all excellent, *smorgasbord* is the logical calculation of Swedish life.

Being a Swede, Swedes tell me, is not easy, because it means being a repository and practitioner of the best that has been taught, felt, discovered and done in all the countries of the West, Sweden itself included. Being a successful Swede means that you have to be dynamic and static at the same time, tolerant and critical at the same time, jealous and magnanimous, virile and unaggressive all at once. The static intensity natural to Sweden can be observed in a Stockholm restaurant by anyone who watches a group of Swedes, grave and judicious, not so much attacking the *smorgasbord* as permitting their critical sense to play with this particular example of it. It is necessary for them to be sure whether the *smorgasbord* is as good as it ought to be or could be, and whether it is worthy of them and they of it, and when a foreigner sees a Swede in this condition the kindest thing he can do is to attack the *smorgasbord* himself. His enjoyment of it—or rather the fact that his enjoyment is so obvious—reassures the Swede both as regards the food of his country and his own feeling that he is more self-restrained than foreigners.

Of all the national diets I have sampled, the most portentous is the Russian. Those who eat heartily in Russia are few, or were few until very recently, but this makes no difference because these few are the only Russians who count. In 1937 I spent part of a summer in Leningrad and Moscow, eating in Intourist hotels, and even now when I remember the food and the people who enjoyed it, I tremble.

Russian food is almost exclusively protein, with a limited interlarding of fat. At breakfast, which is served any time between nine and noon, I was offered five or six boiled eggs along with caviar, bread and tea. At lunch, which dragged on from two in the afternoon until four-thirty, caviar was followed by *borscht* and topped by several courses of meat and fowl accompanied by tea. Dinner was more of the same except that it was much more, and the Russians who came to the hotel to eat generally settled down to their tables about midnight. After consuming huge slabs of pressed caviar, they worked their way through more *borscht*, more meat and fowl, and were offered (I can't remember whether it was before or after the meats) ponderous side dishes of head cheese, plates of smoked sturgeon, eels and herring, and salmon pressed into shapes enriched with devilled eggs. While they chewed onward, they refreshed themselves with innumerable cups of pale tea, and most of them drank vodka and sweet Crimean champagne, and somewhere around two-thirty in the morning they at last stopped eating and went on their way. Only a people of colossal ambition and lack of subtlety could exist on such a diet, much less invent it. Churchill warned the world what to expect of Russia when he told us that Stalin, after eating a meal much larger than the one I have just described, settled down in his private quarters to an extra dinner consisting of a roast sucking pig. After eating the whole of it, he went back to work.

During all my time in Russia—this is the most significant note of all—I never saw a leaf of lettuce, or even a leaf of cabbage, that had not been turned into a heavy soup. One morning I woke up with the insides of my cheeks so swollen I couldn't close my jaws without biting chunks out of myself. From my boyhood reading of the life aboard sailing ships I knew this condition was caused by an excess of protein and an absence of fruit and greens. I searched for greens in vain, but I did manage to find some honey-dew melons kept by the *maître d'hôtel* as decorations on his sideboard. I bought three of them at two dollars apiece, and by mid-afternoon I was able to sit up and eat my caviar.

Chinese food, in the judgment of most travellers, is the finest there is, but to me it is decadent. Not in the way of the eating habits of the later Romans, of course; there is no record that the Chinese ever ate nightingales' tongues, or installed vomitoria as adjuncts to their banqueting halls, or that any Chinese emperor followed the example of Heliogabalus in promising a consulship or a province to the cook who invented a new sauce. Yet it is obvious that a man who enjoys thirty or forty courses for dinner, no matter how sparingly he may eat of each, is in danger of declining, even though his final fall may be accomplished with grace and a conviction that his previous life has been well spent. Chinese cooks on the grand scale seem to me not cooks at all, but Toscaninis of food, nor does anything give me more hope for the ultimate failure of Russian ambitions in China than the contrast between the tastes of these two peoples at table. Their incompatibility is total.

Of American cooking, apart from those restaurants in New York which offer specialities from all over the world, what can we say except that it is the most hygienic, scientifically balanced and vitamin-conscious available? It is absolutely forthright, and no American dish above the Mason and Dixon Line ever pretends to be other than what it is. Nor is American food by any means as varied as Americans believe it to be, despite the thousands of recipes published yearly in women's magazines, for variety is bound to be limited when both cook and eater agree that what counts as the final standard of excellence is the quality of the raw materials, and when nearly everybody wants to top off with ice cream. Only in New Orleans, where a Creole tradition in decline united with a climate that often spoiled uncooked food, do you find any exaggerated development of highly flavoured sauces. Throughout the rest of the country steaks from the primest of beeves, chickens guaranteed tender by metal tags, salad-greens and vegetables scientifically grown and Cellophane-wrapped for the market, potatoes mealy and incomparable from Maine and Idaho—American food is as direct as American prose literature and (so say European connoisseurs) American love-making.

Of all the foods I know, the most fascinating is the English, for like everything else English, it cannot be considered apart from history, nor is its message in any sense as simple as it seems. While the empire was a-building, Englishmen ate massive meals of protein and starch, but once the empire was built, the English ruling classes tried to come to terms with a dilemma their knowledge of history told them was critical for their national existence. If they enjoyed the pleasures of the table too much (and now they could utilize all the diets known to man) they would lose their empire for the same reason the Romans lost theirs. Yet what was the use of the empire if it condemned them to living permanently on Brussels sprouts?

The ruling class of England thereupon came to a typically English compromise. Indifferent to the lower classes, themselves accustomed to spending at least a month of every year on the Continent where they could eat the delicious foods of decadence, they decided to outdo Sparta within the home island, nor was any law necessary to guarantee the moral salubrity of English restaurant food. By that extrasensory perception which enables the island to survive, English cooks saw their duty and did it. Hence the boiled meats and fish, the cabbages and sprouts dripping with lukewarm water, the incredible gooseberry fools, the one all-purpose sauce that looks like ground caterpillars and is used to lubricate everything erroneously called a sweet. But those foreigners who believe the English drink the kind of coffee they do because they lack the wit to make it any other way, have as much understanding of the English mentality as the German admiral who believed the Grand Fleet held the seas after Jutland only because the British were too stupid to know they had been beaten.

If a wise maturity accounts for the food of England, masochism must be held responsible for what the Scotch eat. Believe no Scotchman who tells you that his countrymen can afford no better. When Lord Strathcona was a millionaire many times over, oatmeal porridge, so I am told, remained his favourite dish. Believe no Scotchman who attributes the national diet to the barrenness of Scottish soil. Scotland is surrounded by billions of the finest food fish in the world, and the Scotch are skilled fishermen. If they boil their salmon and halibut till no taste remains, if they bake out of their haddock the last drop of moisture, if they serve these ruined fish with a dry, grey potato and (for variation) boiled turnips and sprouts, if they offer for dessert soggy rice pudding with bloated raisins bulging out of it, if they equate a distaste for haggis with disloyalty to Scotland herself—let nobody pity them or wonder why they eat as they do. They prefer this diet because it gives them pleasure of being miserable.

As I neither need nor dare discuss the cooking of France, I come finally to what I would call, were I Jonathan Swift, my own dear country.

A few years ago an article appeared in one of our national magazines which asserted that Canadian cooking, apart from that of Montreal, is the most tasteless in the world and the most carelessly prepared. In a later article in the same magazine statistics were paraded to establish a corollary to the previous hypothesis—namely, that Canadians are the greatest eaters of ketchup known to the Heinz company and that there are many Canadians who eat ketchup three times daily.

The only thing that astonished me about these articles, especially the former one, was the public response they occasioned. The editor was buried under a deluge of letters written by furious housewives and loyal males boasting about their mothers' apple pies. Here, indubitably, was evidence that Canada is in the throes of a moral revolution.

A generation ago most Canadians would have been quietly pleased with a writer who told the world that their food is tasteless and carelessly prepared. Puritanism in Canada was not on the defensive then, and the reading public would have taken "tasteless" to mean "wholesome" and "carelessly prepared" to indicate that we are a people with no nonsense about us, reserving our full energies for things higher than sensual pleasures, of which the pleasures of the table are unquestionably the lowest. Now, it seems, we are almost willing to admit that cooking is an art we may begin to practise one of these days, and that perhaps it might be interesting to climb a few steps up the slippery slope called civilization.

Psychologists have been heard to murmur that the desserts of our childhood are the dishes we most yearn for in our adult lives, and that this is why even middle-aged and elderly Scotchmen continue to eat rice puddings no matter how rich they are. If we don't get our childhood desserts, so they say, it is because our wives do not care for them or they have gone out of fashion. But with all respect for my own childhood, which was not an unhappy one, I harbour no nostalgic longings for the cold baked-apple and tapioca pudding which invariably made its appearance, one or the other, whenever I visited relations or dined out with a boyhood friend. In our own house these were eschewed, at least as a rule, and personally I suffered little from the puritan theory that pleasure in food is a sin. It was the society all around me I am talking about here, not my own home, for the strength of character that made Nova Scotia great was absolutely determined to impress upon children the salutary knowledge that if they really enjoyed what they eat it was probaby bad for them, while if they loathed the taste of it, they were being well nourished. So now, as I can no longer postpone answering those letters asking for my favourite menu, I shall do so in detail and with candour.

For breakfast I like a half-partridge, *petit pois* underdone, some light greens and a half-bottle of hock. For lunch I will make do with a small serving of lobster Newburg or a golden-brown *soufflé* high as a chef's cap and enclosing within its airy mystery a nest of soft-boiled eggs—I ate this once in my life and have never been the same man since. Champagne is a daylight drink with me; I like it best with such a lunch at a table where no politics are discussed. Tea I dispense with unless I am in England, and as I have been in England only for a few weeks in these last many years, let's say I dispense with afternoon tea entirely, for it is a poor preparation for the dry sack I like before dinner but almost never drink. Dinner is, of course, the solace of a hard day, and I prefer it accompanied by a variety of wines mostly white, and a really good dinner I like to see articulated with some of the subtlety one looks for, but seldom finds, in a well-worked novel. The oysters should be Malpèques untouched by any sauce, and the meal should continue through vichyssoise on to Dover sole, airborne to Montreal and cooked so lightly I can still taste the North Sea (so subtly different in taste to the western Atlantic) in its incomparable flesh. For the climax to this dinner I should like roast pheasant or woodcock, and before the *demi-tasse* of Turkish coffee prepares my palate for a few dry *fines*, I choose something light, brief and *flambant* for a sweet, followed by a small but knowledgeable morsel of *brie* or of a soft cheese of rare delicacy native to the Ile d'Orléans. Let psychologists make of this what they will.

3 THE LOST LOVE OF TOMMY WATERFIELD

It was a strange time to grow up, those years of the First World War, and it must have been especially strange in Halifax. What were we like then; what were we like as boys?

I'm not sure I know, the human memory being the salt-mine that it is, crystallizing all the facts and episodes it retains. Yet I'm sure we were more conscious of the world beyond us than modern boys are, those of us who were the sons of professional men as well as those who were not. To this day I can give you the history of almost any important battle in the First War, I can tell you the ships that fought at the Dogger Bank, the Falklands and Jutland, together with their power and tonnage. And I have not studied those battles since; I merely absorbed their stories in childhood. We were scrappier than boys seem to be now, we were scruffier and more untidy, we seldom parted our hair unless it was Sunday and we were going to church, our hands were dirtier than boys' hands are now, we knew nothing about girls and would be ashamed to be seen talking to them, we had no impulse to be in with a gang, no organized games and had not the slightest awareness that it is the chief task of a child to adjust himself to others. At least that's how it was in Halifax.

I asked some McGill students, who were about as old during the Second War as I was during the first, what they remembered about Mitscher, Cunningham, Vian, Fogarty Fegan and a few others of World War II and it wasn't much. Maybe I remember so much about those forgotten admirals of the First War because of Tommy Waterfield and the *Olympic*.

Tommy was a stocky boy short for his age, with bristly hair, buck teeth, big eyes, a pugnacious temperament and a lovely hand on the tiller of a boat. In 1917 I was at home in his house and his parents were friends of my parents, but I never liked to visit him on the Sabbath because it was such a heavy day for him. His parents were charming but they were absent that year and he had an aunt so God-fearing that she always drew the blinds on Sundays so Tommy couldn't watch the boats that were breaking the gloom of the Lord's Day by sailing on the Northwest Arm. In 1917 he was eleven years old and I was ten and I admired him extravagantly.

As for the *Olympic*, I suppose everyone has forgotten about her now and that she has become more remote than the *Flying Cloud*, which at least still appears on calendars. But to Tommy Waterfield, who was abnormal like so many Halifax boys at that time, she was the focus of his fanatical study of naval and military affairs. She was perfection in a naval and military scene in which little seemed to him to be ordered as it should be.

The *Olympic* was the younger sister of the lost *Titanic* and in her day the second-largest vessel flying the British flag. With four high, thin funnels slightly raked, a huge overhanging stern and a high knife-bow, she grossed forty-eight thousand tons and logged at least twenty-five knots.

She transported about two hundred thousand Canadian troops overseas, shuttling steadily between England and Halifax and sailing alone because she was so fast that no submarine of those days could get close enough to put a torpedo into her. Every time the *Olympic* entered harbour there was a quiet flurry through the town, for she was the darling ship of Halifax. Each voyage she looked different, her camouflage being constantly changed. She was always spectacular. She came up the stream with a loud bellowing, moored at old Pier Two and waited there several days while men, victuals and fuel were poured into her. Then she bellowed again, backed out, turned her knife-bow eastward, charged down the harbour and out through the gate of the anti-submarine net.

Never on water have I seen anything more impressive than the charge of this enormous, fantastically painted ship down the harbour with thousands of citizens watching and her decks brown with the khaki of four thousand men, many of them staring at Canada for the last time. More than any battleship or battle-cruiser or the Grand Fleet, the *Olympic* symbolized the war to the boys of Halifax.

By the middle of 1917 Tommy Waterfield had come to a conclusion which the informed public did not reach for another decade. He decided that Jellicoe, though not exactly a brilliant admiral, was nevertheless a maligned one and that he should never have been superseded by Beatty in command of the Grand Fleet. "It was Beatty," Tommy declared, "who let the Germans get away at Jutland. He neglected his signalling. If he'd called in the Fifth Battle Squadron sooner, we'd have blown them to hell." They should have had this boy in the war cabinet to take Churchill's place. "The trouble with the admirals, they aren't out at sea enough, and they lose the feel of it. Now take a look at the *Olympic*—she's out all the time. You want to know who ought to be Admiral of the Fleet? It's Captain Hayes of the *Olympic*. He sails the ocean as if he owned it."

Tommy also sailed the ocean as if he owned it—in a red dinghy twelve feet long with a jagged crack in the bottom which we caulked with oakum and putty once a week. She leaked and in a heavy sea she was tricky to handle, for she had no freeboard. Tommy sailed her and I did the bailing, and as he sailed her hard and in the most open waters he could reach, I used to bail till my back ached.

All through the summer of 1917 we cruised the outer harbour where the winds blew strong and the waves were frequently high enough to conceal the land—if you were in the trough of them in a dinghy. Sometimes we sailed out beyond the lighthouse and even beyond the sentinel sandspit called Thrum Cap, and if the easterlies blew we were practically on the ocean out there, for beyond Thrum Cap there is no shelter from an easterly wind. Sometimes there was target practice and shells from the forts would tear over our heads and we could see them splashing far out. Once we got mixed up with a small convoy and were cursed through a megaphone from a mine-sweeper's bridge. I felt ashamed to be in the way of a war operation, but Tommy's attitude was contemptuous. Cupping his hands he shouted back at the Jimmie on the bridge: "Dontcha know your rules? Dontcha know a sailing ship's got the right of way over steam?"

All of this sailing around turned out to be merely a long build-up for the climacteric of Tommy Waterfield's seafaring career, which came to pass the morning when he and the *Olympic* met together in a contest of wills.

It was early October, cold with an easterly blowing and building up into a storm. We put out from the Northwest Arm with billycans, pork and beans, tea and sugar and headed as usual for the broad reaches of the outer harbour.

Tommy's objective was a stretch of McNab's Island between Thrum Cap and Meagher's Light. To get there we had to sail on a long tack close-hauled beyond York Redoubt, then tack directly across the shipping channel to McNab's on the other side, the width at this point being something over two miles if my memory serves me right. As we got out, the sea built up until the incoming rollers were the highest we had ever tried to weather. They marched into the harbour like long lines of advancing guardsmen, each roller about a hundred yards behind the one ahead, with lesser waves in the trough and some cross-chop because of the whipping wind. In spite of her lack of freeboard, Tommy's dinghy was a pretty dry boat; it couldn't throw too much water without swamping, and Tommy's tiller-hand was exceedingly cunning at nosing her through the cross-chops and up the slope of the slow, advancing combers. But on that day the wind whipped spray off the waves and by the time we passed York Redoubt and came about under Sandwich Point, both of us were cold and wet through. We beat across the channel with the city and the inner harbour concealed by the rollers and also hidden by the sail, which now lay over the port side and yawed whenever we slithered up the side of a comber.

What prompted me to bend and look under the boom I don't know, but I probably peered out involuntarily while I was bailing. The sight that filled my eyes I have seen many times since in nightmares. The *Olympic*'s bow was only half a mile away from us and even at that distance it looked mountain-high. She was camouflaged in a wild pattern of greens, blues, oranges and greys and she was charging seaward at full speed. Just as we slithered into the next trough a huge sheet of white water was hurled out from her forefoot. I cried to Tommy, but he had seen her too, and his bulldog face set hard while his fingers whitened on the tiller.

"Sail's got the right of way over steam," he said.

We came up on another crest and the *Olympic* was growing enormous against the grey sky.

"Keep her balanced," Tommy ordered. "How can I keep her on course with you looking out under the boom?"

I screamed at him: "If we keep on like this, she'll run us down."

"Hayes knows the rules," Tommy said.

We slithered into another trough, and this time when I looked up I could see the *Olympic*'s foremast with her flags blowing hard out to leeward, lurching as she rolled.

"We're so small she can't even see us!" I cried.

"Hayes is a good man. It's his job to see us. If he doesn't, he'll be in trouble."

When we reached the crest of the next roller the size of the *Olympic* was terrifying. Distances at sea are hard to estimate, but she could hardly have been more than two hundred yards away now. I could see the upreach of her bows cutting the rollers and cleaving them apart, I could see her heave to the headsea, lift and come smashing down in a welter of crashing water, I could see the khaki line of the soldiers staring over the railing of her fo'c'sle head. I tried to get the tiller from Tommy's hand but he batted me away.

"Stop that! A sailing ship's got the right of way over steam and Hayes knows it."

We went down into another trough, half rose in a cross chop and I was afraid to look, and then I heard a roaring, trembling sound and opened my eyes and there she was. The bow of the great ship was driving past in a cascade of spray and thrown water. Her camouflaged flank came on and on and past and past, terrible and as high as the sky. Troops looked down from the rail and some of them waved. Then suddenly there was a huge pile of churning, roaring white water and her overhanging taffrail passed and she was clear.

Tommy just stared at her. "The bugger!" he said. "The bugger!"

Our sail, robbed of its wind by the passage of the ship, suddenly cracked out. The moment it did so I saw myself staring up at a mountain of water that had suddenly jumped upward out of the sea, twenty-five thousand tons displaced and lifting, driving outward and just about ready to topple over. We were going to be up-ended. But somehow that dinghy climbed sideways up that humping hill of ocean, staggered on the top while I looked down into a hole in the sea, then shot down into the hole like a toboggan on a slide. Her nose went under, Tommy whipped her half about as the water poured in, wriggled her back on course again to meet the next jumping hill, climbed it and again descended. After three successive waves, each less than the previous one, we rode like a winged seagull in the smooth, undulating, hissing track of the great ship, the water halfway up the centreboard box, the dinghy heavy and lurching with the weight of it, but still controllable and obedient to the helm.

"The bugger!" Tommy said, staring seaward at the receding pile of the *Olympic*.

Then he put the helm over and we lumbered about, the water sloshing and I bailing desperately, and with the wind behind us we ran back to the beach under York Redoubt. I heard the waves sent out by the *Olympic* volleying and crashing along the line of the shore while we drifted heavily in behind them. Now that the crisis was over I was sweating with fear, but if Tommy's knees were shaking he did not show it. We reached shore, heated our beans over a fire in a small cave, ate them and sipped our hot tea. Neither of us said anything until Tommy picked up the package of bread and found it sodden with sea water.

"Hayes was lucky," he remarked quietly. "If he'd run us down, he'd have been courtmartialed."

But something had happened to Tommy Waterfield that day which was never mended, though it was not until 1939 that his injury came to the surface. His love and admiration for officers who wore blue suits with gold stripes on their sleeves had been crushed forever. When the Second World War began, Tommy Waterfield joined the Army.

4 REBELS AGAINST THE AMERICAN DREAM

Just when you think you can't stand the Americans they do something to make you love them. You see them all full of Eisenhower and television and *Time*, you quiver as with organized goodwill they approach to embrace you to death smiling that great big American smile, and then with a single masterful gesture some American individual or some American group gives the lie to everything their opinion-industries insist is the basis of American grandeur. Never is the American greater, never more lovable or worthy, than when he gives a good swift kick to the American Dream.

In his heart the real American never believed in it anyway, but he is a well-brought-up boy and for years he can go along with the crowd without any of the organizers knowing that his heart is not in the right place. Then he kicks. He does not revolt, he does not theorize, he does not excuse himself, he just kicks and does something else. Fed up with producing, distributing, consuming and riding around in a big car to prove he produces, distributes and consumes more successfully than his neighbour, suddenly he stops doing any of these things. He says the hell with the Cadillac and the better home and garden, and he does not even waste the breath necessary to say the hell with the highly paid characters who for years have been telling himself and the world that he is the kind of person he never was.

"So you think Dooey's gonna make it?" said a Philadelphia taxidriver the night of Dewey's nomination in 1948. "Like all you press guys you believe that stuff?"

"What makes *you* think he isn't going to make it?"

"Listen, Mister, you come down here next November and watch us ...... 'em."

On higher levels the repudiation of the Dream by people who are supposed to worship it can be—there is only one word—spectacular in its totality. Walt Whitman said he would sooner go and live with the animals than listen any more to the opinion-industry of his day, which was the puritan theocracy. When Herman Melville had taken all he could stand of the Quaker whaling ship, he calmly left it and went to live among savages. "It was a good country *once*," grunted Hemingway from the greeen hills of Africa and never went back to live in it again. When Sherwood Anderson locked the door of his Winesburg store he indulged in no rhetoric; he simply locked the door and went away to learn painfully how to write the books which said the hell with it so loudly that all the world heard him. Last summer on the lower Mackenzie River I encountered one of these Americans who had had as much of "it" as he could take, and in his own way he was the most total of them all. He was a tugboat chef who had once been a successful business man and a successful army officer; he once had owned a big home with a substantial family somewhere in Texas. "Do you know what's the matter with the States?" he said calmly. "The whole goddam U.S.A. is just one big hunk of baloney."

The American in this mood is an unbeatable man because nobody can argue with him. He has heard it all—but all—and one of the most curious syndromes in the life of that country is the ever-recurring effect of this mood on the minds of its writers. The hell with it is the theme of nearly all the famous American literature of the twentieth century. Dreiser, Lewis, Dos Passos, Lardner, Faulkner, O'Hara, Caldwell, Schulberg, Eliot (don't let his British citizenship fool you), Mailer, Jones, McCullers, Hemingway very frequently, J. D. Salinger, and that strange school of writers designated by a distinguished McGill scholar as the Californicators—Ezra Pound even took to the Italian radio in wartime to say the hell with it to American troops fighting in Italy against the Nazis, and when the officials caught him they locked him up in an animal cage. The technical term for this literary syndrome is revolt, but it is not a revolt *to* anything. It is more like the violent regurgitation of a mind that has imbided one sales-talk too many, has heard one pitch too many, bought one car too many and married one wife too many. "Nothing fails like success," said Scott Fitzgerald with a finality no European has ever managed to match.

Nothing does, of course, and the Americans are the only people with a broad enough experience of success to understand this in a really ample way. "Prosperity," said Bacon about the time the Pilgrims landed at Plymouth Rock, "doth best discover vice." It certainly does in American literature, and that is its limitation, for no American writer these days seems conscious of the truth of Bacon's countertheme, which is that adversity doth best discover virtue.

What prompts these glittering generalities is a motion picture called *Edge of the City*, which was not particularly successful at the box office, but is one more proof of my thesis that the moment you can't stand the Americans, some of them do something to make you reverence and love them. I had reached the place where I thought I could not stand another Eisenhower platitude, another Nixon smile, another American novel in which nobody smiles, another American movie in which the old routines reappear, when *Edge of the City*, quite unheralded, came to town.

The astonishing thing about this picture is that it was made in Hollywood—by Metro-Goldwyn Mayer as a matter of fact—yet it turns its back on almost every attitude on which M.G.M. has built its fortune. The picture deals profoundly and elementally with the three themes Hollywood almost never touches without lying about them—love, violence and the spirit of Jesus Christ. *Edge of the City* (unconsciously, I am almost certain) is the Christ story told by a camera in a modern American setting and in a modern American idiom.

The setting of this picture is so reminiscent of *Waterfront* that most reviewers assumed it was a copy of it. But it is nothing of the kind, for *Waterfront*, excellent though it was as a picture, was contrived and theatrical. *Edge of the City* is not. Most of it seems to have flowed in perfect form right out of somebody's subconscious.

The camera opens on a scene on the North River at night with a migrant workman applying for a loading job in a dockside-railroad warehouse. He gives his name to the hiring boss as Axel North and as the picture proceeds we discover that this is an alias, that his real name is Axel Nordman, that he is a deserter from the American army and a previous deserter from a lower middle-class home in Gary, Indiana. We are shown that home and its authenticity shrivels the heart. It has the inevitable appendages of the American dream: the television set, the washing machine, the big, white refrigerator, the new electric stove.

But Axel's parents, instead of being magnified by these possessions, are reduced by them. The mother is not merely faded; she is washed out, defeated, pitiably crushed by the failure of everything in her life to turn out as she hoped, and by her own inability to understand why. The father, a policeman, means well but has been reared on the legend of toughness and with the best will in the world, he has broken the spirit of a son who tries to be tough when actually he is gentle. This son, Axel, has killed his adored elder brother (who was successfully tough) in a road accident. (Of course the Nordman family owned a car, and of course it was a new car capable of a quick acceleration to ninety-five miles an hour.) Cursed out of his home by his father, cursed out of the army by the sergeant who was simply his father all over again, Axel is much more than a mixed-up kid. He is an American tragedy.

Now he is about to be hired by a foreman called Charley Malik, who soon turns out to be still another version of the tyrant-image the boy is running away from. This Malik is the realest bad man I have ever seen on a screen. He is no stage heavy, scowling, leering and shouting around. He has no gestures and only two kinds of expression on his face, and both of them chill the blood.

That first night Axel sleeps on the dock in order to be on hand for work in the morning, and when he wakes from his sleep what he sees is his saviour. We hear a beautiful voice speaking ordinary American words of good cheer. Axel hears it too and opens his eyes, and his saviour is black.

He had to be. In this modern Roman Empire what else could a Jesus be but a negro, since in white America any man of moderate intelligence and moderate mental balance could not help being too prosperous to know what Jesus knew? But the negro knows it. Just as the cross stood stark in the consciousness of the slaves of ancient Rome, so does the lynching party stand in his. No matter how prosperous the American negro becomes, nobody need tell him that he is not a first-class citizen of the United States, or that he is not despised and rejected of men.

Yet this negro saviour of *Edge of the City* is no more a symbol than he is a stage negro; from his speech we discover instantly that he is a well-educated man, and this is one of the reasons why Charley Malik and the other white workmen on the docks dislike him, for his superiority aggravates their own consciousness of failure to live up to the American dream. In this time of prosperity, what sort of white man is reduced to their kind of work?

The negro sees Axel and recognizes his fear and misery; he sees him and loves him, and the love shows not in his words but in his face. Quietly, so naturally and idiomatically that we believe every scene, he begins his evangel. He teaches Axel not to be ashamed of his own failure to live according to the dream. "But you've got to do something big if people are to love you!" Axel cries in desperate defence of it. He teaches Axel how to protect himself against Malik's sadism, he invites him to his apartment to meet his wife and child, he introduces him to a white girl who is an instructor in one of those playgrounds on the edge of Harlem where whites and negroes mingle naturally. Axel, for the first time in his life, knows a glimmering of Christian happiness, which of course has nothing to do with the sort of thing he has been taught in any church he may possibly have attended. As time passes he tells the negro the story of his life and the miracle of love begins to shine in his tormented face.

"Man," says the negro when Axel is desperate with shame and fear, "Man, I'm your friend. Can't you understand that what happens to you matters to me?"

But Malik, the foreman, is out to get them both. Somehow he senses that his own worthlessness will be unendurable if these two are allowed to continue as they are. He discovers that Axel is an army deserter and he uses this knowledge for blackmail. "Wherever I've gone," cries Axel, "there's always been Charley!" As if the negro hadn't known all his life that wherever anyone goes, there's always a Charley.

The neurotic white boy comes to the inevitable American sticking point where he says the hell with it, and instantly he finds himself face to face with Malik, each of them with a baling hook in his hand, and it is at this moment that *Edge of the City* becomes great.

Of all the crimes Hollywood has committed against truth, the most serious has been its consistent falsification of the nature of violence. Hollywood either glamorizes violence or makes it theatrical. But in *Edge of the City* it tells the simple truth about it, which is this: that no good man ever wants to fight anybody, and that the most terrible thing about a fight between a good man and a bad man is that the good man must be at least momentarily wicked if he is to win.

The negro, seeing that the evil cannot be averted, takes it upon himself. Stepping between the two neurotics with their baling hooks, he says quietly to Malik, "It's me you're after, isn't it, Charley?"

And with a terrible cry of "Black! Black! Black!" while the mob of workmen cluster around with their grey, eroded faces, the duel between the negro and Malik begins, and it is a duel with two weapons by their very nature hideous and degrading, baling hooks. "Charley," the negro pleads when he has Malik at his mercy, "this makes no sense." Malik, expressionless as ever, renews the fight and kills him.

The scene of the negro dying in the arms of the grief-tormented Axel is an authentic motion picture *pietà*, and it is followed by the next scene in the Christ-story, the betrayal. Yet there is no conscious parallel here: it is just what would have happened. The police come to investigate and the workmen, as terrified of Malik's vengeance as Peter was terrified of the Jerusalem mob, deny all knowledge. Axel denies all knowledge, too. Then, as despairing as Peter after the cock crowed, he bursts out into the darkness of New York and seeks the negro's home.

It is here that the Christian story ends. Whether the producers lost their nerve, whether they could not face the full force of their own creation, I don't know. At any rate it is a Hollywood ending. Shamed by the contempt of the negro's wife and the white girl, Axel returns to the warehouse and fights Malik and wins, and the picture ends with him dragging the unconscious foreman to the police. Having trembled on the brink of a new Christian revelation, *Edge of the City* faded in the stretch into something Roman and American.

But it was a great and noble effort just the same, and perhaps the ending was not as false as it seemed. For at the close the Christ was dead, and this American Christ was after all not the only-begotten son of God. He was simply a Harlem negro with a college education.

5 JOURNEY INTO THE PRESENT

By what perfection of irony is the finest train of the senior railway system of Canada known as *The Canadian*? Over the old right of way the pioneers hewed out yard by yard and mile by mile in the years when nobody but a handful of visionaries had any confidence in Canada, this Diesel-hauled *consummatum* of streamlined alloys sways as cool and sweet as the dream of a millionaire soothed by a tranquillizing drug. It is a miracle of comfort and efficiency, this train. It is—dare I say it?—the symbol of this bright new Canada of ours.

The moment *The Canadian* leaves Windsor Station, a machine hidden in its mechanism breathes music into the the ears of everyone inside of it. Softly, insistently and oh so gently, like the Chinese water torture, the music drips into every brain. I left my seat and roamed the train searching for escape, but there was none. The music dripped into the dome where you saw the lovely landscape swaying past. It dripped into the perfectly adjusted seat where your back was massaged by the soft, steady pulse of the engine's power. Blameless music, music the whole world of the common man loves: Romberg, Herbert, Léhar, Strauss and a host of others: *O Sweet mystery of life!*

Oh sad mystery of this country of ours, so determined to be morally superior to the Americans whose every soul-destroying gadget it instantly copies! "I'm so awfully glad I am a Beta!" dripped the mechanical monitor into the dormitories where the children slept in Aldous Huxley's *Brave New World.* "It's much better to be a Gamma than a Beta." "Isn't it nice to be a Delta, a Delta, a Delta, a Delta!"

Through the Lake of Two Mountains, now visible, Champlain had paddled three centuries ago. Through this lake in the river had come the saints who taught the Hurons Christian hymns, the heroes who discovered the Great Lakes, the Ohio, the Mississippi, the American plain. Into the Province of Ontario where this super-train was bound, less than two hundred years ago had come the ragged men and women who had stood for the King, and neither they nor the Frenchmen before them had come to Canada to be soft or make a profit.

Now as *The Canadian* swayed with perfect balance toward the nation's capital, its miraculous, silent speed bringing us in two hours to the shape of things that are, to the bureaucracy which intends to produce a true Canadian culture by creating still another bureaucracy, *Oh, Miss Chloë, I Want to Go Where You Are,* I pressed both index fingers into my ears in a desperate effort to escape the Canada of 1957.

The countryside was so beautiful that day. Never had I seen such a spring as this had been. Even as early as Easter morning, the sun had been a glory over Montreal and the church bells had sung like the bells of Italy. April this year had not been the cruel month it usually is in Canada. In my country garden the jonquils had danced in the breeze a full fortnight before their usual time, and gay little warblers had fanned their feathers in the spring water which issues into the tiny grotto where, twelve years ago, we planted the maidenhair ferns. *I Want to Go Hooaam, Where the Buffalo Rooaam*. Well, nobody had compelled me to travel on the best train in the land. Nobody was compelling me to go on living here. The only reason I did was because I loved the country and felt I had a stake in it.

Opposite me a civil servant tamped together a pile of mimeographed documents, at least five inches thick, and stuffed them into one of the two king-sized brief-cases he had with him. Our eyes met and he sighed. He shook his head sadly at the music and his weary smile seemed to say: "I know. I know everything. I, Tiresias, have foresuffered all, foresuffered even the knowledge that there is nothing you or I can do about this." With a resigned shrug he reached into his second brief-case and extracted still another pile of memos. *Some Day I'll Find You, Some Day I'll* . . .

A farmhouse swayed by against a curving hill and the colours of the hill were Gauguin-green, and I thought of the title of Gauguin's most famous painting and felt the mystery of the plastic forms he had created after he had, for a few years, escaped from economism into life. *Whence Come We? What Are We? Whither Go We?* But surely these are questions for Norman Vincent Peale, not for the successful, tranquillized citizen of our bright new Canada? *When You Have Found Her, Never Let Her Go, When You Have Found Her* . . . I thought of some of the men who had tried to save their souls by enriching humanity out of the water and soil of their own sorrow and loneliness, and especially I thought of Mozart, and of Einstein's wondering words when he was asked what would be the result if the supreme accomplishment of modern civilization were actually used. "But Mozart's music will still be here. It will still be here, but there will be nobody left to listen to it."

What a failure Mozart was: no business sense at all, completely impractical and a squalid end. His wife was sick, his children were in want and he himself was dying in poverty and knew it. Yet in that last year, in the presence of death, he composed the B Flat Piano Concerto, *The Magic Flute* and the *Requiem*, though he got so little money for them that he was buried in a pauper's grave. My mind groped for a pattern of his woodwinds, but it had no chance. The machine in *The Canadian* was piping in the "Merry Widow" waltz, and the author of *that* tune was no failure.

Like a metal snake supple and glittering in the sun, the train flickered on toward the city where post-war Canadian nationalism has come to rest in the burgeoning bureaucracies. *I'll Never No Never Say Never Again*, said the machine. Or did it? Or didn't it? Or did it say something else? *The Canadian*, perfectly sprung, swayed smoothly around a curve, and as it righted itself the heads of the fifty consumers in front of me swayed like a single head back into line.

Another tune began, with a wince I identified it, and reminded myself that everyone on the train was normal but me. Public relations men, advertising men, salesmen and psychological engineers had made careful scientific studies which proved to the management that this mechanical music was what the majority of the consumers wanted. *Vox ventri, vox dei*, which could be translated as, "The voice of the consumer is God's voice", and how pleasant for everyone that the voice of the consumer can be made 95 percent predictable in this modern Canada by public relations men, advertising men, salesmen and psychological engineers. All through Canada this machine plays its blameless, soul-destroying tunes to the happy captives in the train. Through the rock and scrub of the Shield, under the slow prairie sky, up the Kicking Horse and down the Fraser Canyon—but no, it will stop when it is time for all good consumers to fall asleep. It will stop in order to give the seconal a fair chance. And soon it will stop altogether. For the day cannot be far off when the super trains will flow across Canada with their windows sealed in order that the consumers, just as if they were in their own living-rooms, may enjoy the television from coast to coast. And after the ordinary television will come the coloured television, and after that the three-dimensional, and after that the scented, and if our Canadian engineers are unequal to meeting the challenge of installing it, the country is now rich enough to hire Americans who can.

Reading might help, I thought, so I reached up to my suitcase, snapped it open and took out the first book my hand closed on. It turned out to be the Bible and this was the first time I was ever to read the Bible on a train. By some weird accident, the Good Book fell open toward the end of *The Acts* with St. Paul before Felix, and what a perfect parable that was for a man on his way to meet a section of a government department.

Bureaucracy in the western world was a Roman invention, and Antonius Felix, procurator of Judæa in 60 A.D., was one of the ablest bureaucrats of his time. Otherwise he would not have been procurator of the most notoriously troublesome province in the whole empire. For the Jews not only despised the Romans; they believed the spirit was more important than the *panem et circenses*, the consumption of groceries and entertainment spectacles on which the bureaucratic Empire rested. The Romans, of course, were tolerant. They were even in favour of religion; as a matter of fact they were in favour of *all* religions. They believed in the law, in production, distribution and consumption, in organization, roads, aqueducts and sewers, in housing restrictions, insurance and a good standing army. Antonius Felix, procurator of Judæa in 60 A.D., had his general instructions: he was to keep Judaea as cosy as possible, and if his public relations went sour, he would be held responsible. And since he was a good bureaucrat, being held responsible was something Felix was very adroit at avoiding.

That is the whole point of the last chapters of *The Acts* —Paul, inconveniently a Roman citizen, was making a nuisance of himself in Judaea and nobody in authority wanted to be held responsible for what was done, or was not done, in his case. And nobody was.

Felix's solution was to stall things around for two years during which no decision was made, knowing that in two years he himself would be transferred to another post. So Paul, like a Jehovah's Witness awaiting a verdict from the Supreme Court, was neither in nor out of jail. The two years elapsed and Felix went back to Rome, where he was very nearly liquidated for something else he did or did not do in Judæa, and escaped only by the intercession of his homosexual brother, who was a favourite of the Emperor.

The next procurator was Porcius Festus, and in the middle of his stalling around I was reminded that there was no stalling on *The Canadian*.

"This is the conductor speaking," said a mechanical voice. "We are now fifteen minutes from Ottawa. This train is on schedule."

I could almost hear the lift of surprised pleasure in the voice of Festus when Paul spoke the famous words that got the bureaucrat off the hook.

"Thou hast appealed unto Caesar? To Caesar thou shalt go!"

Caesar, far off in Rome, was well away from Festus' department, and as Festus well understood, it would be years before the case would ever reach the higher court.

Then entered the last modern touch in the person of Herod Agrippa, whose family for more than a century had been the Chiang Kai-sheks of the province. The Jews hated the Herods, and the Roman bureaucracy insisted that the Jews loved them. Agrippa had a different angle. If Paul were set free, would he not become a divisive force in the synagogue, being both a Jew and a Roman? "Almost thou persuadest me to become a Christian," Agrippa purred to Paul. And to the procurator he added hopefully: "This man might be set at liberty if he had not appealed unto Caesar."

But Agrippa had no chance, for the papers in Paul's case had already gone Rome-wards, the bureaucratic machinery had been set in motion and Festus could do nothing about it. After another long delay, shipping space of a sort was found for Paul, and though his ship was wrecked on the way to Rome, the apostle finally reached the capital of the world.

There, of course, he waited for years. He waited long enough to convert so many people that when Rome caught fire and Nero needed scapegoats, he had a supply of Christians that lasted him for weeks. Paul's case was heard, indecisively it seems, and he was sent back to jail pending a decision, but in the end they executed him. It probably seemed the most mature and statesmanlike thing to do.

But the Roman bureaucrats in their efforts to avoid responsibility, the Roman governmental machinery in its majestically slow movement, had permitted something to start which was too big for its successors to handle. The bureaucrats took so long making up their minds about Paul that he had time to found the Christian Church. Three centuries later a special department was set up—or rather, an old department was re-vamped—to take care of Christianity, but it was still too late. The character of the Church had changed out of recognition from the days of Christ, but it was distressingly opposed to the idea of the economic man. To produce, distribute and consume—no, the Church saw no sense in this as a chief end for humanity. And as the only thing the Roman Empire was capable of doing was producing, distributing and consuming, the Roman Empire perished.

6 MONTREALER

Of all the cities of Canada except Quebec, Montreal seems to me to have changed the least in its character in the last twenty-five years. The cities of the plains and the coast, so their chambers of commerce inform us (and I wonder why they think it is anything to boast about), have altered out of recognition. Mackenzie King has turned a tough old lumber town into a city of civil servants, and a ghost returning to Ottawa would mourn for Eddie Gerard and those glorious nights in the arena when the citizens bombarded visiting teams with frozen lemons and empty beer bottles. Only yesterday the largest built-up area on the north shore of Lake Ontario was an overgrown Port Hope and proud of it. Today it is unmistakably Toronto, flooding past recall over the plain under a forest of television masts.

But Montreal, despite the new apartment buildings and the crazy living costs, has changed little. When I first arrived in the mid-thirties its character was more palpable than it is now, because it was not covered with the veneer of internationalism which has hidden its soul from strangers since the war. I learned to know it then, and since knowing it, I have learned to cherish it. It is my haven in a nuclear world. Deep in its heart, Montreal's spirit knows that H-bombs exist and can annihilate life on this planet; deep in its heart, it does not take this aspect of nuclear development seriously. Shrewd in the ways of men, it assumes that the real purpose of nuclear research is to maintain scientists and technologists in the style of living to which Hitler's war has accustomed them.

I came to Montreal in the mid-thirties with the usual freight of misinformation outlanders still have about the place. It was gay and it was wicked. On the sophisticated level of André Siegfried it was an English garrison enclosed in an overgrown French village. Montreal did not seem very gay to me when I first encountered it, nor did it seem wicked, for there was so little aggression in its corruption, and in those days so little violence in its vice, that the phrase which seemed best to fit the frame of its mind was amiable cynicism, with equal emphasis on both words. In those depression days the unemployed were everywhere, but they looked a little less wretched here than in London and Berlin and less acridly bitter than in New York. Nor again did the city remind me of any French village I had ever seen. Indeed the so-called French section east of Bleury Street is more suggestive of some sections of Victorian London and Southampton than of any community in France, and it occurred to me that both these English cities, after all, had grown out of a mixed population of Saxons and Normans.

V. S. Pritchett, writing of London in *Holiday* and comparing it to Rome, said that while Rome reminded him of violence with murder lurking red in a thousand doorways, London made him think of experience. That is what Montreal has always made me think of. Quebec with its Citadel and noble past has the air of grand tragedy turned into a monument, but in the great days of New France Montreal was never noble, being friendly to fur-smugglers from the earliest times. No matter how glorious were the aims of the colonial governors, or how ascetic the aspirations of Bishop Laval, Montrealers even in those early days seem to have regarded both with the same appraising eye they now turn on the rarest bird in modern Canada, a Montreal civic reformer. Nothing is more typical of the kind of experience Montreal enforces on her citizens than the career of the Old Woman of Saint-Antoine Street, *The Gazette*. I suppose it is possible to find in North America a paper more conservative than *The Gazette*, but I don't know where to look for it. Only one other paper on the continent, and two others in the whole world, are older. It always pleases me to reflect that *The Gazette* began its career as a revolutionary sheet, and that its founder, Benjamin Franklin, discovered in Montreal that friendly resistance which has ruined the aspirations of every reformer since his time.

This city of ours has always been shrewd in the ways of men, which is not quite the same thing as to say that she has always been wise. Wisdom could remind her that history abounds in examples of men who have not invariably made *des arrangements* with city halls and the prince of this world, but shrewdness tells her that these are on the whole exceptional men and that their descendants tend to lack the stamina to keep up the good work. Life is excellent, so why should a man be tragic? Tragedy is alien to the character of Montreal, and for an elementary reason. Does not experience avoid or absorb a tragic situation? Hamlet could never succeed in Montreal, nor could he be taken seriously, but Falstaff could become the mayor.

Before the war Montreal had a tutelary genius; it still has, though he is harder to find these days because so many of his friends stay at home with their television sets that sometimes he is forced to stay at home himself. In the

1930s anyone could find him who knew where to look. He haunted the central city and made occasional excursions into outlying regions. He knew all the taverns off Dominion Square, a few choice lunch counters and off-beat restaurants like Chez Son Père, and when he wished to expand he occasionally dined in the Ritz and the St. James Club. In Leacock's heyday he belonged to the Faculty Club of McGill, but he dropped his membership in the 1930s when the political and social arguments seemed to him to exceed the limits of ordinary common sense. Nôtre Dame de Grâce he entirely avoids, also the Town of Mount Royal, and about Westmount he has grave reservations, though he admits that some of his friends live there in a furtive fashion. When seeking adventure he is not above visiting The Main, in midsummer heat he likes the Chalet and Lafontaine Park, but on the whole he prefers sitting with the neighbours on the steps of those outside staircases where the whole street relaxes until the heat-wave ends. The Forum he likes in the winter, though he feels less at home there since the old millionaires' section fell a casualty to post-war prosperity and his old cronies in the flat cloth caps and the red jerseys no longer can afford the price of admission. He would not be caught dead reading *Le Devoir*, though if he has nothing better to do, he will occasionally glance at *Midnight* to make sure that none of his acquaintances have had the misfortune to be found in during a police raid, or found out during a business deal. But he still likes the city and he insists it is much as it always was, nor was he fooled for an instant when Jean Drapeau became mayor with the declared intention of cleaning the city up. I met him once during the second month of Drapeau's régime and he did not even wish to talk about it. "I can't go to City Hall any more," he said, "they won't let me in." But then he added grimly: "Don't worry. I'll be back sooner than some people think." And in the next election he was.

The first time I met the Genius was in October 1935 on a St. Catherine Street tram after midnight. As we were the only passengers we fell into talk, and he expressed himself in proverbs. These are a few I remember.

Ideas are useful, but the moment you take them seriously they become a bore.

Religion is the backbone of a community, but don't put too much strain on it, or you will rupture its disks.

A good reputation is like a precious ointment, but it won't build you a house on the side of a mountain.

It is better to be liked than admired, and best of all to be admitted into the right club.

Time is like snow. It obliterates traces, and quickest of all does it obliterate the traces of how a politician obtained his power, or a rich man his money.

Everyone ought to know that he can be sued for almost anything he does, but if he has the right lawyer the judgment can be reversed by a higher court, and if he has the right friends the suit may never be heard at all.

The Genius went on like this at some length, and as I was a serious young man in those days, and prudish as well, I was shocked by him. I pointed out the window of the tram at an unemployed man and gave him a lecture.

"How can you talk like this when the whole city is filled with men like that?" I said. "Earlier this evening I was walking along St. Catherine Street and one man in every four that passed me was out of work. I saw a crowd of men in front of a restaurant where chickens were roasting right in the window, and some of those men were slavering. One of these days there's going to be a revolution, and then you'll find out a thing or two."

He looked at me and nodded. "I'm sorry about the unemployed. Some of my best friends can't even afford the price of a beer."

"And what are you doing about it?" I asked.

"Nothing." He shrugged. "What can *I* do? I didn't make the depression. If my friends in St. James Street had been running affairs in Wall Street, there'd never have been this depression."

"But your St. James Street friends are rich, and those men out there are hungry."

"They're all my friends," he said. "I like all of them. But there won't be any revolution. Not here, anyway. My unemployed friends will soon be joining the army."

"Before they do that they may rise in mobs. They may burn your rich friends' houses."

Again he shook his head. "They're not that kind of people."

"They're hungry."

"No, they won't do a thing like that. You see, my rich friends all live on the side of a mountain. It would take a mob half an hour to reach them, and the streets are pretty steep. In summer it would be too hot, and in winter it would be too cold. A mob is like water, it flows downhill. Anyway, they're not that kind of people."

"They'll change into a different kind of people."

"You lack experience," said my friend. "Nobody ever changes, not if he likes to live in Montreal."

He left me then, and apparently he was so disappointed in me that he avoided me for years. The war began and the unemployed—just as he predicted and just as Gabrielle Roy described them in *Bonheur d'Occasion*—joined the army for a pair of shoes and three meals a day and a suit of clothes. The war ended and the boom began, after a time the beer recovered its lost savour and once again there seemed enough of it to go around.

"You remember?" he told me in the late 1940s. "Montreal didn't change after all."

Outwardly, he admitted, it had changed a little, but not

in many parts that interested him. He admitted that the old farmland between Snowdon and the Back River had come to resemble most of Toronto, but as he never went there he didn't really mind. The factories? Yes, it was regrettable that they filled the city with smoke, but at least everyone could afford to enjoy himself on account of the factories. One couldn't live without money. Dorchester Street, one of his favourite haunts in the old days, no longer had the furtively wise air of a well-bred lady who has taken to prostitution and drink in her old age, but he could put up with its loss because he disliked traffic jams and the new Dorchester Street seemed to relieve the congestion a little. What he missed most of all was the old Square Mile.

"It seems only yesterday," he said, "that an old dowager whispered to me that she never expected to see the day when a daughter of hers would have to live in Westmount."

He expressed sorrow at the disappearance of apartments at fifty dollars a month and garage space at two dollars and a half. And to myself he was flattering.

"You've learned quite a lot since you came here in the Thirties. You were a crusader then, I seem to remember. But you stayed. In the long run I like anyone who stays here long enough."

The last time I met the Genius he spoke to me through the mouth of Montreal's most famous mayor, who had just retired from public life. We were talking of old times, and Mr. Houde spoke feelingly of the depression, and amusingly of some of his old adventures. I asked him how he accounted for a fact that seemed ironic to me, that he, who had begun his career with anti-English speeches, had ended it more popular in the west end of Montreal than in the east.

"That's easily explained," he said. "The English like a good loser, and I was a very good loser. Besides, I was around so long they got used to me, and anyway, I didn't really lose very much."

Then he gave me one of his most seraphic smiles.

"The mayor of Montreal," he said, "must be a broad man." Placing his hands on his hips he drew them wider and wider apart. "While I was mayor, I became broader and broader and broader."

7 THE CLASSICAL TRADITION AND EDUCATION

Just after New Year's in 1960 I was asked to read a paper on the subject of the classics in education. I was astonished. Truly I believed I had sat through the death-watch on the classics twenty-five years ago; had listened to the symptoms of a once-great personality expiring from malnutrition, contempt and disappointment. I was aware that what is called "the Latin requirement" still lingers in a few curricula, but this survival had seemed no more significant than the retention of the little residual piece of steel, still called a bayonet, on the end of a rifle of a soldier in an atomic army. When somebody remarked that only a third of today's college presidents can translate the texts of the degrees they hand out at convocations, I had believed the figure exaggerated. You see, I once taught Latin and Greek myself.

But the subject began to fascinate me; chiefly, I suppose, because somebody was still around who remembered the classics and wondered whether more had been lost than gained when they were allowed to perish from the system. Although I work with the young three days a week, like them and admire them, I have tried to avoid thinking about theories of education these many years. In my time there have been as many of them as there have been theories of economics, and the successful ones, by which I mean the ones which were adopted, all trend in the same general direction: they conform to the producer-consumer cycle. But lately we have been hearing a peculiar whirring sound ("... the thunder rumbling in the sky, it was Hitler over Europe saying 'they must die' ") emerging from the young people, and quite recently it has become articulate in three terrible words which should make older people tremble: "We are cheated!" The young not only understand, they are beginning to say openly that what has cheated them more efficiently than anything else has been the educational system they are offered. The best of them transcend it as the best transcend almost anything, but the best also say that the average student today is graduated naked to his enemies.

There is a vacuum in the system and the young know it, and there are probably millions of older people who know it, too. It occurs to me, perhaps wrongly, that this vacuum began to appear when the classical tradition began to die out. So I brought myself—and 'brought myself' are the *mots justes*—to think back a little on what has happened, and this is what I am going to try to do now. Though I do not care much for Aristotle's personality and know that the scientists abhor his favourite question, I have never found it profitable to dodge that question very long. It is, "What is the purpose?" So what is the purpose, the overall purpose, of the educational system which almost every articulate young person today believes is cheating him?

I don't know. Modern educators (the noun is theirs) profess so many different purposes I could not enumerate them, but I find it hard to believe that education is the most important of them. Perhaps it is, in nooks and corners. But within the system itself I can discover no overall purpose clearly understood by students and faculties, no focus similar to that of a novelist creating a book which will not fall apart in a dozen different places, no clear line of thought comparable to that of a mathematician understanding precisely why he has moved from one place to the next.

On the university level in North America the casual observer takes it for granted that the chief purpose of the system is the teaching of a variety of skills, many of which have no direct connection with each other. The faculties with the highest prestige are the skill-teaching ones: medicine, engineering, commerce, law, dentistry, and in some more comprehensive institutions: farming, hotel-keeping and the like, together with as many contingent schools and institutions as the establishment can support, or be persuaded to support. Oddly enough, most first-rate universities still proclaim that the Faculty of Arts and Science is its core, and that the Faculty of Graduate Studies and Research its finest flower. Lip-service to the arts is paid in proportion to the degree of neglect from which they suffer, but the fact remains that on this side of the ocean the majority of students registered in arts courses are girls.

Therefore I think it no exaggeration to say that since the war the universities have been half-educating a substantial number of girls, and have been training, at least in terms of the respective assignments, a somewhat larger number of boys to qualify for the higher income brackets. Science is encouraged because it is essential to most of the skill-teaching courses, but for one genuine scientist in the student bodies there must be thirty who take the courses only because they are required as preliminaries to whatever skill-teaching faculty they are registered in. Science, it is admitted, is still regarded as essential. But arts is not. An increasing number of students, doubtless repeating what they have heard from their parents, are now uttering new versions of the old question the Latin teachers used to await with the sensations of a man in a dentist's chair anticipating the moment when the dentist would reach for the drill: "Sir, what is the *use* of English?" "Sir, what is the *use* of French unless you live in the Province of Quebec?" "Sir, what is the *use* of history and philosophy?"

The students, it would seem, are more honest than the educational officials. They are certainly franker than the American engineering dean who stated (and in the same speech) that the ideal of his faculty was to produce a broadly educated man, and then proceeded to boast that the reason why more students were enrolled in his faculty than in any other was because engineers, in that particular year, were enjoying the highest per capita income of any professional group in the country.

When we look lower down in the system, when we get to the foundations on which all really depends, the picture varies from state to state and from province to province, but its general features become more uniform every passing year. No doubt of it, the school authorities have at last persuaded the public to spend more money on education than the public ever spent on it before; or, to be more precise, to turn over more money for the educational authorities to spend as they see fit. The continent has blossomed with shiny new high schools homogenized out of glass, brick and plastics, full of light and air and concert halls, and these are improvements on the grim old structures which often were mistaken for the town jail. But so far as the instruction is concerned, I don't see how anyone can argue (at least not without laughing) that the principal purpose of the modern grade school is to turn out educated men and women. Perhaps its purpose is more humane. Education is not a thing designed for comfort, but for survival and for the development of a personality our ancestors believed was valuable in itself, and moreover (their evidence may have been inadequate) valuable to the God who counted every hair on the personality's head. Perhaps it is cruel—certainly many psychiatrists thought it was, at least for a while—to encourage individualism in a world like ours, or for that matter in any world. Adjustment is the word. So it would seem that the overall purpose of most primary education in modern America is to turn out friendly people free of neuroses and the critical sense which makes its possessor gnash his teeth at the calculated insults to the human intelligence perpetrated by politicians and advertisers in a television-consumer society. Nice work if you can get it; even nicer work if you can get away with it indefinitely.

Anyway this is the general picture in the schools, and I believe its modern perfection required the total elimination of the classical tradition, which first was attacked by the educational revolution of the mid-nineteenth century. This revolution, however, had some results which its instigators, most of whom were honourable men, did not foresee.

From the moment education came under the control of the state, it was inevitable that two developments were certain to follow. Education would enter the area of democratic politics; the educational system sooner or later would betray the usual symptoms of a bureaucracy. In the nineteenth century this seemed less dangerous than it does now, because then democracy was more of a living reality. Its issues were competently debated in small towns and on the hustings. Politics had not yet become a branch of the advertising business.

It has now, with the results that political success depends more on popularity than on ability, and that the easiest way to become popular is to take the road of least resistance.

Applied to education, this has meant that the officials in the system who were ambitious to rise were generally the ones who told the public what the public wanted to hear. By modern methods (remember the propaganda of two decades ago?) boys and girls could become educated without having to work. The play-method would teach them all the grammar and arithmetic they required to know; democratic citizenship habits would be acquired in the schools, as indeed they were, if we understand them to mean what they do now; the teacher would teach better if he or she were careful to be popular with the class; discipline must be relaxed so that no neuroses could develop; standards must be lowered lest a stupid child acquire the inferiority feelings that breed neuroses. By now the story is so familiar it needs no repeating; we are left with the results of it. And the educators who introduced this system have created a pattern in which education, instead of leading society, follows a blindfolded society wearing a double blindfold of its own.

Meanwhile within the workings of the system the bureaucracy burgeoned. In the past the teacher and the administrator was one and the same man. The college provost gave lectures and tutorials, the headmaster taught in the upper forms, administration was reduced to bare essentials. This seldom happens any more in a school or college because the chiefs are too busy to teach, and in many cases even to see students except on convocation platforms. On the school level we see the teacher, better paid than formerly but without prestige, coping with the age-old job of teaching the young. But he does so in a system in which he has no authority, in which his wishes and experience are little more considered than those of a private soldier in the army. Above him we see the successful "educator", who is usually a teacher graduated to the administrator's desk, a man somewhat privileged, and in his office he is an executive giving directives to teachers he barely knows, a business man dealing with boards of external business men on more or less equal terms of prestige. But whether he likes it or not, these outside boards are his final courts of appeal. It is they on whom he depends for his success, his advancement, indeed his professional existence. People being as they are, he is generally compelled to deal with them on their terms and not on his own, and their terms are miles apart from those of the teachers who do the actual work in the schools and colleges.

In the days when the classical tradition reigned there was nothing like this. The purpose of education was simple then, and the schools and colleges were so system-less that to the modern executive mind anything like them would be intolerable. Not only were there no IBM machines; there were not even typewriters. The purpose of education was merely to teach the student to read, to write, to learn basic mathematics, to work in a disciplined way, and finally to expose him, while doing this, to the best minds in civilization and to let the classics become a part of him and the clarity of mathematics enter his thinking. The overall purpose of education in those days was precisely as Bacon described it:

"Studies serve for delight, for ornament, and for ability. Their chief use for delight is in privateness and retiring; for ornament, is in discourse; and for ability, is in *the judgment and disposition of affairs.*" If I emphasize this last statement it is only to remind the reader that in the days when our civilization was growing, judgment was valued more highly than any particular skill, and the ideal man of affairs was not a specialized executive but Aristotle's *phronimos*, the prudent, experienced man of goodwill with a wide perspective of men and events.

Bacon goes on: "For expert men can execute, and perhaps judge of particulars, one by one; but the general counsels, and the plots and marshallings of affairs, come best from those that are learned."

And again, because it was the essence of the classical insight that life is a fleeting thing and a rare privilege; that life must be *lived:*

"To spend too much time in studies is sloth; to use them too much for ornament is affectation; to make judgment wholly by their rules is the humour of a scholar. They perfect nature, and are perfected by experience: for natural abilities are like natural plants that need proyning by study; and studies themselves do give forth directions too much at large, except they be bounded in by experience.

"Crafty men condemn studies; simple men admire them; and wise men use them: for they teach not their own use; but that is a wisdom without and above them, won by observation."

Here, with unparallelled clarity, is contained the entire philosophy behind the old classical education. And for the technique and curriculum, Bacon is equally specific:

"Reading maketh a full man, conference a ready man, and writing an exact man. Histories make men wise; poets, witty; mathematics, subtle; natural philosophy, deep; moral, grave; logic and rhetoric, able to contend." And he concludes this famous passage with the Ovidian line my old school used for its motto: *Abeunt studia in mores*. Hence it appears that the purpose of the old education was to produce a certain kind of man.

What manner of man he was, how remarkable was his variety within a coherent system of knowledge and values, the history of European, and especially of British and French society, shows very clearly.

He must not be judged—God forbid—by the German and American pedants of the Ph.D. mills which developed in the decadence of the tradition and aided its enemies in extinguishing it. During the Renaissance, he was the "new man" of his epoch, and he led the people of Europe out of a priest-ridden medievalism into the light of knowledge and discovery. Indeed the chief word associated with the Renaissance is *illumination*; not comprehension, not the deep and precise understanding of particulars which comes from science, but illumination of thought, life and society expressing itself in language, literature, music, architecture, art, life-values and—this above all—action.

In the modern connotation, a man trained in the classical tradition is obviously an amateur, and as such he is judged inadequate. He cannot fill a tooth, perform an abdominal, fire a rocket to the moon; he is relatively useless to the specific producer-consumer-repairer tasks which now have become nearly the whole content of life. But when we look at his record in the past, we must admit that the classical tradition did quite a lot for civilization.

It enabled Dante and Petrarch, followed by the writers of every other nation of Europe, to mould the vernaculars by translating into them the light, knowledge and methods of the mother cultures which had died. The classics underlay the literature and thought of the West as surely as Roman Law underlies the Code Napoléon. In England they nourished nearly every genius of which the nation is proud. The classical ideal of clarity, applied to the clumsy and confused prose of the seventeenth century, enabled Dryden, Addison, Steele, Defoe and Swift to forge the peerless linguistic instrument which made England's eighteenth century the most lucid period since Pericles. Inheriting a language purged of obscurities, Jefferson was able to frame a most complex constitution so clearly that ordinary men could understand it without a lawyer's help. No complex system produced these results. They came from hard-working teachers who stood no nonsense, who taught the mathematics and the languages, and knew that clarity would come as a matter of course to anyone capable of becoming educated.

For how could a man be unclear if he had mastered a language in which it is impossible to be ambiguous without being ungrammatical, and who applied the Latin tenets of clarity to his own speech? Nor was this all: people classically trained had acquired a sort of human geometry which now has been lost. They understood the past not in detail but in its broad outlines; they knew that certain actions are bound to produce similar effects no matter where or when they are performed. The eighteenth-century gentleman may have been callous to the sufferings of the poor, indifferent to the cruelty of the laws. But he was tender to civilization itself, which he knew had not come from the masses but from a very small number of gifted individuals. It is impossible to imagine a statesman of Pitt's time dropping an atomic bomb, if he had one, on a city of an already defeated enemy. It is impossible to imagine him giving the orders to have one made. Above all, the classical tradition taught this: that the road of least resistance is sure to become the hardest road in the end, and that this road is usually followed by people whose minds are fragmented, who judge of particulars without relating them to the whole. Ruthless though the eighteenth-century politicians were, before the French Revolution they seldom deceived themselves.

If our statesmen today constantly deceive themselves it is because they are too ignorant to understand where the road of least resistance leads. Most of them appear to know nothing of the human geometry. Imagine, for instance, a modern revolutionary statesman addressing the people with the words of John Jay, first Chief Justice of the United States. Speaking only ten years after the constitution had been drafted, it would have been easy for Jay to proclaim that a new era in humanity had dawned, that the old evils had been conquered by the glorious revolution, that mankind (pick any cliché you like) was now marching shoulder to shoulder into the broad uplands of prosperity, brotherhood and justice for all. But what Jay actually did utter makes strange reading today: "I do not expect," he said, "that mankind will, before the millenium, be what they ought to be; and therefore, in my opinion, every political theory which does not regard them as being as they are, will prove abortive."

The classics can still teach this kind of human geometry to anyone who acquaints himself with them. Even when I was a boy there were vestiges of the tradition left in daily life. My father was one of them. He was a doctor who spent much of his earlier life in a very hard practice in a Cape Breton mining town, but thanks to his classical interests he was not isolated there. He read Latin and Greek for pleasure; he read the philosophers. In retrospect I see him as one of the least provincially minded men I ever knew, even though he was full of Scotch and Calvinist quirks. He was democratic in his human dealings; not familiar, not a gladhander, not a winner of friends and an influencer of people, but democratic enough, apparently, to make a hundred-odd workmen want to follow his hearse to the grave through a snowstorm. I used to think him hidebound pretty often, and I also used to think him intolerant, for he was full of scorn at most of the things that were going on in the educational system, and he developed an increasing contempt for the mentality of politicians. I see now that though he entirely lacked modern social techniques he was not often wrong. He objected to modern education because it failed to educate, and he objected to modern politicians not so much because they deceived the people as because they first deceived themselves. This self-deception he ascribed to the fuzziness and confusion of their language, which they used in an automatic manner which in time could do nothing else but cloud their thinking processes. My father died just before the Hitler war began, and he died knowing it was inevitable and why it was inevitable. This he understood not so much from reading the papers as from reading Thucydides. I have often wished he had lived a year and a half longer, for in 1940 he would have seen a classicist of genius rally the decent people in the world with no weapons but language well used and a vision of essentials as clear as a relief map. I know that Winston Churchill boasts that at Harrow he was a bad Latin scholar, but he was a product of the tradition. In his more reckless moments he talks fustian, but never when the matter is important. Then his language is the sparest and most classical in measure of any writer in the last century. Churchill did not have to read Cicero and Demosthenes in the original to obtain his style; he got it by direct inheritance from Gibbon, Burke and Chatham, who in turn got it from the primary sources.

It is gone now; to repeat, the classical tradition is gone so far beyond reasonable controversy that it makes no more sense to regret it than to regret the time when bankruptcy was considered a disaster, and not a technique used by shrewd men to avoid their obligations. But we still want to live somehow or other, and so many people are beginning to think that our survival depends on an improvement in the educational system that it may be worthwhile to examine *why* the classical tradition died. Nobody can think sensibly about today's educational needs unless he understands this, for the classics were attacked and defeated for reasons which do not obtain today.

It is commonly believed that the classics failed because they could not meet the competition of science. In a sense this is true, yet science was never hostile to a tradition which originated in the Greek scepticism whose greatest thinker inscribed over the doors of the first academy: "Let no man enter here who knows no geometry." Bacon and Newton wrote their scientific books in Latin; in our own time scientists like Einstein and Oppenheimer were versed in the classics. No, it was not science which killed the tradition, for in a sense science is a part of it, an outgrowth of its entire attitude. It was democracy which killed it by insisting that education should abandon its role of illuminator of life in order to convert itself into a tool-maker for democracy's material needs and a healer of democracy's bodies. In this insistence I don't see how anyone can deny that nineteenth-century democracy was entirely right.

The primary needs of nineteenth-century democracy could not have been other than material, and at that period of history it would have been criminal to have denied them the satisfaction they craved. Though adventurous minds were exhilarated by the prospect of exploring the new possibilities in science, the ordinary citizen's interest in science did not lie in the exploring of mysteries and the accumulation of knowledge. He wished to apply scientific aids to increase the wealth, to mitigate and finally to abolish a poverty no longer unavoidable, to conquer what Mark Twain called "the ancient dominion of pain", to open as many new avenues of opportunity as possible. None of these aims could be satisfied by a tradition whose chief end was to produce a wise man with a sense of perspective and time. Around the middle of the last century, the classical tradition appeared to the *avant garde* of educationists as a luxury which society could not afford, and by the end of the century it appeared a luxury to almost everybody. Many of its defenders were branded as cold-hearted obscurantists, as some of them probably were. For what was the use of wisdom if it was only for a privileged few? What was the use of culture if the handful who possessed it was supported by the patience of a culture-less poor? Also there was greed—where was the profit in Latin and Greek? The greed of the business community on the one hand, the humanitarianism of the liberals on the other insisting that poverty and disease must be conquered—these two mighty forces united in the nineteenth century to rout the classical tradition almost everywhere in North America.

But human society—in another essay I quote Montaigne to the same effect—goes very incompetently about healing its ills. Humanitarians, like so many liberal revolutionaries, are apt to have extremely provincial minds. They are—Montaigne again—so impatient of what vexes them at any particular moment that they seek to get rid of it reckless of the cost. They also like to succeed, and the path to a quick success is usually the path of least resistance. If you are an administrator or a politician, it is almost always that.

As I look back on the educational revolution of the last century, its most typical instigator does not seem to have been T. H. Huxley, Eliot of Harvard or even Jeremy Bentham. My man is Sir William Dawson of McGill, who had a freer field than any of the others and was faced with conditions especially appropriate for what he sought to do. Dawson's is a career and personality worth knowing if you want to understand the forces which originated the educational system we have now.

He was a Nova Scotian of great character, kindliness and integrity. He knew enough science (his subject was geology) to become a member of the Royal Society of London. He loved the young and in turn was loved by them. He was a prodigious worker, modest, pioneering, a man who was eager to take on two dozen jobs at once: so hard did he work it is small wonder that he had no time for reflection. He was also a fundamentalist Calvinist.

That Dawson opposed the arts as the basis of education is well known to anyone acquainted with the McGill story. It was assumed, correctly, that he considered them impractical. But in his chapter on Dawson in a recently published history of McGill, Edgar Collard gives us a fascinating piece of information about the great principal who led the educational revolution in Canada. It appears that Dawson's main reason for opposing the arts was not his belief that they were impractical, but his conviction that they were wicked.

Mr. Collard writes: "Accepting, as he did, the theological dogma that man is a fallen creature, he believed that man's work must share the corruption of his nature. Would not the humanist studies, for that reason, be tainted even at their best? How could a man hope to raise himself through education if he were to steep his mind only in what must be discoloured by the sin of Adam?"

Why Dawson did not apply the same argument to the sciences, which are equally the product of human genius, is a mystery a psychologist might find it profitable to explore. Though unselfish in his personal life, Dawson was an extremely rugged character and he played to win. He was not a vulgar politician in any sense of the word, but he was a master politician nonetheless. Montreal was becoming a rich community, and the industrialists and business men were mostly people who had worked their way up, who knew nothing of the old humanist tradition and were becoming, some of them, rich enough to buy out dozens of people with B.A. degrees. Most of them were also Calvinists. It must have been welcome news indeed to hear from a college principal, a fellow of the Royal Society, that the humane education they lacked was not only impractical, but was immoral into the bargain. It must have been even more welcome to have a principal who spoke out with defiant boldness for the very interests and beliefs they held themselves:

"If we offered the arts," said Dawson, "we would be offering something for which the palate of a new and young society has little relish . . . We have no mass of educated gentry trained in the method *to support us*." The italics are mine because these last three words seem suggestive of at least one of Dawson's motives: at all costs, he was determined to make his college succeed. When he justified his decision to found McGill's reputation on practical studies (again the italics are mine) he resorted to an argument which every politician would agree is the most cogent one possible in a commercial democracy: "These subjects, *by being more popular*, increase *the value* of the education offered." There, in that word "popular", in the context virtually equated with the other word "value", is the little cloud the size of a man's hand which in a later age was to cover the whole educational heavens.

But I am not done with Sir William Dawson yet; this singular Victorian is too precious to be forgotten before we know more about him.

Though Dawson was highly in favour of subjects like physics and chemistry, he applied the adjective "practical" to them on every possible occasion. A scientist he may have been, but the evidence proves beyond question that he understood very little of the scientific attitude. The scientist he most admired in his early years was Charles Darwin, and it was Darwin who had sponsored his election to the Royal Society. But when Darwin published *Origin of Species*, Dawson was appalled. The only thing about *Origin of Species* that was significant to Dawson was its implicit attack on his belief that every word in the Bible is true. He accordingly spent the rest of his scientific energies on composing an enormous tract aimed at confuting Darwin and re-establishing the Book of Genesis as the final explanation of the origin of species. Nor did he stop there. On another occasion this ardent champion of applied technology led a party of sixty-five Montreal gentlemen out of the old Erskine Presbyterian Church because an organ had been installed in it. Together they founded a new church with a constitution laying it down that if there were one dissenting voice, the church should have no organ. Dawson, eager for machinery everywhere else, called organs "praising machines", and because music was tainted with Adam's fall, they should therefore be banned from places of worship.

In thus writing about Sir William Dawson I am not attacking him. He was a great man who laid the foundations of a great university, which also happens to be an extremely civilized one. His successor, Sir William Peterson, though detested by most of his board, did much to restore the balance at McGill, and significantly it was Peterson, the classical scholar, who brought to McGill the two most eminent scientists ever connected with the university: Rutherford and Soddy. But Dawson's influence, and that of others like him, played right into the hands of the rising middle class whose philosophy was becoming more and more narrowed down to the modern concept that the chief end of man is to produce, distribute and consume material goods. Dawson would be appalled by the morality of a society like ours at the present time, and if I have dwelt on his career it is only to emphasize that it was not the scientific attitude which killed the classics, but the immediate material needs of the nineteenth century, together with the provinciality of the leaders of the educational revolution.

Now I think the time has come when we can return to the basic question. Since a vacuum has been created in education by the death of the classical tradition, is it possible to discover anything with which the vacuum can be filled?

It is not possible, I should say, unless there is a large general understanding that the needs of modern democracy have changed out of recognition since Dawson and other educators like him set out to satisfy the needs of a century ago. Their success is attested to by our present condition. Education has most certainly produced the tool-makers, the healers, the accountants, the distributors, the consumers; the totality of its success in doing this is now recognized on all levels. The old hostility of commerce to the academy has changed from an hostility to something it considered snobbish and impractical to a vague feeling that too many professors are likely to harbour socialistic theories. Why commercial men should believe this, or worry about it if it is true, is a mystery to me, because if a modern nexus of corporations is not a collective under another name I don't know what it is. But the old hostility is virtually gone now, and no wonder. Not long ago at a debate conducted by the McGill Humanities Association, a representative of the Manufacturers' Association said that his body had come to the conclusion that higher education deserved all the support from business that it asked. According to him, consumer research efforts had turned up the interesting conclusion that college graduates are the best consumers we have. Yes, the situation is very different now from what it was in Sir William Dawson's day.

Democracy in the last century was poor and partially in rags; its condition was similar to that of what we now call an "undeveloped country". But western democracy is now so Croesus-rich that its most characteristic industry, advertising, must keep the producer-consumer wheel turning by constantly creating what it calls new needs. Nineteenth-century democracy could not afford the humanities, as we have seen. But now the question is different. Now the question is: can mid-twentieth century democracy dare *not* to afford them? Its officials do not want them, do not admit they are valuable, and most of them know nothing important about them. But can they *dare*—and this is the right word—to tolerate much longer a system in which the humanities live the anaemic existence of underprivileged beggars in the bad old days of old?

I would argue that they cannot, and for what seems to me a reason pretty hard to disregard. Specialized skills we now have in abundance, but hardly anyone in authority understands how to use them for any other purpose save the production, distribution and consumption of goods and services. On international levels we are floundering from one confusion to another, and are getting scared. The West has reached the place where its leaders *want* to be able to fear Russia. The truth is that they, and we, are more afraid of ourselves. We are terrified inside by the galloping corruption produced by a now meaningless routine of production, distribution and consumption. And this I know, because I teach the young.

When I said earlier that the young feel cheated I meant just that, and from talking to dozens of them I know why, because they know why. When they read that the chief economic adviser of the American President says that the chief goal of the American government is "to maximize consumption", they feel those words in their nerve-ends. They ask themselves: "Has life no more purpose than the dreary round of mating, raising families which will live as our parents do, working endlessly to make ends meet in a constantly more expensive society, unable really to enjoy ourselves, passing on the responsibility of doing something better to our children?" If the majority of young men avoid the humanities in the colleges, it is not because they are hostile to them. It is because their fathers urge them—indeed the whole organized voice of modern society commands them—to install themselves in paying jobs at the earliest possible moment. Staring them in the face in the centre of the treadmill is the Organization Man, and not one young person in a hundred likes him. How can he, when the Organization Man is unable to like himself?

So I believe that the revolution may now be nearing the point of full circle, and I think this because of the example of Russia.

No country on earth has been more firmly wedded to faith in material progress than the Soviet Union. Unlike ourselves, who do not let the right lobe of the brain know what the left lobe thinketh, the Soviets for years were unashamed materialists. Yet in recent years a new phenomenon has appeared in Russia: students, male as well as female, are being urged to enter the humanities, and at the moment no less than fifty-five percent of them in the state-supported system are engaged in these studies. Evidently the Russian leaders, more intelligent than the self-salesmen who have propelled themselves into the so-called leadership of the West, have concluded that a time has come when material requirements will be satisfied more or less automatically, and that there is now a need for the kind of education which will produce people capable of thinking in perspective. "The general counsels, the plots and marshallings of affairs, come best from those that are learned"—quite possibly the present leaders of Russia go all the way with Bacon on that point. Doubtless the history taught in the Russian system is even more mythological than in ours. But if Russian students are now learning thoroughly at least one foreign language, if thousands of them are encouraged to study Latin, if fifty-five percent of them are becoming acquainted with the old humanistic disciplines, then it is certain that within another generation Russia will be much more civilized than North America. As she will also be stronger in the materialistic sense, and have a better morale, it requires no feat of the imagination to see what this is going to mean for our descendants. They will (probably without conquest because conquest will be unnecessary) become a tired-out province in a world-state dominated by Moscow.

So the question would seem to be more urgent than most of us think: can anything be substituted for the classical tradition which is gone? Since men a century ago asked themselves what were the prime needs of democracy, and sought to satisfy them by building a new kind of education, we might do the same now. And it seems to me that our present needs can best be understood in terms of losses. What qualities, abilities and attitudes have we lost as a result of the abandonment of the humanistic tradition?

The first loss, I should say, is the virtual disappearance of the old belief that life is a coherent experience.

The second loss—the result of the first—is of the collective and individual self-confidence our forefathers knew, and which we ourselves knew for a brief while under Churchill's leadership in the last war.

The third loss—the result of the second—is the ancient respect for truth as something valuable and unassailable in itself, as something hard to find but precious, as something which cannot be juggled with by advertisers and politicians without regard to the final consequences, as something more important, however austere it may be, than conformity for the sake of comfort to any marketplace necessity of the moment.

The fourth loss—the result of the third—is the old belief that education cannot be easy, that it does not lead to material security but to struggle, that at its best it is a pilgrim's progress to the heavenly city.

Therefore I would say that education on all levels should get back to the primary business of education, which is to create an atmosphere in which these four losses will slowly be restored. In the long run the most important question, for a man or for a state, is simply this: "What is the will of God?" I use this latter word with apology and sometimes I think it should be retired from the language; it has been so debased that the people who use it seldom know themselves what they mean. Use "Creator" instead if you like; use "the Life-Force" or "the Prime-Mover of Motions"; use "Nature", so long as you understand that nature in this sense is something more than the provider of static raw material for laboratory research. But what is truth? What is the purpose of life? What is God's will?—what matters here is not that these questions can never be adequately answered. What matters is that they must be *asked* if a society is to survive. And my reason for stating this categorically is based on experience and on nothing else; it rests solidly on the recorded experience of the human race.

In order to create an atmosphere in which questions like these again become important, some drastic steps will have to be taken, especially on primary levels in the system. On the one hand the philosophy of "adjustment" will have to be thrown on the junk-heap; on the other, the schools will have to stop smattering and seek to prepare students for the marriage of the two basic disciplines: theoretical science on the one hand, on the other the humanities properly studied. This marriage can never become an intimate one; at best it can be only the marriage of Rilke's two solitudes which protect and touch and greet each other.

If this general philosophy of education is accepted, the next step is to stiffen the curriculum all the way down the line. I do not believe it is possible to restore the classics to the position they once occupied, though in a changed atmosphere I know that many more students would come forward to them than most people believe. But certainly the great books of our own and other languages which are the classics' inheritors can be used, as in some cases they are used even now.

But in order for them to be used properly, students must be taught to read, and by this I do not mean (in the phrase of Albert J. Nock) merely passing printed matter through the mind. Nobody can read and understand a book unless he himself knows how to write after a fashion, and to express himself in print with reasonable clarity. Reading still maketh the full man, and writing the exact one, and the reason why eighteenth-century people expressed themselves almost effortlessly was because they were trained to do so in the schools. They learned the use of their tools early in those days, and this brings me to another point in which it is a pleasure to call science itself to witness.

The neurologists have now proved that the old educational methods were better than ours for a reason beyond, apparently, any contradiction. When children are very young, their memories are excellent—better than they will ever be again—but their reasoning powers have not yet developed. This is not for psychological causes; it is for reasons purely physical, for reasons connected with the growth of the brain itself. By a method of trial and error, teachers in the past insisted on a vast deal of memory work in the lower grades. As a result, it was not difficult to produce a student aged fourteen who wrote passable Greek verse, who knew all his basic mathematics in his sleep, and at least one modern language.

If the cart had not been put before the horse in our educational system, the same results could be obtained now. With no hardship a good student could reach high school in reasonable command of two other languages besides his own. He could know his grammar and spelling. He could know his basic mathematics up to the stage of the calculus. He would have at his disposal the tools which a developing reason could then employ. As only a small proportion of the human race seems capable of thinking rationally, not all of the pupils could proceed much further. But the vital élite could, and the rest would be no worse, and much better, for the knowledge they had acquired. If Russian students have mastered one language and the calculus at the equivalent of our tenth grade, and as few of our present college graduates have done either of these things, it would seem that the case against the present system has been pretty thoroughly laid.

I will now follow Sir Philip Sidney's example and come to you with a tale. It may not hold children from play or old men from the chimney corner, but if all of its implications are taken in, it may give you the interesting sensation of mice dancing up and down on your spine. It certainly gave me that feeling when it happened, and still does whenever I remember it.

Shortly after the first election of Dwight D. Eisenhower to the presidency of the United States, I happened to be in Washington speaking at a luncheon held by the people who were backing the Seaway Bill in the Senate and Congress. I still don't know how I happened to get there, but somebody asked me and I went. After the speech was over, I realized that some of the audience had acquired the impression that I was a kind of trial balloon sent down unofficially to express the real views of the Canadian government on the matter. Nothing could have been farther from the case; I was even more private a person than I am now. But I soon found myself at a table in the bar of the Statler Hotel surrounded by politicians and lobbyists who fired questions at me, and who did not believe what I told them.

While the questioning was going on, I happened to look over my shoulder and see Dr. Robert Oppenheimer enter the room in company with another nuclear physicist. I guessed (correctly as it turned out when I had time to read the evening paper) that he was in Washington on atomic business, for he was at that time head of atomic research in the United States and the H-bomb was being built.

In order to change the subject, I said to the politicians: "I notice that a genius has come among us."

One of them glanced at Dr. Oppenheimer, did not recognize him, and when I told him the name, did not recognize that, either.

"What does he do for a living?" he asked.

"For a living, I suppose he's still director of the School for Advanced Studies in Princeton."

"A professor, ugh?"

I said that Dr. Oppenheimer was not a teaching professor, at least not principally, and that the Institute was no part of Princeton University. Then, assuming that everyone knew who Einstein was (he was still alive at the time) I added that the Institute was where Einstein had worked since his arrival in the United States.

The politician then looked at me, and with the sincerity of total innocence, he asked: "This Einstein, has he got anything real on the ball, or is it all theory?"

The politician, as I learned by looking up his record later in *Who's Who*, was a graduate of an American middle-western university.

8 REMEMBRANCE DAY, 2010 A.D.

The time has come, the President feels, when it is essential to pay the homage of a day of remembrance, and what we are required to remember is the period of our history, and especially the men who lived in it, which made possible the world we inhabit now.

Those men are so remote that in our eyes they seem almost like primitives, yet it must be understood that they had few of our advantages. In their time education by conditioned reflex was confined only to the elementary schools and to the outer selling fringes of commerce; they were burdened by a great weight of superstition from the pre-scientific past which made thinking such a dangerous activity that their most successful men found it impractical to think about anything above the level of a technical problem; wherever they looked they were surrounded by reactionaries who sapped their vitality by telling them that if they continued on the path they had chosen, they would destroy all human life on the planet Earth.

But they did continue; they defeated reaction by refusing to be reactionary; they did not call a halt. The President therefore feels that a tribute to these men of the sixth decade of the twentieth century is long overdue, and he has given me the assignment of telling their story.

As in most truly creative periods of history, events in the sixth decade of the twentieth century followed so fast on one another that the leaders had no understanding of what they were doing. They, too, were handicapped by superstitions inherited from the past: they went to church and they mouthed the old platitudes. Yet somehow they contrived in one part of their brain to live in the past and in another to live in the present. But whatever they may have said to the contrary, there can be no doubt that they acted according to the two great principles of psychology on which our present civilization rests and draws its power.

The first principle they accepted and made operative—one which today every conditioned child regards as self-evident—was simply this: *Man would sooner die than be bored*. The President feels that the acceptance of this principle at that particular time was the most remarkable leap the human mind had made since it accepted the earlier principle that the world is round and not flat.

Recall how people talked in those days. The reactionaries still babbled about the delights of peace, and insisted that true happiness comes only to the man who lives free of fear and anxiety. They even talked in hushed voices of the peace of God which passeth understanding, and failed to recognize that what passed their own understanding was that for men who lived as they did, and as we do, this so-called peace of God would far better have been named Hell. For how can a man whose nervous system has been conditioned by progress to repeated shocks, dislocations, surprises, terrors and wonders be happy if these stimuli are taken away from him? It is incredible, but the reactionaries of that time pretended that peace was what progressive man truly desires!

It was the manner of our grandfathers' acceptance of this dynamic principle, the President feels, which sheds a peculiar glory on them. On the other side of the world the Russians were behaving in their chronically efficient way: they had liquidated their reactionaries and closed those fonts of superstition, the churches. They had banned or rewritten the moral teachings of the pre-scientific past, and had compelled their satellites by brute force to live as they did themselves. It was easier for the Russians then, just as it is easier for them now. For our grandfathers, like ourselves, were compelled by their morality to obtain their results by the processes of democracy. They could not tolerate the idea of a satellite country; the countries in their orbit had to be their friends. They closed no churches, on the contrary they proclaimed it their duty to defend the principles on which these institutions rested. They jailed no reactionaries; instead they so honoured them that in a popularity poll two religious teachers called the Pope and Albert Schweitzer ranked close in esteem to the President himself. They listened with respectful attention to every negative argument advanced by men like these, they made available to them all the usual channels of publicity, and yet, without ever departing from the principles of democracy, they achieved the necessary results. With a rapidity which seems astonishing even to us, they advanced to the acceptance of the second great psychological principle which our children take for granted, the one we now call *The Love-Hate Syndrome*.

We have proof (so obvious that every child recognizes it) that the two most mighty forces in the world are love and hate: not love by itself or hate by itself, but love and hate working together like a pair of legs underneath the body. On the leg of love a nation can stand almost indefinitely, but it stands still; on the leg of hate a nation twitches so violently that it falls flat on its face, as happened to a country called Germany, now extinct, in the reign of a leader called Hitler, now forgotten. But if one leg is love and the other is hate, the nation advances on the run, and it accomplishes miracles under the spur of the chain reaction this syndrome sets in motion—pride and contempt, hope and despair, terror and relief. Under the Love-Hate Syndrome these psychic hormones are daily pumped into the national bloodstream, and progress not only becomes possible, it becomes irresistible.

To us the truth and value of this syndrome are self-evident, but not to the men of the sixth decade of the twentieth century, and that is one more reason why the President feels that it is essential to give you some more information about them.

The chief of their many superstitions was the one they called Christianity. Democracy in those days was so committed to defend the Christian religion that its leaders never dared to make a public speech without mentioning God, never went to war without claiming they did so to preserve the spirit of brotherly love and never did anything without being quick to inform the people they would have been unable to do it without God's guidance. They still honoured a book—though few of them seem to have read it—called the Bible, and at the President's suggestion I myself obtained a copy from the inner vault where it is kept side by side with the Constitution and the old Declaration of Independence. Let me tell you a little about this book.

To begin with, it is the most dangerous book ever compiled. If it were widely read and supported today, and if people believed even a fraction of what it contains, civilization as we know it would not endure as long as a single year. The chief author of the official superstition was a man who possessed astonishing powers of language—far greater,

I freely admit, than those of our present Minister of Education. This man, who was liquidated by some ancient government so long ago it does not matter when, declared that it is impossible for a human being to serve two masters, his theory being that he will love the one and despise the other. He said that nobody can serve both God and Mammon, or gain the world and save his soul, or be happy and miserable at the same time. Repeatedly he talked about the beauties of peace and brotherly love, even carrying his argument to the point that we should love our enemies. So pervasive was this man's propaganda in the sixth decade of the twentieth century that even the Russians—this is almost incredible but it is true—paid constant lip service to it. Whenever the Russians of that time made a war, their leaders never failed to say they were establishing peace. Whenever they butchered a satellite, they announced they were coming to the aid of the peace-loving citizens within the satellite.

The Russians, we may believe, were cynical in these statements as they are in the statements they make today. But our grandfathers were not cynical. They really believed that they desired peace and they really believed that they were acting according to Christian principles when they made those great decisions which resulted in the Love-Hate Syndrome becoming operative once and for all in our democratic society.

The President feels, and so do I, that if we are to pay our grandfathers the proper meed of respect we must fully appreciate the appalling technical problem they faced. For consider some of the facts.

Then, as now, the world was divided into the two systems. Our grandfathers loved their system as no system had ever been loved before, and they hated the Russian system as no system had ever been hated. The Russian attitude was ours in reverse. And when the Love-Hate Syndrome became operative, the tension it set up, the creative tension, drove both systems to achievements greater than its citizens could comprehend.

Our system built a bomb which annihilated a single city in a minute; the Russians matched it a few years later. The Russians then built a bomb which would obliterate a whole province; we matched it in a matter of months. We built a submarine which could fire a rocket from the floor of the ocean and hit a target hundreds of miles away; the Russians countered with an earth-satellite useless in itself, but terrifying in its implication that they possessed stronger rockets than we. We fired off a fusillade of rockets into space, some of them so far we lost track of them, and then set frantically to work catching up with the Russians in this important department of technological culture. Within a matter of a year and a half, progress on both sides was so rapid that thousands of rockets were zero-ed in on every important city, air base and military target in the world.

Think what a technical problem this situation created! For a time of several years not only the life of every human being, but technical progress itself, hung on the balance of a hair-trigger! Imagine if you can the nerve the people of our grandfathers' day possessed to live like this and act like this!

It was of course easier for the Russians than for us, for the Russian leaders were not democratic and had silenced all their reactionaries. But our reactionaries were not silent, far from it. "Call it off!" they howled. "Call it off before we're all dead!" In their response to this final challenge, the President feels, our grandfathers saved civilization. For to the cry, "Call it off before we're all dead!" they answered, in effect, "We'd sooner be dead than call it off!"

Without their being able to understand it, the Love-Hate

Syndrome was saving them. By making it impossible to yield to the Russians in any particular, it was already transforming their entire society in such a way as to eradicate all traces of the reactionary superstitions which hitherto had held it back. Under the spur of love of country and hate of the enemy, of fear and competition, of hope and despair, of all these emotions which are now our common spiritual food, our grandfathers reformed their whole educational system. They scrapped every element which did not directly pertain to science, engineering and propaganda. They let their old so-called humanists and religious teachers wither on the vine. They bred a generation—us—so progressively-minded that nothing has been able to hold us back.

At the last moment, in the very nick of time, their faith was justified. For at the very instant when their nerves, and the Russians' nerves, were at the snapping point, the progress which had been set in motion by the Love-Hate Syndrome crossed a new frontier. The moon was occupied by human beings.

The President feels no shame in having me admit that it was the Russians, and not ourselves, who established the first actual base on the moon with flesh and blood humans in it, for the establishment of this base was important only in so far as it proved that it was now possible for both systems to continue doing what they liked doing and survive. It outmoded the old technical problem of how the Love-Hate Syndrome, plus progress, could continue to operate full blast without annihilating all life on the planet. It made it not only possible, it made it inevitable, that we could now engage in the all-out war for which we had planned and prepared ourselves for years.

Within three days of the establishment of the Russian base on the moon, we established one of our own about five hundred miles distant. A meeting of international lawyers, quickly convened in Calcutta to argue points of ownership and establish a treaty whereby our system could share the moon with Russia, broke up with mutual abuse, and before the lawyers were half-way home the rockets were moving moon-wards and our base and the Russian base were simultaneously obliterated. In the political sense the First Battle of the Moon ended in a draw, but in the technical sense it did not. After computations had been made, our scientists were able to prove that the force of our explosions exceeded those of the Russians by some half a million megatons.

The first space war was now on, and try to imagine what a feeling of release, what a sense of joy swept through the minds of men when they realized that the wonderful devices they had been stock-piling for years could actually be used! Instead of outmoding them before they were employed, now each new model could be sent instantly into action. More than this was proved by the First Battle of the Moon. It was proved that our way of life could now go on indefinitely and that progress would never cease.

The decade following the First Battle of the Moon was the most spectacular in the history of the universe up to the present time. In less than a year and a half, working on two separate crash programs, our electronic engineers and lense-makers beat the Russians in producing telescopic television which relayed from space platforms the planetary expeditions from the moment of their setting out to their final obliteration when the rockets found them. Our democratic ingenuity enabled us to overcome what had hitherto seemed an insuperable obstacle, that of transmitting sound through space itself. But we beat the Russians to it, and by the first decade of the present century we had in operation twelve different channels which enabled our citizens to follow the planetary wars and even to hear faint echoes of the explosions. We beat the Russians in sound by two and a half months, and our programmes were always better than theirs because they were more democratic, while the Russians stultified theirs by interrupting them constantly with mechanical voices which repeated propaganda from empty space.

Now I must change the key of this message; I must tell you the real reason why the President feels it necessary for us to observe a day of remembrance in honour of the men who made possible the world we now inhabit. It is because he thinks the time is at hand when we, too, will require all the nerve and courage at our disposal if we are not to fail. He feels, and I agree with him, that now is the time to remember that if our ancestors could keep their nerve, so also can we.

The government of Russia—the possibility had long been foreseen, despite the election propaganda of the President's opponent—is now in the hands of a lunatic. How he got there cannot be explained beyond mentioning that in Russian history there has always been a high frequency of insanity in the higher echelons of government. This creature now threatens to blow up the world unless he gets his own way. And the President, who has always been frank with the people, feels that it is right and proper that the situation be laid fairly before them, in order that the people may decide for themselves on the course of action they will follow. He has full confidence that the people will decide rightly.

As you know, the Russians have been established on Venus for a year, a move which was inevitable after we decided it was necessary to blow up the moon in order to provide ourselves with a sufficient number of adequate space platforms for further scientific experiments, and also for an improved television service. The Russian advance to

Venus made it inevitable that we should advance to Mars, where we have been established for five months. Both of these outer bases have been inactive up to the present, pending completion of television stations on the fragments of the moon which will enable us to follow the operations farther out. Military operations are scheduled to begin, however, the moment our super-television service is ready, and they will begin on schedule about nine months from now unless the Russians beat us to it, which hardly seems probable.

But now, owing to the state of mind of the Russian leader, we are faced with the gravest crisis in a quarter of a century. He has stated that unless we withdraw from Mars, he will attack us in our own heartland. When the President first learned of this threat, he of course made the routine answer that if the Russians annihilated us, we would also annihilate them. But intelligence has since confirmed that the Russian leader is a genuine psychotic, and not merely the emotionally unstable brute we assume all Russian leaders to be. His answer to the President's message must be taken with extreme seriousness, and his actual words must be reported. What he transmitted to the President was the briefest, crudest, and most uncivilized note in the history of diplomacy. It was this: "I don't care whether you get me so long as I get you. Get off Mars."

I don't think it necessary to say that the President does not contemplate for an instant yielding to a threat of this nature. But he feels, and surely he is right, that the public should understand that the threat is real. This lunatic really means what he says. He has literally put the rocket to our heads.

That is why the President believes that we should observe a day of remembrance in honour of our grandfathers who outfaced a danger equally great, and a future equally uncertain, and did not fail their destiny. At that time, ignorant though they were, they knew if they showed a moment's weakness they would merely encourage the worst elements in the Russian government. The situation is precisely the same now. If we withdraw from Mars, it will mean only one thing to Russia: that our nerve is failing. But if we stand firm, even knowing that this lunatic means literally what he says, who knows what may happen? Our grandfathers stood firm, and just at the moment when their obliteration seemed inevitable, they were saved by the Russian action in occupying the moon. There are a variety of ways in which we can be saved now, provided we stand firm. This Russian will not lose his nerve, because lunatics never do. But is it unreasonable to suppose that he will be liquidated by his own cabinet? Horrible though the Russian cabinet members are, they are not lunatics. And they are—we might as well admit it—as progressively-minded as ourselves.

Here, then, is the political reason for our day of remembrance. If, at the height of our present crisis, we take out a day to honour the men who made our civilization possible, we will give to the Russians the clearest possible proof that our nerves are staunch and that we will never yield. And the very stars in their courses will fight on our side, for they are up there, billions of them, waiting to be visited, exploited or blown up by us. Our technology is more lovable than the Russian technology, and in the end it is bound to prevail. We are only beginning. We have just reached the outer fringes of the Solar System. Can any sane man possibly argue that we should stop there?

9 CONFESSIONS OF A WOOD-CHOPPING MAN

Pleasure, profit and beauty from a single afternoon's exercise—what more could a puritan ask, especially when the profit will not be reaped till next year, and the beauty harvested for years to come. As for the pleasure, merely to be alive on an Indian summer afternoon in my part of the country is as close to heaven as my imagination extends.

After the first frost has turned ferns to brown dust and the birds have flocked south, the woods around my house in the country are filled with the living presence of silence. My feet crunch outrageously in the dry undergrowth as I make my way to the heart of the grove. My jeans are stiff with ancient sweat and my jersey is out at the elbows, the red paint has long ago been rubbed off the bow of my Swedish saw and my axe blade, several ounces lighter than when I bought it nine years ago, is honed sharp enough to sever a hair on my forearm. Looking up to the sky through the leaf-patterns I shame my environment by the academic thought that this scene is the equal of Sainte-Chapelle, but the comparison lasts only a few seconds. A hardwood copse in the Eastern Townships of Quebec in Indian summer can be compared to nothing else on this earth, being itself an absolute.

By some recurring good fortune I am here; I am here with the axe, the saw, the wedge and the determination to alter the landscape a little. It is a moment that involves every aspect of the slow change in my whole view of life over the past decade and a half.

I was born and raised in a part of Canada where nobody is able to change the landscape. Along the Atlantic coast of Nova Scotia you grow up with the conviction that everything in nature here is as it is forever, and that man, living with the shifting immutability of the ocean and the unshifting immutability of granite rocks, can never dominate his fate, never play artist with nature, but must take life and the world as he finds them. The glacier that set the mould of the Nova Scotia coast (and the coast set the mould of the Nova Scotian character) so denuded the rocks of topsoil that for evermore only a spruce will thrive there. From childhood I accepted the belief that summer, spring and fall are much the same. One is grateful for a spruce if it is the only tree one really knows, but since any spruce is much the same as any other, and since no spruce ever changes its colours, the trees of my childhood helped the granite and the ocean to confirm me in the belief that nature can neither be altered nor improved.

It took me a good many years to respond to the soft luxuriance of the Eastern Townships, where the eye, the ear and the sense of smell are played upon gently and with subtle variations. It took me no time at all, however, to learn that here the landscape can and must be altered from time to time because it is continually altering itself to your disadvantage. A house in the country for summer living must be tied to the earth by close plantings of shrubs and trees, to give protection from the winds and to take away its aspect of being a brash intruder. But a maple sapling grows eight feet a year in this rich, rainy land, and a small fir that looks like an incipient Christmas tree when you transplant it soon becomes a dense screen breeding swarms of blackflies. Where there was one butternut there is soon a grove, and within a decade the pasture in which your house was built has been taken over by a stand of maples, oaks, poplars, wild cherries, honey locusts, old appletrees, hornbeams, birches, beeches and even some stray pines. Their roots are now under your cottage, their branches are joined over your roof, and they have made your home as dark as an animal's den.

The year I bought my house, I cut away every cedar, pine and spruce that crowded it. This was an act with a double meaning for me. I intended to let the sun filter down through the branches of the great hardwoods farther back, and I also needed a symbol of emancipation from the stern acceptance of my youth, I suppose.

"You'll feel naked without some kind of protection, won't you?" said a neighbour. "Now there's only the garden and the lawn between you and the road."

He meant that *he* would; I felt as though cobwebs had been swept from a dirty window. What good to keep other people from looking in, if at the same time I was prevented from looking out? Anyway I live high on a hill away from the village, on a dirt road that leads to nowhere, and the passers-by are few and friendly. Since my land slopes at a twenty-five degree angle and the road is below the house, I can overlook any activity on the road and let my eye take in a view that extends for ten miles over a deep lake indented with bays that lap the feet of thrusting hills. I can look across wind-blown farms and red pine headlands and the shining roofs of new cattle barns.

I began to cut in order to get sun and air into the house and I continued to cut in order to get sun and air into the surrounding woods. The second year I was mildly surprised to discover that the wood I cut had saved me many dollars. Then I bought a lot across the road and down the hill to protect our view. But the view gradually disappeared behind a wall of rapidly growing trees. They were a fine mixture of greens in summer and an unbelievable blend of colours in the fall, but living with them in front of me was like living behind a seventy-foot hedge.

So, over the years, those rapidly growing trees have given a pattern to my life in much the same way that his rotating wheat fields pattern the life of the farmer. Come the fall and I must get to work on them.

I have a neighbour who thinks it a crime to cut any oak, but what do you do if you have two oaks within six feet of one another? I run my hand over the smooth, olive-green trunk and feel the hard muscles inside the bark. An oak, especially a young one, feels human when your hand strokes it. But more than any tree in the forest, the oak needs room to grow. Its roots spread wide and lie close to the surface of the earth. I look up at this pair and see that they have grown like basketball players, tall, thin and not much good for anything else but growing tall and thin. Their lowest branches are at least twenty-five feet above the ground, since it was always dark in here before I got busy cutting out the saplings, and the trees had to thrust high in order to reach the life-giving sun. I feel the trunks of both and decide that the spindlier one must go, to give the other a chance to fulfil the destiny of an oak.

So I go down on both knees, set the saw at the trunk of the victim and get to work. In such a close-grained tree the opening made by the slim saw-blade is almost invisible once the saw has buried itself in the trunk. White dust spurts out, to become brown as the blade reaches the darker heart of the tree. Then comes the crack—hard, solid, vibrating up the entire length of the trunk and echoing through the silent copse. There is a shiver, a twitch in the pinky-brown plumage, a moment of hesitation. As I stand up and watch, one hand on the trunk, the tree nods in the direction I had intended it to fall, then goes down in a swooshing, stately plunge. There is a flash of scarlet as a maple is brushed on the way down. Inevitably the oak comes to rest at an angle, its cascading upper branches caught by the interlocking branches of neighbouring trees.

In the new silence I consider my next move. A fallen tree, even one as modest as this, creates a sizable wreckage. I think of Mr. Gladstone, who used to slay giant oaks, Royal Navy oaks, to relieve his emotions. When Disraeli was extraordinarily witty or the Queen ordinarily rude, another oak on the estate of the Grand Old Man was doomed to fall. And then there was the labour of cleaning up the mess, a job that I know from experience must have taken days. So far as I can discover from my reading, the Prime Minister gave little thought to this aspect of forestry. He was able to sate his aggressions and stalk off, sweaty under the armpits but with his Victorian waistcoat still in place, while humbler men took over the long task of trimming the oak, sawing its trunk into logs, splitting them and trundling them into the woodshed. Humbler men without the need to sublimate a libido must have stacked and burned Mr. Gladstone's slash.

Perhaps the psychiatrist who lives below me on his own tree-enclosed acreage, hearing the crash of my falling oak, thinks I am ridding myself of aggressions, too. He may even think I am slaying a father-image. But no matter what he thinks, my oak has merely been severed at the base, it has not been transformed into cordwood.

It was cold last night. It was colder still at six this morning when I peered out at the thermometer and saw that the mercury stood at twenty-seven degrees. When I got out of bed at eight and built a fire there was still rime on the lawn. The day was fine and clear, but it was so cold my fireplace consumed ten logs before one o'clock. This year a short cord sells at seven dollars, a long cord at anything from fifteen to twenty depending on what kind of wood it contains. No matter what my woodpile represents to a psychologist, it gives me an intense pleasure to use it for warmth, even though (as the countrywoman remarked yesterday when she came in to clean the house) it takes a lot of sweat to build a woodpile.

I think, sometimes, that Mr. Gladstone missed the best part of tree-cutting. Each fallen tree presents its own problems, and the man who walks off and leaves them is as bad a tree-butcher as the one who murders a copse with a power saw. This oak of mine is entangled with two other trees and of course the simplest thing to do is cut them both down so that all three are prone. But the tree supporting the oak on the left is a rowan, a fugitive from an old garden, probably, and under no circumstances, under absolutely none, will I cut a rowan tree in my own woods. The other is a rock maple, a tree which still fills me with wonder and joy because it was scarce in Nova Scotia and in England almost non-existent. I always have a twinge of conscience when I cut down a maple. But here the maples grow like weeds and this particular one is so close to the rowan it will rob it of nutriment as both try to grow. So the maple goes, and the crack of its fall echoes over the hill.

Still the oak is suspended; when the maple went, its weight was taken by more stuff beyond. There is nothing for it but to cut the oak down to size in the only way left. I start sawing the trunk in eight-foot lengths, each cut about four and a half feet above the ground, which is as high as I can drive the saw. With the entire tree exerting hundreds of pounds of pressure on the saw blade, I must use the wedge. And this means that for the rest of the afternoon these two trees, the oak and the maple, are going to keep me busy.

Towards sunset the logs are piled and split and fragrant, the slash dragged off into a great angular pile to dry and await my pleasure on a future moist day. I come out of the copse and look to see what effect my work has made on the landscape. A little, and the beginning of a lot, because a splendid butternut has now been uncovered and must be given its chance. With that poplar out of the way the sun will slant deeply into the copse and I will have the beginnings of a woodland nave. A forest without sun is like a church without God; I reflect that the thought is corny, but I don't care. Disposing of the poplar will put no burden on my conscience. Along with a ragged spruce, it exists to be destroyed, for if the axe doesn't get to it the insects will, and after the insects will come the flickers and the pileated woodpeckers. Tomorrow afternoon's work is now planned, and it, in turn, will lead to the work of the day after and the day after that. Carving out the raw material of a forest to create a civilized wood is like making a picture or writing a book. One vista suggests another and there is no absolute end to it in a country like ours. But when the season's cutting is over after Thanksgiving, and I go muscle-bound back to the city, I feel as Melville did when he finished *Moby Dick*, as pure as the lamb.

10 A DISQUISITION ON ELMER

Ever since I was a student and occupied a seat next to a boy called McCunn I have been fascinated by some of the names human beings are known by. There is history in them; there is romance in the thought that from obscure semi-bronze-age origins presidents appear; in some names there is evolution, in others devolution. How strange that the seed of a cowherd should blossom centuries later in the playwright of *Private Lives*. The original Turnbull, who turned a bull from the pants of King Robert the Bruce, fathers a clan which culminates in the inventor of the variable pitch propeller. Daniel Boone, that noble American primitive, almost certainly carries bluer blood in his veins than he ever guessed, for the original spelling of Boone was Bohun, and the Bohuns were Norman barons as aristocratic as they were wicked. Even my own name has a history, albeit a sordid one. It started as Logan, but a chief of that name was killed by the Frasers in an unsuccessful rustling expedition, his son was captured and the Frasers broke the boy's back lest he grow into a warrior able to avenge his father. So young Logan entered the Celtic Church, married (as many Celtic priests did at that time), chose as his patron an obscure Gaelic saint called Finian, and left behind him a little brood which later proliferated into one of the weakest clans in Scotland. Their tartan was on the loud side, but even among the Scotch their motto was notable for its lack of optimism: *While There's Life, There's Hope*, they said in Latin on their crest, and their war-cry, translated from the Gaelic, was "The Ridge of Tears". Few of us ever amounted to much, and the only one mentioned in the *Britannica* is an Edinburgh Victorian who wrote a book on the sexual habits of savages. I have never learned whether he left Scotland in order to do it.

You can play the name-game indefinitely if you stick to surnames, but there is not much point in it because nobody can help his surname. Given names are more informative. Especially are they informative in the United States, where they tend to be either fantastic or to prove something about their owners.

Why an American admiral was called Husband Kimmel, an American press agent E. Toxen Worm, an American ad-man Orison Swett, an American baseball commissioner Kenesaw Mountain Landis, an American outfielder Tyrus Cobb, an American Judge Learned Hand—these are mysteries which can be dissipated only if you know the families involved. But there is no mystery about the politics of Franklin Delano Roosevelt Jones, about the religions of Calvin Coolidge and Urban Shocker, about the uniform worn in the Civil War by Abolition Smith, or the feelings entertained towards Truman's State Department by the father of little Joseph McCarthy Czluzewski. More than any other people on earth, the Americans think a given name should signify something.

The Americans have also been much influenced by ideological and social fashions in the giving of personal names. Of all the nations theirs is the most principled and commemorative, the most determined to show where it stands on basic issues. From Plymouth Rock until now, there has been a strong American tendency to enlist personal names into the service of right opinion. In puritan New England it was right opinion to oppose Episcopalianism in all its forms, and as most Episcopalians and all Roman Catholics called their children after saints, the early New Englanders repudiated all the saints except the Twelve Apostles, St. Paul and his helpers. This saved a lot of time and trouble. There was no need to ask Jedediah Brown how he felt about bishops; you simply asked for his name in full and then you knew how he felt about almost everything.

A century after the witch-burnings it was the right opinion in the United States to be hostile to kings and in favour of written constitutions. So Greek and Roman names came into style, the Americans of the period having the quaint notion that all Greeks and Romans were good republicans. Hence Ulysses Grant and Romulus Lycurgus Hanks. You did not have to ask either of these men where they stood in politics; their names proclaimed it. The Civil War produced its army of little Shermans, Sheridans and Lincolns in the northern states, while a counter army of Beauregards, Lees and Jefferson Davises burgeoned in the south. Now the full gamut has been run from the prophets to Hollywood, from Abigail to Shirley. If you meet a young American woman called Shirley today, you can be pretty certain that her age lies somewhere between twenty-three and thirty-one.

Whether these changes of fashion in American nomenclature represent a decadence is a matter I leave to Arnold Toynbee, but the decadence has clearly not gone the whole way, for there is one American given-name which has survived all changes in fashion from Cotton Mather to Eisenhower. That is Elmer. There have always been Elmers in the United States, and there are none anywhere else except in a few Canadian families of United Empire Loyalist extraction.

Why Elmer? From the first time I heard the name I have wondered.

"I don't know," one Elmer said to me. "I guess there's always been an Elmer in our family."

"I never even thought about it," said another.

"Elmer is a rube name," said a New Yorker who wasn't called it. "Haven't you ever heard W. C. Fields' joke?"

As time passed, Elmer began to haunt me, nor did a search through historical records do anything but deepen the mystery of its origin. There aren't any Elmers. No Elmer (the surname, I mean) appears in the Testaments Old or New, none in the passenger list of the *Mayflower*, none among the Roman and Greek regicides, none among the signers of the Declaration, the early Abolitionists or the Civil War generals. Moreover, none of the people of the name I have ever met seem to have the slightest notion of how the name got into their families.

Yet the idea persisted in my mind that Elmer, in the American beginning, stood for someone or something which seemed pretty important to the first Americans who bestowed it on their sons. It was basic; it was uniquely American and always had been. All the Elmers I knew had names derived from the British Isles. All of them seemed to be sectarian Protestants. There were more of them in the north than in the south, and more in the corn belt than anywhere else. Find the principle behind Elmer, I thought, and you will solve the riddle of Elmer.

If you stay with an idea long enough you are bound to learn something about it, and this is how I finally learned about Elmer.

A few years ago I drove across the United States west to east, and on the second day out of Los Angeles I stopped for the night in a small town on the Arizona plateau called Flagstaff. In the bar of the only hotel was a considerable crowd of people in western dress, both real and phony, and one of them who looked at least half-real was making a great deal of noise. He was huge, fat and wore a ten-gallon hat, he was a braggart and his voice sounded like a cement mixer working unnecessarily hard. He left after half an hour.

Beside me at the bar while all the noise was going on had sat a tall, thin, silent man about sixty years old with a face eroded by wind and sand. He turned to me and said: "Yew like thet fella?"

I said I was a stranger and didn't know that fella.

"Yew don't hev to know a fella," the lean man said, "to hate his guts."

After this exchange he was silent for ten minutes. Then he turned to me again.

"Year ago," he said, "I shot thet fella. Sideways. Through the ass."

I expressed appropriate surprise and the man was silent for another five minutes. Then he spoke once more.

"Yew like them auto-mobiles with four-note hawns?"

"Not particularly."

"There's a lotta things I don't like, I guess."

Another silence ensued before he started again.

"Thet fella thet was in here, he had an auto-mobile with a four-note hawn. Used to go around town nights a-blowin' of his hawn and awakin' of people outer their beds and feelin' mighty big."

Another silence.

"Third night he done thet, I sed to my wife, 'I guess I don't hev to stand fer this.' So I tuk my rifle and I opened the window and there he was, a-leanin' on his car and a-blowin' on his four-noter and feelin' mighty big. So I tuk a bead and I guess thet stopped it."

Another silence, but a little shorter this time.

"Sideways," the thin man said reflectively. "More across the ass than through it. Didn't chip the bone any. Jest kinda stung him up a bit."

I looked at the grim face, the lantern jaws, the sand-pitted skin, the pale blue eyes, the crisp white hair.

"One little thing I don't get here," I said. "You say you shot this man. How can the two of you drink in the same bar after that?"

Another silence.

"Maybe we couldn't at thet, if he knew who done it. But he don't. Folks knew though." Silence. "Folks was pleased." Silence. "I never did like them four-note hawns. There's a lot of things I never did like, I guess."

After this we got into a general conversation during which he learned I came from Canada and I learned that he didn't think the Russians were so tough. Finally he gave me his card and in large, uncompromisingly plain lettering I read the name of Elmer Z. Stebbins. So the hunt for Elmer was on again.

"No," he said, "I can't say I know where the Elmer come from. The zee is easy. It's for Zebadee and Zebadee is in the Bible."

"Were you born in Arizona?"

"Arkansas," he said. "My dad was born in Missouri and his dad come down from West Virginia, for our family keeps movin'. My grandad tol' me there are Stebbinses back east thet are big shots with dough, but us, we don't have dough and we never bin big shots. Guess we never stuck around long enough for the moss to grow. Take my son. A lot of things in Flagstaff he didn't like, so he moves on to L.A. Take his son. Wouldn't be serprised if his son ends up in Honnaloola."

"Is your son's name Elmer too?" I asked.

"How'd yew guess?"

"I don't want to seem curious, but did your family come west from New England?"

"How'd yew guess? Salem. My grandad was a great one fer history, and he tol' me us Stebbinses were original Americans from the start."

"And there's always been an Elmer?"

"I guess most of the time yew'd be about right about thet."

"It's a name I've always liked," I said. "And I've been wondering where it came from. I was wondering if you'd know."

His grim, impassive face looked into mine, pleased, but eager not to show it.

"Thet's mighty interestin' you bein' interested in thet. Elmer was a preacher, my grandad said, and a mighty fine one."

And so help me, Mr. Stebbins turned out to be right!

A few weeks ago I happened to be searching a little-read American reference book for a word to fit a double-crostic and suddenly—I would have missed it had I not been subconsciously primed—I saw what I had been looking for these twenty-five years. "Elmer:" the book said in black print. "See Aylmer." So I did see Aylmer.

John Aylmer, the man responsible for the fact that hundreds of thousands of American boys are called Elmer, was indeed a preacher and his name (in the seventeenth century it would have been pronounced Elmer) was a famous one in the history of early church controversy. Born in 1521, born to trouble as the sparks of his own cantankerous character flew upward, he went to Cambridge and later became tutor to the unfortunate Lady Jane Grey, and Jane's father, the Marquis of Dorset, thought so highly of his work that he obtained for him the archdeaconry of Stow.

It was then that John Aylmer sealed the fate of those hundreds of thousands of unborn American boys. For he discovered there were a lot of things about the Established Church he did not like, one of them being the current view on the all-important matter of transubstantiation. He was against transubstantiation, and said so, and since being against transubstantiation at that time was a burning matter in England, Aylmer fled for his life to Calvin and Knox in Geneva. There were a lot of things he did not like in Geneva, one being John Knox himself, and by the time Mary Tudor died and Elizabeth ascended the throne, Aylmer was glad enough to escape from the Calvinists. He returned to England, in the course of time he was advanced to the see of London by the Queen, and in that capacity made more enemies than any bishop in the history of that stormy diocese. He ended hostile to everyone, the Puritans included.

But what difference did that make to the founders of New England? John Aylmer had started the ball rolling that finally rolled across the sea into Massachusetts Bay. He had been an authentic puritan hero before the puritan movement even began. And besides, he had a name much more pleasant and pronounceable than Jedediah.

I was so fascinated by this discovery that I almost wrote to Elmer Z. Stebbins in Flagstaff to tell him about it, but I reflected that I would not be able to find him in Flagstaff.

"There's a lotta things about this town," he had told me before we parted, "thet I dont' like."

"You'll be moving on?" I asked him.

"Guess so," said Elmer.

11 SIR JOHN

It was with a mixture of feelings that would be amusing to an Englishman and incomprehensible to an American that I finished reading Donald Creighton's superb two-decker life of Sir John A. Macdonald. In these volumes *(The Young Politician* and *The Old Chieftain)*, our greatest citizen comes alive again, and when I put the book down I felt that bugles ought to be blowing all around me. I was annoyed that they weren't and chagrined to the point of teeth-grinding because I knew why they weren't. For Macdonald's country isn't England or the United States; it is Canada. And in one respect above all others, Canada is dismally like the Scotland from which so many of our ancestors came.

There is no group of people anywhere on the earth's surface that think more highly of their collective selves than the Scotch do, nor any other in which the great native individual is reduced by public opinion to a mere Lilliputian size. Not since John Knox have the Scotch, in their innermost hearts, been able to believe that a native-born Scot can be much more than a native-born Scot. Whenever a Scotchman becomes a world-figure, his own people lose all capacity to understand him or even to believe he is real. When foreigners praise him they will admit to a certain pride, and the pride is genuine, *but* . . . that word "but" is endemic in the soul of Scotland.

It is also endemic in the soul of Canada, for otherwise how could Canadians have been so consistently blind to the true position of Sir John Macdonald in world history? Not merely in Canadian history, but in world history!

Another of my feelings when I finished Creighton's book was sadness. How few of the truly great ones live long enough to see time justify their vast expense of spirit and genius! Rare indeed is Winston Churchill. Shakespeare died thinking himself a passing shadow on a stage, Lincoln wondering whether the surgery he had performed on his country might not still kill the patient from the after-effects of shock. In the last days of his final exhaustion, Sir John Macdonald knew that he had finished his course and done his best, but as he claimed no intimate communion with the Beyond as Mackenzie King did, he could hardly have guessed how superlative and far-reaching his best had been. All his life he had been called a colonial leader, and the British and most of his own countrymen took it for granted that a colonial leader who eschews revolutionary courses must automatically be regarded as a statesman of the second class. Honours he had received from England in abundance, but the kind of honours an exceptionally good colonial steward might have expected. He never received the supreme honour of a total understanding of what his life's work was going to mean to future generations in countries scattered all over the earth. He could not possibly have guessed that a time would come when he would be ranked among the three or four supreme statesmen of the entire nineteenth century.

That time has not come yet, not even in his own country,

for we have allowed him to become too remote from us. Between ourselves and Sir John have intervened two wars and the remorseless tedium of Mackenzie King; a public style has been set which makes his gallant, gay and tragic humanity seem a little in bad taste, a little—how shall we say it?—not quite the thing one expects to find in the head of state in Ottawa. Also since his death in 1891 the art of biography has made prodigious strides in nations with mature literary traditions, with the result that the illustriousness of the famous dead has come to depend as much on their biographers as on their own achievements. By a process of literary osmosis we Canadians have absorbed the great ones of other lands and have allowed the best of our own to become mere names, because the best of our own have lacked biographers with the art to bring them alive. We know Lincoln, Gladstone and Disraeli, some of us even know Melbourne better than we know Sir John Macdonald, so if ever a book were needed in this country, it is Donald Creighton's, for if it does nothing else, it will give Sir John back to us again. It will make us understand that our public life was not always the dry-as-dust thing it became during the interminable reign of the Incredible One.

Not with a chip on my shoulder, least of all in a spirit of boosting jingoism, but rather with the sensations of a boxer getting up off his stool expecting the next round to be a repetition of the ones already fought, I am going to stick out my chin for Donald Creighton and Sir John and stick it out as far as it will go. Creighton is too wise an historian to make the kind of comparisons I am going to make, but in these days of national and international rankings perhaps the only way to make people take Sir John seriously is to throw down a challenge that will startle them.

If a statesman's stature is to be measured by the magnitude and difficulty of his task, by the beneficence and durability of its results, by the weight of the responsibility he has had to carry, by the style with which he conducted himself—for surely in politics style is as important as it is in art—then who else can you find in the whole roster of nineteenth-century statesmen who can rightly be ranked ahead of Sir John Macdonald?

Abraham Lincoln certainly. But Gladstone and Disraeli mainly on the ground that the weight of their responsibilities, subjectively speaking, was greater; they had empires on their hands and the balance of power in Europe. Yet neither of them had Sir John's clear vision of the future and both, Disraeli especially, were spokesmen for an era's end. Palmerston simply does not rate at all, not if you subtract from his reputation the noise he made and the self-satisfaction he gave to millions of English clerks who thrilled to the news that another British gunboat was teaching the Chinamen wot was wot. Bismarck? Since the chief result of Bismarck's activities has been the career of modern Germany, why bother even considering him in such a context? No, my friends, it is not easy to dig out of nineteenth-century history the peer of the first prime minister of Canada.

This frail-looking man with the immense and rueful patience of the Celt combined with the Celt's nervous fire, with an eighteenth-century lust for life and an eighteenth-century frankness in showing it; this utterly masculine man with so much woman in him that in old age his face—as do the faces of so many great old men—began to resemble a grandmother's of strange and incalculable powers; this lonely man flashing gay out of his inner solitude yet driven at times by private grief and his own insights to drown his senses in brandy; this statesman who understood that without chicanery statesmanship is powerless, yet never for an instant mistook means for ends or hypnotized himself by his own powers of hypnotizing others—Donald Creighton has restored him to us after many years, he has restored him alive and breathing, and now that he is alive and breathing we can see from a new vantage point of history the magnitude of his achievement.

Confederated Canada and the British Commonwealth of Nations—both still growing, both with their greatest days still lying ahead, both, we trust, beneficent to mankind—these were his achievements, and with the single exception of Lincoln, what other statesman of the nineteenth century can match that record?

It can be argued, indeed it is almost assumed, that without Sir John's genius Canada and the Commonwealth would have come into being anyway. But the more you study the mass of evidence compiled and arranged by Creighton, the more impossible it becomes to accept the theory, flattering though it be in this epoch of the Common Man, that bumper political harvests grow naturally like weeds, or that skilfully contrived edifices build themselves. Quite a number of enlightened British statesmen, together with leaders of Australia, New Zealand, South Africa and latter-day Indians, Ceylonese and Pakistani, even Mackenzie King himself, have united in increasing the harvest implicit in the Commonwealth idea. But Sir John was the chief gardener who planted the seeds, cultivated and fertilized the soil and nursed the young shoots. Nor for a moment did he think that the Commonwealth idea would have a chance of success if Canada, the first Dominion, failed.

The more one reads of those early days, the more certain it is that Sir John was the one indispensable man. Loyal helpers he certainly had, some of them governors-general who came to understand that he was far more than a mere colonial steward. In Cartier he had an invaluable and loyal lieutenant, in Tupper a vigorous one, but neither of these men was in the class of the Old Chieftain. Perhaps one can measure his quality best by considering the only other contemporary Canadian who equalled him in magnetism, Joseph Howe. For all his courage and intelligence, Howe was a far smaller personality. As he grew older he became a crippled personality; crippled by his vanity and perhaps by slights suffered in his youth. He lacked patience, and though he may have had the vision to grasp the Commonwealth idea before Sir John himself grasped it, he could never have turned that vision into reality. Faced with the attitude towards colonials shared by the English ruling classes of the day, Joseph Howe would have blown his top time and again. And in so doing he would have blown young Canada right into the waiting arms of the United States.

We forget so easily what a merciless teacher history is. The England of Sir John's day, the workshop of the world with a navy that could defy those of all other lands put together, was not the England of now. Ever since the late seventeenth century, snobbery had been endemic in England's public life. The Great Victorian liberal was perhaps the greatest snob of them all; he was convinced that God Himself had chosen Gladstone as His instrument. When a colonial statesman approached members of the English ruling classes, he had to accept the fact that hardly any of them would accept him at his own face value. The note of patronage creeps constantly into the references made about Sir John by English politicians. "He is a considerable man," admitted Disraeli—but not "considerable" in the sense that even a half-forgotten member of Disraeli's cabinet would be counted considerable in the London of the day. Creighton's book contains a fascinating photograph of Sir John in company with the Joint High Commission that sat in Washington in 1871. He was the first colonial ever to be appointed to such a commission, and his English colleagues, courteous enough at first, soon felt themselves outraged when they discovered that he was unwilling to agree to their convenient plan of putting Canadian interests up to barter for England's gain in the matter of an American treaty. "He has acted with a pretty strong degree of treachery toward us," wrote the chairman of the Commission, Lord de Grey, to the Colonial Office. Lord de Grey felt it intolerable that a colonial should forget that he was a colonial, and it was quite beyond his limited powers of imagination to guess that the only reason why he himself would be remembered by posterity was Sir John's presence on the Commission he mismanaged. No, Joseph Howe could never have dealt with men like de Grey without losing his temper. But Sir John, who had that inner aristocracy that enabled him to rise constantly above situations in which he was underrated by mental inferiors, invariably kept his temper. None knew better than he that the English leaders of the day had little interest in Canada so long as Canada did not become a *casus belli* with the United States. Perhaps the greatest of all Sir John's achievements was his astonishing power of perspective. What, after all, is harder to retain than self-confidence when the other men around the table take it for granted that even if you put down four aces, their value (simply because they came out of your hand and not out of theirs) can be conveniently assessed by old members of the club at the value of a pair of sixes or sevens?

But the life of Sir John Macdonald is far too rich, complex and varied for discussion here. Creighton is the man to go to for that, and all I want to do here is to express my pride in him and my gratitude. The scholarly biography is perhaps the most difficult and exacting of all the literary forms there are. To marry accurate learning to a narrative that never lags, to retain the dramatic timing of a great human story without ignoring the multitude of disorderly historical facts that clutter the dramatic highroad like rubble in the street of a bombed town—it is only in the present century that this art has been mastered, and it is a measure of our growth to literary maturity that we have produced in Donald Creighton a writer able to meet its merciless demands.

So let the trumpets blow—not too obstreperously, because that would make people think we exaggerate. Let them blow with a discreet Canadian sennet for Sir John Macdonald and his latest and best biographer!

12 BOY MEETS GIRL IN WINNIPEG AND WHO CARES?

The writing profession has many advantages: no boss breathes down your neck, nobody cares if you are late to work so long as you are not late *with* work, you don't have to co-operate with anyone except yourself and maybe the occasional editor. Along with the uncaught criminal, the artist is, as Somerset Maugham long ago pointed out, one of the few remaining species of *homo sapiens* who can roughly be described as free. Not even the Russians have been able to organize him without making him useless.

For this freedom the writer pays, and with each passing year he pays more, because in any technological society freedom almost prices itself out of the market. The price you pay for freedom today is a total lack of security.

While a book is in train, life can be so exciting for the writer that he never thinks about money unless the bank tells him he is overdrawn, and he thinks about his security only in those ghastly moments when the book bogs down. But all this changes after the book is completed and sent off to the publishers. Publishers are more human than writers in their cycles: a writer's period of gestation may range from ten days (Earle Stanley Gardner) to five years (myself with the last novel) to the lifetime necessary for the man who intends to produce a masterpiece the moment he can get around to it. But publishers, from the time they receive a script to the time they deliver the first edition to the bookstores, usually consume from seven to nine months.

Nine months can seem pretty long to a waiting man, and during this period I always swear I will reform. I remember my father telling me not to gamble, and I realize that if I have not gambled with money (never having had enough to gamble with) I have certainly gambled with my life, and have done so deliberately with the odds against me. The writer's usual gamble is to bet on hitting the jackpot somewhere along the line, his idea being that if he keeps on writing long enough the probabilities are reasonable that he will do so at least once, and then he can invest the money and attain his security. In the old days this worked pretty well, and in one or two countries it still works up to a point for the very lucky few, in spite of the tax gatherers necessary for the support of the welfare state.

But in Canada the gamble doesn't work at all; in Canada the odds against the jackpot are what they would be in roulette if every tenth slot was a double-zero. I have known this for years, and yet I have contumaciously gone back to the tables again and again. While it is true that our population is rising fast, at least a third of it is not presumed to read English literature in its spare time. A best seller in our market is exceptional if it tops 10,000, and the royalty on 10,000 copies is about $4,500. On the other hand in the United States, where the population now exceeds 170 million, all of them over five taught to read and write and all of them over two to look at television, a best seller cannot only hit the half-million mark but later, and for this very reason, be sold to the movies and television people for sums of money which fatten the tax gatherers as a dead elephant fattens the vultures that roost on Kilimanjaro. But even after the publicans have picked you, if you hit a jackpot like that you have a sizable paycheck to bank.

This simple arithmetic I have always disregarded whenever I have been in train with a novel. To hell with figures, I say, while genius pretends to burn. I write English, I say, and the Americans read English, and as long as I build a better mousetrap the world is sure to beat that famous path to my famous door. Again and again American reviewers, who are more generous to outsiders than any other reviewers in the world, urge their readers to read Canadian books. But in spite of all this goodwill, grass still grows green and thick around the doorsteps of our better Canadian mousetrap builders.

Why shouldn't it? If we insisted on electing Mackenzie King for twenty-two years, why should Americans think us an interesting people? In any case, literature has always been mixed up with nationalisms and popular assumptions. Citizens of new countries are supposed to break sods instead of typewriters, and Europeans coming to live among them are supposed to furnish them with such culture as they can imbibe. A century ago Melville and Hawthorne had as hard a time crashing the international market as we Canadians have now, and it did their pockets little good, nor did they know about it during their lives, that in our day Harvard students turn out about a dozen theses a year on their work. In the last three generations the United States not only broke through into the international market; for a time it came close to capturing it. But the American writers who developed a mature native literature had an advantage the critics have seldom noted: a huge and growing native population. It was this native population which supported them in the years when they were growing up, for it is natural for people to find their own societies more interesting than the societies of strangers.

Facts such as these I have stubbornly disregarded for more than twenty years. I have known them perfectly; I have known them ever since I received a telegram informing me that two Hollywood studios were interested in my first novel. I saw dollar signs all over the Windsor Station the night I boarded that train for New York, and there were still more of them hanging from the skyscrapers when I drove in a taxi to the old Ritz-Carlton to meet the representative of the studio which was the more interested of the two. He was a man exceedingly affable, though somewhat boiled-looking about the eyelids, and before ordering a thirty-dollar lunch he gave me two cocktails. He also told me the deal was off.

"It's like this," the man explained. "This book of yours, it's about this town Halifax and who's ever heard of Halifax down here except as a word nicely brought-up kids say when what really they mean is hell? 'Go to Halifax', is what nicely brought-up kids down here say. Well, of course, this wouldn't make any difference if this was an ordinary book. We could work a switcheroo. But the trouble is in this book of yours Halifax gets itself blown up in the climax of the story. We fooled around with a switcheroo even on that. We thought of the Johnstown Flood, but that happened so long ago that who cares, so we canned the whole idea." He looked at me in sincere friendship and said: "It's tough, but that's how it is. All you've got to do next time is set the scene in the United States and *then* we'll be really interested."

Being naïve in those days, I asked what difference the locale of a story makes so long as the story is good.

"Well, take Paris," he said, "that's okay for one kind of story. Take London—that's okay for another kind. But take Canada—that's not okay because what do Americans think when they hear that word 'Canada' except cold weather and Mounties or maybe when they hear it they don't know what to think. Now this is not the way it ought to be and it's tough, but look at it like this. A boy meets a girl in Paris, one thing leads to another and they—well, it's interesting. But a boy meets a girl in Winnipeg and they swing into the same routine and who cares? I'm not saying it's not just as good in Winnipeg as it is in Paris. Maybe it's even better because in Winnipeg what else is there to do? But for the American public you've got to see it's a fact that Winnipeg kind of kills interest in the whole thing."

I protested (I was *very* naïve in those days) that my books tended to be serious, what you might call social novels.

"That's exactly what I've been trying to say," he explained. "The way you write, if you want a big market down here, you just haven't got much of a choice. The way you write you've got to make it American. Now let me tell you a little tale to illustrate that point."

One Monday morning on the Coast, he related, in the days of the silents when Hollywood magnates were real magnates and not Organization Men, one of the very biggest of these magnates padded into his office, seated himself behind his twelve-foot desk and pressed down all the buttons it contained. Within five minutes most of his executives, script men, continuity men, cameramen, directors, idea men, editors and press agents were arrayed before him. He advanced his dimpled chin, stared at each of them in turn, and barked:

"Why do I pay you guys one—two—three thousand dollars a week and from you what do I get but strictly nothing?"

After the necessary quarter-minute's silence had been observed, the magnate continued:

"Over the week-end I was with high-class people and they told me of a very wonderful book, the most wonderful story of this century, and from you what do I hear of this story but strictly nothing?"

After the necessary ten seconds of silence, the chief story editor asked if the title of the book might be revealed. It could be, and it was *The Well of Loneliness*. The editor shrugged and said he had read it long ago.

"Then why," stared the boss, "don't I see this *Well of Loneliness* in lights?"

The editor sighed and said it was impossible. The magnate scowled and said the word "impossible" was a word that nobody in his studio was permitted to understand. The editor agreed that this was true, but argued that the censors would not permit *The Well of Loneliness* to be shown in American family theatres, not even with the "Adults Only" sign on the door. The heroine of the book, he explained to the chief, was a Lesbian.

The dimpled chin advanced further across the desk, the wonderful little eyes gleamed.

"Why do I pay for brains when evidently brains is what you do not like to use? So the girl in this story is a Lesbian? So what if she's from Peru? So what if her home is in Costa Rica maybe? In this studio we make her an American!"

The man from Hollywood looked at me mournfully and said: "So now you see the way it is."

Oddly enough I saw exactly how it was, just as I see how it is now, for right here in Canada the situation is little different. Suppose you try to sell a serious social novel about Peru or Costa Rica in Canada, how many Canadians are going to storm the shops to buy that book?

Yet I, fully understanding this situation years ago, have continued to squander my dwindling hopes of security by continually writing books about Canadians living in their own country. Can anybody be stupider about his interests than that? Now, with still another long novel due this month (due as a matter of fact on Friday the Thirteenth of this month and no kidding) I feel like the gambler in the garden at Monte Carlo solemnly telling himself "Never, never again." For five years I have been assuring myself that this novel is by far the best thing I've ever done or dreamed of doing, that its Canadian setting is worked into it like shot silk, that here is a story that should sound just as good in London or New York as in Montreal. Maybe it will; maybe it will! But my Scotch instinct also says, "Maybe it won't!" And as I await the results with Scotch fatalism, I again remember the words of that man from Hollywood, and this time I swear I'm going to act on them the next time I write a novel.

"The thing for you to do," he said, "being a Canadian, is make the best of *both* your worlds. Mix up the English and Americans in the same package, and fix it so somehow this Englishman in this book comes over to the States with certain ideas and he changes them, understand, when he finds out about American women and democracy." He shook my hand warmly as we left the Ritz. "Now just one more little thing and it shouldn't be too hard to do. Try to work Lincoln into the story somehow. Work Lincoln in, you as a Canadian work Lincoln into it with this Englishman, and something very nice ought to come out."

He paused as we passed through the revolving door, wrinkled up his face into a confidential question-mark and spoke again:

"How inhibited are you on sex?" he asked me. "This last book of yours, it had some hints of sex but not half enough in my opinion."

"How much sex do you think I need?"

"Pretty well all you can put in. Of course, it's got to be

moral. I mean, if people get it extra-curricularly they've got to pay for it, but you can describe them getting it, and while you're at it, let yourself go. A book with no sex, the reader feels cheated. But you know all that anyway."

Dumas *fils* once told a neophyte the three basic rules of the novelist's trade: "First tell them what to do. Then do it. Then tell them you've done it."

Now, being determined to atone for a mis-spent life before it's too late, I'm going to tell you what I'm going to do, then I'm going to do it, then I'm going to tell you I've done it.

My next novel is going to open in London just as the Hollywood man said, with Lord Peter Sandwich (can't you see him: tall, saturnine and a soldier?) conversing with Lord Palmerston beside a window looking down into the Horse Guards where some very pretty guardsmen are trooping the colours. As everyone knows who knows his Civil War literature, Lord Palmerston is a villain, and if it had not been for the Good Queen and Prince Albert, together with the spirit of English democracy (this book has to be sold in England as well as in the States), Palmerston would long ago have turned the might of the British Empire against Lincoln's embattled Union. So this novel of mine will begin with Lord Palmerston giving Lord Peter Sandwich his instructions, and these instructions, when followed out, are going to be the storyline of the book.

In case you have not guessed it, Sandwich has just been given a secret mission: he is to sail to Havana where he is to proceed immediately to a certain address. There he will be told how to find the transportation which will convey him through the northern blockade into Charleston, whence he is to proceed inland through the Confederacy to President Jefferson Davis whom he will promise (verbally, of course) that if the Confederacy can make one more major successful effort, if it can strike out of its lines into the heart of the Union, the right-thinking people in Her Majesty's Government will be able to sweep aside the protests of the liberals, the milksops and the Good Queen herself. The Royal Navy, the Royal Navy, sir, will be ordered out to sea, and Boston and New York will be blockaded. Then, while Lee strikes north through the Shenendoah, that army of redcoats will strike south from Canada to plunge the dagger into the back of the Great Experiment. "History," says Palmerston in effect, "from now on depends more or less on you."

Lord Peter has still a few days left in London, and these he occupies as a young man does when he is about to set forth on a secret mission. The lady's cries (she is of course nobly born) will be duly recorded in my novel, and Lord Peter's prowess in the culbatizing exercise will be described with what the critics now call clinical accuracy, and rightly too, for "clinic" is derived from a Greek word meaning "bed". This will be the first sexual commercial on my programme, and as it will occur around page 20, the reader will be assured at the very beginning that this is a novel in which he will not be cheated, for if the spacing continues at that rate, at least twenty more similar scenes will follow, and he can feel by the weight of it that this is not a short book.

Once this scene is over, Lord Peter takes the train to Southampton (some pretty descriptions of Hampshire scenery, some moral reflections about the immorality of his current life) and thence to the frigate, aboard which Lord Peter is impressively piped.

As nothing can be more monotonous than the description of a sea voyage on a neutral man o' war, this frigate on which Lord Peter sails must encounter a few incidents which will liven up the log. I am not sure of all of them yet, but there are a variety of possibilities. *H.M.S. Atrocious* (the name must exist somewhere on the navy list) may quite possibly run down a Yankee merchantman and create an international incident. Or perhaps a woman has stowed away on board and Lord Peter can discover her? Or perhaps the captain can go mad, and Lord Peter can save the ship from him? As I said, and as you well know, there is a variety of possibilities here. But there is one thing of which I am certainly not going to cheat the reader and that is the flogging scene. A sailor is going to be seized up in the gangway and the bosun is going to give him two dozen with the cat, and the screams of the sailor are going to be recorded and the sound of the cat whistling through the air and snapping against his bare back—first with a dry sound and later on with a kind of splash—are going to be described with all the vividness at my command, and this should put the reader into exactly the right mood for Lord Peter's next amatory adventure, which he consummates with the Cuban lady who arranges his transportation to Charleston.

In Charleston, of course, Lord Peter sees a proud aristocracy on its last legs, its flowers at their prime, and several of these he adds to his collection before finally he goes inland (descriptions of the Confederacy feeling the pinch of the Northern blockade) where he not only meets President Davis, but also shakes hands with General Lee, and although General Lee's nobility makes him uneasy about his own character, the result of Lord Peter's meeting with him is what it has to be: the march to Gettysburg.

By now, as the reader will understand, the mysterious something in the New World has begun to work on the mind of this hard young aristocrat and it occurs to him that he may be a bit of a heel. The first messenger of grace is an American woman. He seduces her, but this time the scene is a little different, for in the deep of the southern night she breaks into tears and reminds him that her husband is in

Lee's cavalry and here she is being disloyal to him in her own bed. Nor is this lady at ease as regards the righteousness of the Southern cause, or in the inevitability of war. In fact she is confused all around. What will she do with herself if her husband finds out about her? What will she do if her husband is killed? What will the South do even if the South wins? And what will happen to the South if any more men are slaughtered in this insensate war? War, she informs Lord Peter, is not quite the manly sport he seems to think it is, and it is with these words ringing in his ears that Lord Peter reaches the field of Gettysburg.

The Battle of Gettysburg has been described so often that it is necessary to re-describe it every February when Lincoln's birthday rolls around. You may be sure it will be described in this novel I am going to write, for it is the turning-point in the life of the novel's hero. We see Lord Peter standing on the knoll with Lee's staff and the other foreign observers; we hear the horses scream and neigh; we see the men fall; we see the mask of tragedy settle on to the face of General Lee as wave after wave of his men die before the Northern sharpshooters; we see the moment approach for Pickett's charge. The bugles blow, and then we see Lord Peter suddenly run away from the knoll and mount a riderless horse, and because he is a superb rider, soon we see him heading the charge against the Union lines.

He gets it, and wakes up with the kindly twang of a Yankee voice saying: "Waal son, I guess you've lost a little bit of weight."

The weight Lord Peter has lost is his left leg, and as he cannot be moved for a while, it is quite consistent with the probabilities that he should still be hanging around Gettysburg when the Presidential party arrives from Washington, and when Lincoln makes that speech, who is present to understand it except this tired, wounded and humbled English aristocrat? The Gettysburg Oration settles almost every problem in Lord Sandwich's guilty, troubled mind, and the little confusion that still lingers is taken care of when the Great Emancipator, visiting the wounded of both sides, puts his hand on Sandwich's shoulder, looks into his eyes and utters a few words. What those words are I do not intend to tell you. You must buy the book if you want to find out.

So there, friends, is the plot of my next novel, and there is only one thing which can prevent it from being written. That is for the Canada Council, which has been established, as everyone knows, to promote the arts in this country, to persuade the Government to agree to pension off every novelist who can prove he has written at least five novels in his lifetime. If the Government of England in the eighteenth century gave John Cleland a lifetime pension after he wrote *Fanny Hill*, its provision being that *Fanny Hill* should be withdrawn from the bookstalls and that Cleland should never write anything else so long as he lived, why should not the much richer government of twentieth-century Canada do something of the same sort? I have warned them fairly what the alternative is, so the next move is surely up to them. If the Government, however reluctantly, kept a Peter Breughel out of the country in the interests of economy and social security, why should it not, in the same interests (or more or less in the same interests) keep this proposed book of mine out of existence?

13 NEW YORK, NEW YORK

The first time I understood that New York taxi-drivers are a unique tribe within the human family was in 1929 on the occasion of my first visit there. I was with my father, who hated New York and never missed an opportunity of saying so, who dreaded New York not for its own sake but for all of our sakes, because New York by its very colossality seemed a constant temptation inviting Providence to get to work on it. On the way to Penn Station, my father grumbling with some justification about the way the traffic was not being handled—they used cops then instead of lights and prohibition had softened the cops up—the driver stopped his car and turned around.

"Listen mister, you wanna know what is the trouble with New York? It is very simple. New York is the trouble with New York."

At the time this struck me as a courteous way of suggesting that what was the trouble with my father was my father, but I don't really think this is what the man meant. He simply meant that New York is New York, and as such that it is so transcendent, so irrefragably self-confident, that for most of us it has an unrivalled capacity among the cities for arousing extreme sensations of love, hate, admiration and nausea. I don't know what your experience has been with this city, but mine is nearly always the same. I arrive full of excited anticipation; I depart frustrated and with my pockets empty. I can't imagine a world without New York; I find it increasingly difficult to imagine the world surviving indefinitely with New York a part of it. New York, for years, has been my Great White Whale. Year after year between my first visit and 1952 I kept going down to New York and once I lived there for eight consecutive months, during which it seemed entirely different from the city I knew when I visited it. Then for five years I stayed secure in Montreal and left the Whale to itself and the rest of humanity.

But a time came—it always does—when I had to return to New York, and on this occasion it was because I had finished a novel on which I had been working for five years. I was tired and with reason. During the previous five months I had been working night and day in the most intense creative drive I had ever known. So I slept for a week, then bought a ticket for the Great White Whale because it seemed essential that I consult my agent. "With this little book," whispered a little thought in the back of my little mind, "I will stick my little bodkin into the Whale. This little book will make the Whale admit that I exist."

So I slept soundly on the train, and with the usual feeling of expectant excitement I stepped out of Grand Central into a cab driven by Joe Przwyk, to whom I carelessly mentioned that I had not been in New York for five years.

"Where you bin?" said Przwyk. "In jail?"

There it was again: that cheerful, humiliating, friendly assumption that if you are absent from New York you are not alive, and that only the most ignominious failure or the direst calamity can keep you away until, after having been preserved on ice, you return. No wonder Moby Dick heaped Ahab; no wonder the Whale was his wall. Ahab was a whaler by trade; I am a writer by trade, and New York, among other things, happens to be the centre of the book market.

Przwyk drove with a competent insouciance delightful after the paranoic behaviour of Montreal taxi-drivers, and the familiar kaleidoscope unreeled, historical climacterics of a quarter century flashing past as he drove from Grand Central to my hotel. There was the corner on which I had stood, that November night in 1932, when Franklin Roosevelt was elected president and the New York crowd, anticipating 3.2 beer and everything else that happened during Roosevelt's régime, sang *Happy Days Are Here Again*. There was the barbershop where I read about Dollfuss' bombardment of the Viennese workers in 1934. Coming out of that theatre I had seen displayed in banner headlines the news that Adolf Hitler had become the master of Germany. In this block my shoes were shined while I looked at a *Daily News* photo of Hitler doing a jig in the Forest of Compiègne. New York had certainly appreciated the news value of the war, but it was from another member of its taxi-driving tribe that I learned what I believe was its real attitude towards that half-forgotten conflict.

"This town," the man said, "is pretty big for the war."

The news in New York on this particular occasion was widely analysed elsewhere on the continent and will be analysed in special circles long after New York has forgotten it. In Brooklyn, which might be described as the belly of the Great White Whale, a prominent school authority had just committed suicide; a famous judge had just been accused of calling the Superintendent of Schools a bastard; a grand jury had announced that the schools were rife with "hoodlums, rapists, thieves, extortionists, arsonists and vandals"; the mayor had ordered policemen into some of these schools to protect the teachers against their pupils.

"Naw," said Przwyk, "that stuff has *always* been here. I could tell you a story."

He deposited me in front of the hotel where, in the spring of 1933, I had lived on credit for eight days while the nation's banks were closed. The hinterland had trembled, several Wall Street bankers had contemplated a choice between suicide and the penitentiary, but the Great White Whale had basked blissfully indifferent and carried on as usual while the world panicked. The most disreputable strangers were given almost unlimited credit in the hotels. New York, after all, had to continue being New York just as it now had to continue being New York in spite of the blackboard jungle.

"Yeah," said Dominick Tintoretto as he drove me that night to a remembered jazz-spot in the Village, "definitely and strictly it is a very wonnerful thing people like you coming from all over here. You see how things is done here, you go home and you make your improvements. It is all very wonnerful. Seeing how things is done here, you *gotta* make improvements or how can you odderwise live? Up in Mo-ree-al how are things?"

I asked him how he knew I was from Montreal, since I had not told him.

"You talk like an English fella," said Tintoretto, "only you don't talk like an English fella, so I figure it is from Mo-ree-al that you come."

I asked how he knew how an English fella talked.

"I bin all over. First World War Wincheser, Durby, Oggsferd, Wales. I guess England's okay if you like the Village. The Mayor is gonna do something about the Village. Now take the Mayor."

He arrived at my destination before he had time to take the Mayor, and I entered the familiar place to find it with a new decor, a quadrupled cover charge, but the same sprightly, spring-fresh jazz played by young negroes who looked just like the ones I had first heard a quarter century ago before they became middle-aged and famous and much duller than they had been when they played here. Next to me was a couple holding hands sitting opposite another couple doing the same, and they all seemed so intimate I thought they were old friends until the second couple departed for the bar and I overheard that the first couple had met them only half an hour before. The girl, speaking a beautiful English in a Dutch accent, was explaining something to her inarticulate American escort.

"But New York is the *only* place where people don't have to live with *each other*. They only have to live with *themselves*."

Her escort, who admitted that his home town was Washington Courthouse, Ohio, opined that New York had everything, and the Dutch girl said she wasn't sure about that, but she was certainly sure—a glance from lowered lids into the eyes of the Washington Courthouse man—that New York was a place where the most delicious things could happen to a girl night after night.

"You know what's the trouble with Arnold Toynbee?" said Isadore Goldberg three hours later as he drove me back to my hotel.

I have been driven through New York by a student of Immanuel Kant, by several Marxian scholars, by one anthropologist, by a variety of ex-pugs and bootleggers, but now, in Goldberg, I had discovered someone who outmoded the lot of them.

"What's history," said Goldberg, "but psychology, and

what's psychology but the ree-searches of Sigmund Freud? Toynbee writes history like Freud was not in it. That's what's the trouble with Toynbee."

New York, which is everything, is also the Metropolitan Museum, and I spent four hours there on my second day, my chief purpose being to revisit the Rembrandts and the Grecos. They were there, they were cleaned and they were wonderful, but once again I found that the White Whale had continued its habit of surpassing and outmoding even itself. I left the Museum overwhelmed, not by Rembrandt and Greco, but by the colossal, nude, bronze statue of the Emperor Trebonianus Gallus, who was the greatest man in the world between 251 A.D. and 253 A.D., when he was murdered by his own soldiers. Black, terrible, huge and naked —the nakedest statue I ever saw—this awful apparition dominates the atrium of the Metropolitan, his face and horrible labourer's body telling more about the decline and fall of the Roman Empire than Gibbon and Toynbee put together. Was it always there in the Metropolitan and I had not seen it? But New York had incorporated Gallus now, and Goldberg, who as a Freudian understands that history is a prolonged process of gods eating gods, religions eating religions, civilizations eating civilizations, might possibly agree with my terrified apprehension that the Great Whale has now swallowed the Roman Empire along with the British.

The Whale, I discovered a few hours later, had swallowed and incorporated another big fish: Franklin Roosevelt, together with his whole family which has survived him and still lives, I understand, interesting and exciting lives of their own, had been legendized into a show off Broadway with Ralph Bellamy in the lead. Mr. Bellamy had never seemed to me to resemble Franklin Roosevelt in any way whatever, but there he was, and I had the odd sensation that so far as the Whale was concerned, the Thirty-first President had never been quite real until he was dead enough to be converted into The Roosevelt Story. The Whale was browsing as usual on a large variety of sexual shows (when will it outmode sex?) and also on the dramatized versions of two novels which seemed to me to have been contemporary only yesterday, but were treated by the critics in the manner adopted by fashionable shops to the dress styles of a year ago. *A Farewell To Arms,* a novel which seemed to me to have been written only yesterday, was playing in a movie at the Roxy, and one of the Whale's special correspondents found it interesting because it demonstrated how out of touch was the writing of the early 1930s with the reality of Now. "Catherine Barclay," the writer complained, "*used* to be every man's ideal girl." That other anti-war novel of the Thirties, *Paths of Glory,* was also on display in a movie version and I saw it and found it tremendous. But the Whale's press was uninterested in it, and the taxi-driver James Westerley (his foreign-sounding name attributable to the fact that he was a Negro) had the final word on its importance.

"They don' fight wars that way no more," said Westerley. "No, sir, not any more do they fight wars that way."

The next morning I decided I could put it off no longer and went to see my agent with the manuscript, which I delivered just before lunch. As we sipped our coffee after lunch I asked him a few questions about the book trade and his answers did not sound cheerful. He told me what I knew only too well: that the general market for cloth-covered fiction was away below the level of what it had been a dozen years ago. Paper-backs had changed the entire shape of the market. Television had cut heavily into the time available for reading. Some eighty-five percent of American families now owned television sets and the average burning time of a set in America was more than five hours in twenty-four. According to some fairly reliable opinion-samplers, only one American in five read even one book a year and only seventeen percent of Americans *bought* as many as one book in a lifetime.

I left my good friend feeling that the effort of the last years had probably been wasted, and walked around for a while trying to forget that in my little mind my little bodkin was broken.

My favourite part of Manhattan—I am obvious in my tastes—is the stretch of Fifth Avenue between the Plaza and Forty-eighth Street and this stretch I now began to pace. My favourite shop in New York is Scribner's, which has the finest window of any bookshop I have ever seen. Mr. Van Duym, who dresses it, is a famous man in the trade; he loves and understands books, and if he really likes a book he has the art of setting it out in the window in such a way that you realize it is a thing much more precious than the diamond tiara you just looked at in Cartier's. I first saw Scribner's window in 1932 and I have looked into it on every visit to New York since that time. I used to think that if ever a book of mine were given even a modest corner of that window, all the work and strain of half a lifetime would have its reward. So now I spent ten minutes studying the window, went inside and browsed, bought a book and emerged for another walk. Ah well, if not with this novel, perhaps with the next. The Whale had never been interested in anything Canadian, and this novel of mine was set in Montreal.

That night I took my departure with the Whale scintillating as he always does on a clear night, and as I rode to Grand Central and saw the towering television masts on the top of the Empire State and the Chrysler, I asked myself why this place seemed to annihilate the value of everything

I had ever learned to do in my entire life. But encouragement came in this dark moment from an unexpected quarter.

"This TeeVee," said Steve Svoboda, "ain't gonna last much longer. People all over is getting very weary indeed of Tee-Vee."

At a traffic light Svoboda pondered further: "They'll come up with sumpin new. When they gotta, they do."

I paid him off, counted the money remaining in my wallet, discovered as always that the Whale had swallowed more than I had expected that even he would be able to swallow, got into the train and slept well. The white snow of Montreal looked comfortable after the White Whale and I muttered that it would be never before I tempted him again. But I knew I was fooling myself, for I always go back to New York. So does everybody. And this brings me to a postscript to the story of my dealings with the Great White Whale.

My forebodings about the book I had written turned out to be well founded, for six weeks after my return I was informed that the publisher to whom the novel had been sent did not wish to publish it. This was a shock, for it meant that for the first time since I became a professional novelist I was without an American publisher. After a very minor revision, the book was despatched to one of the Whale's most ancient and honourable publishers, and there it reposed while the editor considered it. By this time spring had broken out and when my work in the university ended for the season, I boarded a freighter and sailed to England on the first holiday I had enjoyed in a dozen years. The ship took twelve days getting there, and I reached London on a Saturday night. When I picked up my mail at the bank in Cockspur Street the following Monday morning, the first letter I opened contained the news that the second publisher had also rejected the script, his reason being that the prose was turgid and the characters uninteresting. Prospects now were beginning to look alarming. It is worse than grim, it is like writing on the wall, when an established novelist gets two rejections of a script in succession. It is worse still when this happens to what he believes is his best book, for he has always known that at any moment he may cease to please, and that a time comes in the life of every writer when such talent as he possesses fails. Generally he himself is the last person to understand this, just as a faithful wife is often the last person to know what her husband has really been up to on some of his absences from home. Well, I thought, let's forget it and get on with the vacation. So I spent six weeks in England and Scotland and then flew home.

The first letter I opened on my arrival in Montreal was also from my agent, and it told me that the manuscript, as he had all along predicted, was now in safe hands. Scribner's was going to publish it some time in the course of the next year. The months went by and in a rush of new work I pushed the novel into the back of my mind. Proofs arrived and I corrected them, but I diligently kept away from the Great White Whale and professed incredulity when some interesting rumours about the novel floated north. The book appeared on the luckiest day of the year: Friday, the 13th of February, and still I kept away from New York. I was afraid of spoiling the pitch, for no writer, least of all a foreign one, could possibly have received more generous reviews than I was getting from the Whale's special correspondents at that particular moment. My publishers finally invited me down, and down I went.

My mind was confused in that month and I forgot my dates. When I began walking that Monday morning after breakfast the ghastly thought occurred to me that once again something unaccountable might have happened, for at 10.30 the streets were almost deserted and all of the shops were closed. Had the Whale suffered some unexpected disaster during the night? Had the next depression begun? Had Wall Street collapsed? Was an atomic attack impending? As anything is possible in that city, none of these ideas seemed entirely unreasonable.

Then I began noticing that in window after window there was a picture of George Washington, and at last I understood that this was the man's birthday. It is true that the Whale had done no fighting for Washington during the Revolution; indeed, such effort as he expended in that war was mostly on the side of the King. But when the King lost, the Whale of course contrived to make his arrangements with the new government and now he was celebrating this. The holiday would mean a crowded Metropolitan in the afternoon, but it would also mean fairly empty streets. The air was brisk and I continued walking down Fifth until I reached Scribner's window. Honestly I had expected to find nothing there, but what I did find nearly knocked me out.

The entire window had been given over to that little novel of mine, and in my prejudiced eyes Mr. Van Duym had performed the finest work of art in his career. Stacks and stacks of the book were arranged in patterns; in addition there were five large photographs of Montreal, one of Ottawa and another of a Canadian lumber camp. Blown-up photostats of reviews from the *Times* and the *Herald-Tribune* were in the window, and two strangers were bending forward to read them, while every fifth person who walked by stopped to stare.

For myself, I stayed there no longer than fifteen seconds, and when I bolted around the corner I was afraid that I had stayed at least ten seconds too long for my safety. The beastie was at my heels and my father's ghost was on the heels of the beastie. He was reminding me of the winter

Sunday years ago when I had come home from a walk and discovered, absolutely out of the blue, that a telegram had arrived informing me that I had won a Rhodes Scholarship months after I had believed that I had lost my last chance of getting one. My father had risen to this occasion in the spirit of his ancestors. "Go out and shovel the snow," he said, and it was the only occasion when he ever ordered me to work on the Sabbath Day. So on that Washington's Birthday, as there was no snow to shovel in New York, I walked and I walked and I walked.

14 LITERATURE IN A NEW COUNTRY

It would be easier to talk sensibly about literature in a new country like Canada if more people understood that literature, unlike science, is an activity neither importable nor exportable. It must grow out of society itself. In reproof to Canadian writers it is constantly said that our literature has lagged behind our science, and though in a sense this statement is true, it has no significant implications whatever.

Certainly Canadian science compares favourably with the science of all but a very few countries in the world. Osler is generally regarded as the founder of modern medical practice. The work of Banting, Best and Penfield has been seminal, and our nuclear physicists were able to play a part in the Manhattan Project. Marquis wheat was a Canadian development, and in every major university in the country there is at least one scientist internationally known.

But it confuses our picture of reality if we infer from this that the development of scientific techniques is any real indication of the collective spiritual growth of the Canadian people, or for that matter of any other people on earth. Osler learned his basic medical techniques in Germany, he developed them in Montreal, and later he took them with him to Baltimore and Oxford. His Canadian birth was quite incidental to his career, which would have been the same no matter where he had been born provided that his birth-place had given him the opportunity of receiving an education. Rutherford was the son of a New Zealand shepherd. He learned his mature techniques in Cambridge and took them thence to McGill, where he laid the groundwork for his theory of the atom. After a few years with us, he returned to Cambridge. Penfield learned his techniques in various countries before he established the Neurological Institute in Montreal, and now in the Institute men are trained from all countries, some of them primitive, and sent away to teach the art far afield. Science, unlike literature, is an international activity and its techniques can be imported and exported with nothing lost.

But literature is not an international activity in any sense, and though new visions and new techniques can flow across international borders, the substance of any living literature must come out of the society to which the writer belongs. Once the era of the epic has passed, it is only from a mature society that a literature worth reading has emerged. No colony in its formative years can ever be a mature society; it may produce mature *individuals*, but that is not the same thing at all. In a colony the very spirit of creative literature is cut off from its source, and this has been true wherever colonies have been planted.

In Canada it so happened that the early days of growth coincided with one of the most mature periods in all European history, the eighteenth century. At that time in Canada the only prosperous trade was the fur trade, and the lives of the river men were too remote, too epic, to provide material for the kind of literature which then was in vogue in Europe. Alexander Mackenzie and Simon Fraser both wrote fascinating journals which were published abroad, but these were the factual records of voyages, they were not translations of the voyages into art, nor was it possible for the few acres of snow which was Voltaire's notion of Quebec to have provided a literature which would have seemed significant to a Johnson, a Gibbon or a Chateaubriand. The literary time is always out of joint for a colony, and if any colonial has an impetus to write and possesses the means of escape, he always takes the first ship back to the motherland.

In considering the growth of a nation's literature, I think it possible to state a general law. A colonial literature can at best be but a pale reflection of the mother-literature, without authority of any sort, until the colony has matured, and the history of American literature is the best possible example of how this law operates.

It was in the mid-nineteenth century, more than two hundred years after the first landings in New England, before the United States produced its Melville and Hawthorne, and American literature was recognized in Europe as the product of a mature and significant society. When we consider this fact, it is obvious that the growth of art and literature in Canada has not been so slow after all; on the contrary, it has been astonishingly rapid.

English-Canada is no older than the end of the eighteenth century, and in its early years there was no country on earth where the obstacles to a literature were greater than here. Our first writer of merit was Haliburton and he was not even a Canadian; he was a British colonial living in Nova Scotia. While nearly all the poetry written in Canada in the last century was either bad or imitative, at least some poetry was written, and more than one poet tried to deal with the Canadian landscape if not with the Canadian people. By the end of the first decade of the present century

Stephen Leacock was celebrated both in Britain and the United States, though not as a "Canadian" writer. It is significant that in only one book did Leacock specifically and unmistakably set his scene in Canada, and even more significant that in the early novels of Morley Callaghan, published, it seems, only yesterday, the author did not feel the country was recognizable enough to make Toronto a character in his stories, as Toronto in fact often was. It was not until the First World War that a Canadian public was willing to accept a specifically Canadian city as a credible and interesting setting for a novel, and the dates involved here are significant. From 1800 to 1940 is exactly one hundred and forty years: in other words, it is the same length of time which elapsed in the United States between the landing of the Pilgrims and the first tentative "American" writings of Benjamin Franklin.

Canada, I believe, was ready to produce a reasonably mature literature before 1940—indeed, in the work of Callaghan and Ringuet it did produce mature work. But at this time Canadian writers suffered one further handicap: the great themes which engaged everyone's attention could not be handled here with the same authority as elsewhere. A generation ago the world was in flux and chaos, and though every facet of Canadian life was affected by the Russian Revolution, the between-wars crises, the depression and the rise of fascism, Canada was not at the vortex and Europe was. In those days Canadians had either to be local in their choice of subjects—and in that case they were bound to be local in their appeal—or they had to leave home and write in and of a *milieu* they could never hope to understand with the inner authority essential to the creative artist. The work of writing *emigrés* always lacks the drive and compulsion of genuine native work, and there is no short cut to universality. No writer can jump the gap until his society has grown across it like a bridge; until the spirit of his society has merged with that of the world. The impatient young writer in a new country does well to remember that time is the essence of his and his country's problem, just as he should also remember that although on occasion his province may be a hindrance to him, it is literally all that he has behind him. Shakespeare's England was once a province, too; so was Tolstoy's Russia. One of literature's chief tasks is to bridge the gap between province and heartland, to merge the spiritual and moral life of the province with that of the core. But he cannot do this single-handed. He cannot do this until the time is ripe and the province, outgrowing its old spiritual dependence, becomes old enough to consent to be its own judge.

Perhaps I am guilty of wishful thinking, but I believe that in Canada this time has finally come, and that the necessary social growth has been completed. There are many evidences that the Canadian scene at the moment can provide themes as significant to old countries in Europe, and to the United States, as can be found anywhere. If this is so, there is no need any longer to ask whether there can be a Canadian literature. There is one now, it is growing in power and acceptance, and the problems of its writers are therefore the same as the problems of writers everywhere in this scientific age.

15 THE FUTURE OF THE NOVEL AS AN ART FORM*

Somerset Maugham's *Cakes And Ale* contains a passage every professional novelist should recall when tempted to make pronouncements about what is valuable and what is not valuable in literature. Ashenden, the narrator of *Cakes And Ale*, himself a novelist very like Mr. Maugham in character and taste, remarks in one passage:

"I read *The Craft Of Fiction* by Mr. Percy Lubbock, from which I learned that the only way to write novels was like Henry James. After that I read *Aspects Of The Novel* by Mr. E. M. Forster, from which I learned that the only way to write novels was like Mr. E. M. Forster. Then I read *The Structure Of The Novel* by Mr. Edwin Muir, from which I learned nothing at all."

As most of us have read at least something about the art of fiction written by Somerset Maugham himself, it would be indelicate to point out that if he has described Mr. Forster's attitude correctly, he and Mr. Forster have at least one attribute in common.

---

*Address given at the Golden Jubilee of the University of Saskatchewan, in October, 1959.

The moral is that no writer should be trusted when he makes value-judgments about other men's literary styles and attitudes. For that matter nobody can be. What is criticism, after all, but the finding of reasons to justify your personal likes and dislikes? Often these reasons are valid, but if an author's vision is totally alien to your own, it takes a superhuman objectivity to be fair to him. On the other hand if the author is congenial to you in temperament, you are very likely to overrate him. In *The Green Hills of Africa*, Ernest Hemingway makes the laconic statement that all American literature begins with *Huckleberry Finn*. Most of us were under the impression that Melville, Hawthorne, Irving, Emerson, Dana and Whitman were senior to Mark Twain, but for Hemingway the statement is probably true. For him American literature really does begin with *Huckleberry Finn* and for him that settles the matter.

In talking about the novel I am like any other writer: I cannot be superior to my own tastes, experience and problems. If I like another writer and have been helped by him, I am grateful and think he is important. But all I mean by this is that he is important to me.

The reverse is equally true. In my early days I was under the spell of some brilliant friends who believed that if anyone refused to recognize that *Ulysses* was the master-novel of the twentieth century, he was unfit to make a literary judgment in a kindergarten. I got so much fun out of thinking myself a member of the *avant-garde*, it was so delightful to spend long hours in smoke-filled rooms ridiculing every author admired by the bourgeoisie, that for two years I cramped my style by trying to write like James Joyce. But I never honestly liked *Ulysses* well enough to read all of it, and when I got older I noted a peculiar thing: only a handful of the very people who claimed to admire *Ulysses* extravagantly had ever read it through consecutively from cover to cover. As far as I could tell, what most of them read was the first three chapters and what all of them read was the last chapter about Mrs. Bloom falling asleep.

The reason why *Ulysses* has been such a stumbling block to critics of all sorts, it seems to me, is the discrepancy between Joyce's aims and quality as a writer and his actual achievement in this and later works. In *Ulysses* he sought to write an absolutely new kind of novel and in this he surely succeeded. Inevitably the *avant-garde* loved him for his example. But the question for practising writers is not whether the method of *Ulysses* is original, but whether it is useful.

Last summer in the Alexander Graham Bell Museum in Nova Scotia I found myself thinking of James Joyce. He and Bell, utterly dissimilar in character, had at least one thing in common: their early work was more successful than their later work. The young Joyce wrote two beautiful, lucid books; the young Bell invented the telephone. But the older Bell, turning his interest to aeronautics, lost himself in a maze of complexities. He left behind him a series of the most intricate kites, and they display a mind of astounding ingenuity. The work was not useless because it explored many wrong theories of flight to dead ends, but the principles of flight as we know them are beautifully simple and now Bell's kites are in a museum, built in memory of the inventor of the telephone. The analogy between the older Bell and the older Joyce seems pretty clear to me. The novel may be mysterious, but its mystery is not that of a jigsaw puzzle or a private language.

It has been said of the police that they never overlook the importance of the obvious, and I think literary judgments would be clearer if literary men respected this element in the policeman's mind.

A novel, to say something extremely obvious, is a communication in story form. Hence it follows that if a book does not communicate and does not tell a story, it is not a novel.

A novel's chief value lies in its capacity to entertain and in its characters. If it lacks interesting, vital and important characters, not all the style and grace in the world will prevent the public from rejecting it.

A novel is neither a play, a poem nor a social dissertation. It may contain poetry, drama and social revelation, but if it does not contain these ingredients legitimately within the story, it bores the public and fails. No writer can survive if he fails to realize that the most fatal sin he can commit is to bore his readers.

The novel is, of all literary forms invented, the most sensitive and subtle, and until recently it was also the most accurate. (I do not say the most memorable, valuable, intense or important.) As these claims may not be self-evident, I suppose I should offer some evidence to support them.

The novel is more sensitive than the play because its form can contain many more nerve-ends and open up many more varieties of experience within a single book. A successful play seldom has room for more than one plot, and a successful poem, at least since the demise of the epic, becomes tedious if it is long. But a novel can run to more than a thousand pages, contain a dozen interconnected plots, a continuing rain of accurate detail, and yet, if the story-line is firmly directed, hold the reader from beginning to end.

The novel's subtlety is dependent partly on this rain of detail and partly on its length. It has room for analysis. Shakespeare can *reveal* psychological depths better than any writer who lived, but if he had tried to weigh and analyse motive with the precision of a Dostoievsky, he would have emptied his theatre. Nor can any playwright permit himself the series of delayed-action climaxes which makes the novel, in a master's hand, so true to life. Though Shakespeare can give us the young Juliet, he cannot give us the mature Juliet within the same play because his form forbids him that luxury. But look at Tolstoy's Natasha! In the beginning of *War and Peace* she is a child; in the middle a marvellous, wayward girl falling in love. But at the end she is a mother feeding her latest baby without a thought of romance in her head. Then we realize with a start of wonder that Natasha's driving force, all along, has been exactly the same as Juliet's. It was simply the mother-instinct.

It is this true-to-life aspect of good fiction, this freedom from the tyranny of the theatrical climax, which is responsible for yet another of the novel's values: its power to become an active agent within a society. The novel can make social situations live; it can clothe political and economic forces with flesh and blood. T. S. Eliot is probably a better artist than George Orwell and Arthur Koestler, but *The Wasteland* is a poet's lament, not the kind of social revelation which causes thousands of people to change their attitudes on public questions of moment. Novels like *Darkness At Noon* and *1984* are masterpieces of the novelist's art, but they are more than this: they have been, and still are, social forces.

One of the words used by people of novels they like is "satisfying". Though it has become a cliché of the advertisers, the word is still useful. Novels we feel to be satisfying do certain things for their readers.

First, the satisfying novel must entertain them; it must so grip them that when they enter the book they cannot be easy until they have finished it. Then it must make the reader a part of the world of the novelist's creation, and this it does by creating fictional characters more real than the reader's personal friends. In order to make characters like these, the novelist must also create the backgrounds and locales in which the characters move, and make them consistent and vivid. A satisfying novel must also hold all of its characters, all of its descriptions, dialogues, ideas, arguments, scenes and actions, within a whole which is harmonious, within a whole where the surprises are seen in retrospect to have been inevitable. And in the supremely satisfying novels, as in all good works of art, there is finally a mystery.

For all these reasons *War And Peace* is still the greatest novel ever written. It begins clumsily and is slow to get off the ground, it is probably too long and in places it is certainly too diffuse, but these defects vanish when the reader has absorbed its total impact. For *War And Peace* is a whole, coherent world. It includes peasant and emperor, saint and murderer, families and lonely individuals, politicians, generals, soldiers and business men, children and old men. It has more than a dozen different life-stories interwoven either with each other or within the texture of the novel itself. And all these incidents, lives and stories are comprehended within the author's vision of history and religion.

No other literary forms can produce a miracle like *War And Peace*. Other miracles they can and have produced, but not this particular one. On the basis of *War And Peace* alone, I could rest my case that the novel is the most sensitive and subtle literary form ever invented, and to these claims add yet another. It is also the most mature.

Now I must change the key. The novel, which has bestrode the literary field for more than a century, which has ruled almost without a rival, is now in jeopardy and is coming into disrepute.

Around the year 1950 people with their fingers on the

pulse of the literary market began to note a new phenomenon. The public was turning away from the novel in droves. Non-fiction, never a serious competitor before, was outselling fiction in cloth covers at the rate of close to five to one. So uncertain was the future of any novel that publishers were loath to introduce new writers, and many established novelists were forced to turn to other work in order to earn a living. Why and how did this happen? The question is still being pondered by writers and publishers; it is even being pondered by critics.

To some extent this change in the market was caused by new methods of selling literature, of which the development of the paper-back book was an important one. Many readers were unwilling to pay four dollars for a novel, the subject of which they did not know in advance would interest them, and preferred to wait a few years and buy the same book for fifty cents. But there is more to the novel's decline than this. There is the sure fact that what are called satisfying novels have become rarities, and to some extent the novelists cannot help this. Anyone who writes fiction today knows ruefully that the public is harder to satisfy than it ever was. But the important question is why it is harder to satisfy. Why has a situation come about in which people can legitimately ask whether this marvellous literary form may be in danger of extinction?

Institutions—and the novel can almost be called one—pass away for two reasons. One is internal decay, the other is the triumph of its competitors. Because it is easier to identify the nature of the competition than to examine the symptoms of decay, I shall talk about that aspect first.

The chief competitor of modern fiction—of this there can be no doubt at all—is the great fiction already written. There have been so many excellent novels, they have dealt with such a vast variety of themes, they have created such an army of memorable characters that the modern writer would be inhuman if he did not quail before the prospect of competing with the great dead. There is nothing new in this situation, as any musician can testify. The chief reason why it has been so hard to produce a musical masterpiece since 1830 is that Scarlatti, Bach, Handel, Vivaldi, Haydn, Mozart and Beethoven still overshadow everyone else in the field.

The second competitor of fiction is one I have already referred to: it is non-fiction. Ever since Lytton Strachey proved it possible to write a biography in novel form, utilizing all the tricks of the novelist's trade, non-fiction writers have steadily been transforming their art, and already they have defeated the novelist's art in the field of accuracy. I believe that future ages will recognize that the chief contribution made to literary form in this century has not been made by T. S. Eliot and James Joyce, but by writers of non-fiction. Biographies of real people used to be as dull as obituaries; now they are fascinating. Accounts of historical and current events used to be handled in the prose of scholars and reporters; now they are handled with consummate art and a wealth of artifice. The factual, and historically accurate, account of the sinking of the *Titanic* has been reproduced in this modern non-fiction style with far more excitement, drama and surprise than in any of the numerous novels written around the same subject. People say of Walter Lord's *A Night To Remember* that it reads like a novel. So it does. It was intended to.

For all I know, this really is the age of non-fiction. What novelist, after all, could invent a character like Hitler and make him credible? Could even Tolstoy create a Winston Churchill? Could Jules Verne tell a story as astounding as the Russian moon shot? Could any modern Goethe produce a modern Faust with a career as horrifying as that of Nazi Germany?

But this is really beside the point. It takes more than exciting material to make a book interesting; it takes art and craft. The most thrilling story on earth can be made as dull as a board report if it is told by a German professor in the professor's own style. Readers who leave fiction for non-fiction delude themselves when they say that they do so only because they prefer truth to imagination, or because they wish to be informed about history, science and life. Undoubtedly they do wish to be informed about history, science and life, but historians, scientists and sociologists have been publishing for years without the general public storming the university libraries. The real reason why scientific books like Rachel Carson's *The Sea Around Us* become best sellers is that they are entertaining.

The third competitor to the modern novel is television, but its competition, once you examine it, is seen to be more indirect than direct. Non-fiction competes fairly on its own merits, but television does not and cannot. Its success as a competitor of the novel depends neither on its style nor its content, but on its capacity, unwittingly, to employ the services of a mighty ally of which the average televiewer is usually unconscious. On the side of television in its battle for public support is a law of life.

The average organism, be it man, bird, beast or fish, tends to satisfy what it believes, or instinctively feels, are its basic needs with the minimum of effort. If squirrels live near apartment houses containing kindly old ladies who throw them food, the squirrels do not hoard. Of course, if the old ladies stop feeding them, as they did in my district during an abnormally long cold spell when an opened window chilled the house for hours, the squirrels die of starvation. But while food is there, they do not think of this.

The basic need of the average person between dinner and bedtime is usually to be able to sit in a chair in his living-room without being so bored that he can't stand himself. In the past, the period between dinner and bed was the great time for novel reading. Generally what was read was worthless, but it bred the reading habit and sometimes what was read was good.

Television has changed all this because of the law of life to which I have referred: watching television takes less effort than buying and reading a book. It is also easier than to get dressed and go out to the movies. It even seems cheaper, though I doubt if many families spent more money on the movies in the past than they spend now on buying and maintaining a TV set. Television has shaken the economic basis of Hollywood to the bedrock simply because it enables millions to avoid palpable boredom with no effort at all. You can already see its results in some of the students now entering college, who can hardly remember a time when a TV set was not in the family living-room. They associate reading with school and homework, and they don't like it.

But television cannot compete, it cannot even afford to compete, with any form of literature for the serious time of people who have acquired the reading habit and do like it. Most of its fare is, and must be kept, what the lawyers call free and harmless. It can permit the truth to come out in a debate or in the report of a political convention; it can show a ball game happening just as it does. But it cannot permit too much truth to come out in its plays and stories. Hollywood producers always understood that it is fatal to the box-office to offend vested interests, fraternal organizations, or occupations to which large numbers of the public belong. One of Hollywood's perennial problems has been to create a really plausible villain. He cannot be permitted to belong to any known church, to any minority racial group in the United States, to any lodge or labour union that is named. He cannot be a citizen of any foreign country which buys Hollywood products unless it is clearly pointed out that he is regarded by his fellow countrymen with the horror we reserve for an absolute pariah. It is safest for the villain simply to be a villain, with no further explanation offered. And surely one is naïve if one is surprised by this. The bigger the organization, the greater its cowardice. The larger the economic base of an enterprise depending for its profit on the public, the more readily does it succumb to the bullying of pressure groups.

The television industry is not only up against this age-old problem; it is up against still another. It must carry the commercial on the back of every programme commercially sponsored. From the standpoint of the sponsor, the commercial is what the show exists for, and if the show is so intense that its interruption by the commercial annoys the audience, only the most public-spirited of sponsors will underwrite it. A sponsor can hardly be blamed if he takes a poor view of an entertainment which competes successfully with his product.

Whether or not television can reduce the reading habit to the point where publishing becomes unprofitable and dies, only time will tell. My own guess is that it will not, for book publishing never was a big industry and I don't think it can become one. Its smallness enables it to be fairly independent, and if it offends a bully, the bully can't do anything important to get his own back. Its market was always much smaller than book-lovers assumed, and it still is. A Gallup Poll recently published showed that only eighteen adult Americans out of a hundred read even one book a year, and the poll made no mention of the quality of that one book. At a calculated guess, I would estimate the serious book-reading public in the English-speaking world at a little above three million people. This is only a guess and possibly the figure is exaggerated: there is no known way of determining who is a serious reader and who is not. But let it stand. Three million people is about three fifths of the population of Shakespeare's England, and in Shakespeare's time only a tiny percentage of Englishmen could even read their own names. Three million is a potential audience large enough to keep the novel alive and kicking. Even half a million might suffice.

For this reason I believe that the novel's future depends mainly on itself. Relatively it cannot hope to reign over its competitors as it did in Victoria's time, but those who are committed to it have some solid reasons for believing that it should be able to survive as long as people want to read anything.

Non-fiction, after all, cannot entirely supplant the need for good novels because it cannot be so intimate. The non-fiction writer can describe a Churchill, a Hitler, a Wellington, a Florence Nightingale, he can infer their motives and feelings, analyse what he believes to have been their characters and relate with accuracy and excitement the record of their actions and lives. But he cannot *become* them because he has not created them out of himself. Non-fiction cannot hope to give us a Hamlet, an Othello, a Natasha, an Alyosha Karamazov, a David Copperfield. Because its subjects are usually men and women of mark it can seldom if ever deal successfully with the humble. If you want Sam Weller or the old fisherman of Hemingway's book—for that matter if you want yourself—you still must go to some form of fiction.

For these reasons I do not believe that the competition of non-fiction can supplant the need for good novels, though it has already, and properly, persuaded serious readers that they waste their time if they read fiction which presents characters externally, or offers characters which are uninteresting or stereotypes.

That is why so many novelists are in trouble today; that is why it has never been so hard to write a serious novel the public will accept. Not only is it more difficult than ever to make a fictional character credible; it is harder still to make him seem interesting and important. So far as the public for novels is concerned, its threshold of boredom is the lowest it has ever been. Yet a lot of us write, and occasionally we succeed. But we would be stupid indeed if we pretended that our form is not in the position of having to prove its necessity, and even more stupid if we refused to ask ourselves why.

The novel is losing readers because only rarely today does it satisfy the only public it should consider. That public is not a coterie of highbrow *afficionados* of literature nor again is it the mass-man of the television audience. It is the serious reader who knows himself to be an individual and is also a responsible citizen competent to earn a living, raise a family and even to vote. He may be a business man or a worker, he may be a farmer, a fisherman or a schoolteacher, he may be a lawyer, a doctor or a student. More often than not—far more often than not—the profession of the serious reader today, when the reader applies for a passport, is classified as housewife. All of these readers with their various backgrounds have one thing in common: their awareness, often subconscious, of their own uniqueness as human individuals. None of them belong to the amorphous crowd, and most of them are people of goodwill.

Therefore they are ill at ease in this atomic, consumer world which changes so fast; they are ill at ease and are not afraid to admit it. Externally the world is changing so fast that the military power mustered by the United States in 1945, contrasted with that of now, stands about half-way between that of now and the force presented by Henry V at Agincourt. Internally this brave world is newer still, for our knowledge of what Dr. Penfield calls the microcosm of the brain, itself as marvellously complex as the microcosm of the firmament, has altered, among those who know anything about it at all, most of the materialistic concepts of life on which our outward shows of government, economics and practical philosophy are based. Psychology as a science is so new it can hardly be called a science, yet already it has been able to shake our traditional concept of our own inner selves.

And of course (the average organism satisfies its basic needs with the minimum of effort) this new science was barely out of the cradle before it was prostituted, with the result that thought-controllers and psychological engineers, highly paid by politicians and people with goods to sell, have invaded the territory once entered with reverence by poets and prophets.

What wonder, then, if novelists who learned their craft in the Twenties, and acquired their vision of life still earlier, are now out of their depth? In the Thirties some of the most respected men in modern fiction used the Marxist philosophy as a frame for their stories; a few years later most of them realized that deeper causes than any dreamed of by Marx were responsible for the horrors of the twentieth century. Even worse is the plight of some younger writers who have emerged since the war. Facing a situation that frightens them, they either try to escape it or to exorcize it. If they do the latter, they concentrate on peripheral characters, invariably unpleasant, whose very existence is a slap in the face to the conformist society of the advertisers which they loathe. If they escape it, they usually follow one of two courses. They bury a commonplace tale about commonplace people under a mountain of self-conscious symbolism inherited from Eliot and Joyce, or they create a world for two in which an ordinary boy and an ordinary girl spend the first half of the book trying to get into bed with each other and the last half trying to get out. Nobody can blame sensible people for turning away from these clichés. Up to a point some of the novels have been true and honest—I think, for example, of *The Catcher In The Rye* —but compared with the great fiction of the past they have been astonishingly, even alarmingly, limited in their outlook and maturity.

Yet even in the last decade there have been some strong novels published, though few have been written by Americans, and a number of them have even been successful in the market. Invariably they have been books dealing with real people in situations in which the cards were not stacked arbitrarily against them. Some were even books which accepted as a living force an entity dismissed with derision in the Twenties and Thirties. That entity is the mystery the Stoics called the World Soul and Christians and Jews call God. Some novels have even presented decent people as interesting and competent.

I have been a writer too long to dismiss the importance of fashion in literature and criticism. Fashions change like the fashions in women's clothes. But there is one thing about writing I know is true.

No writer can indefinitely get away with it if he despises the public, nor can any writer hold the public if he consistently distorts truth.

The former crime has been committed again and again by the conscious highbrows, the latter by some famous writers who have never been able to shake themselves free of an outworn fashion.

The novel in the Twenties and Thirties often seemed cynical because men of goodwill were in revolt against clichés inherited from the Victorians. One of these was that war is glorious and another was that true love should be disembodied. The realism of this period was like a gale of fresh air, and it produced a vital literature.

But the fashion outlived its usefulness, and cynicism became a habit. Cynicism, after all, is the last resort of the clever, for no cynic is likely to look a fool. But this does not mean that cynicism is more intelligent than faith. It is certainly not intelligent to deny evidence, and there is as much evidence to suggest that the Giver of life did not intend life to be a dirty trick as in Einstein's conclusion that God does not play at dice. A man in despair may cry that as flies to wanton boys, so are we to the gods. But in the end it was Hitler, not Churchill, who went to destruction. Honour is not always defeated by dishonour, and virtue wins in more important fields than in the pages of the slick paper magazines. Decency may, on occasion, even triumph in the state of Mississippi.

I believe that the serious public has bitterly resented this automatic cynicism of so much of the recent literature it has been told to admire. Since the last war the novel, especially in the United States, has failed worst of all in dealing with the very subject in which it should excel. That subject is love. The fact that the human body was kept out of love by the Victorians seems an inadequate reason for keeping the human soul out of it today. Yet it is a fact that in novel after novel the act of love is treated like the description of a problem in mechanical engineering. My heart sinks when I read through a long narrative dealing with the lives of lawyers or business men and come to the inevitable breaks, like the breaks for the television commercial, in which the hero goes to bed with the wife of his best friend and neither gets any fun out of it. I know perfectly well that this sort of thing causes a good many thousands of morons and deprived people to buy books they otherwise would not buy, but I still believe it is a passing fashion. Inside another decade most Americans should be aware of what a naked woman looks like, and they may even prefer the reality to the literary shadow. The novel today is in much the same position as the English theatre at the time of Addison, when playwrights automatically reproduced the stale intrigues of the Restoration dramatists, when the sole purpose of an alderman or a business man on the stage was to provide a wife whom a man of fashion might seduce. What was yesterday's realism is today's cliché and for a simple combination of reasons: men are imitative and life keeps changing.

If the future of the novel lies anywhere, it is in the very fact that modern life is unable to be static. If it were static, I don't suppose we could look forward to any more literature of quality than the Romans got after Aurelius. But where change exists there is life, and where life exists among the educated, there is need of precisely the kind of communication the novel can make to a man reading in solitude.

For the novel, which has developed technically to the point where it can contain almost any symphony of ideas and feelings a writer wishes to pour into it, is still an available form. I am Scotch and by nature inclined to anticipate doom, but I honestly know of no other form of entertainment which can offer the novel's peculiar combination of intellectual satisfaction and emotional catharsis. There will be fewer novels in the future than in the past, and fewer still the public will accept as important. To write a great novel will become increasingly harder as the serious public grows increasingly more demanding. But it can be done, and because it can be done, it probably will be done. For though the novel may not any longer be the most accurate and popular form of literary art, it still has no rival that can be as subtle, wise, intimate, sensitive and mature.

16 THE SECRET AND VOLUPTUOUS LIFE OF A ROSE-GROWER

This moist, cool summer with intermittent washes of sunshine has been poor for grain and vacations, exasperating to tennis players and cruel to mothers who count on summer as a time when the children are out of the house. It has given the cicadas little to sing about, it has sent snails to the lawns and slugs to the lettuce, it has darkened the moon and ruined the haystacks for country lovers. But to one species of lovely life this moist summer has been the kindest I ever remember in this part of the world. Never have the roses been so good.

Roses love sunshine and warmth, but soft nights and moist airs and a little sun are kindlier to them than steady sun and dry nights. Roses love a land like Ireland better even than the Irishmen do, for they thrive there as Irishmen do not. This summer we have had Irish weather all around Montreal. So now, while the second blooming makes in the canes, is the time to wonder why the men who love roses do so with such a voluptuous devotion.

They do so because roses are like women, like all sorts of women miraculously transformed into the abstracted and distilled essence of the ideal woman who vanishes at a touch. Like their prototypes, no two species of rose are ever precisely the same. Each bush moreover is always unpredictable, and from one season to the next its cultivator can never be sure what it will do. Red roses in all their varieties are brunettes in velvet gowns; the yellows are blondes; the pinks and mixed varieties—by far the most numerous—are the women whose colouring and nature can be described by no single adjective, and some white roses are the impossibly pure snow queens of legend.

So there they are with their variety of shades, textures, forms, characters and scents. Scent in a rose is like loving-kindness in a woman, texture her quality of understanding, and an hour in the life of a rose is like a year in the life of a woman after the former has been cut and the latter has known a man she loves. Therefore no one can hope to find an interesting rose in a florist's shop any more than he can expect to meet a beneficent woman in a night club. The florists should not include roses in their business, and I know several sensitive florists who feel on this point as I do myself. Commercial roses are for those who do not understand the genius of this flower: they are bred for the length of their stems and their formless uniformity, they are like show girls with long sturdy legs, matching bosoms and complexions, and an Atlantic City perfection. A man who buys a dozen long-stemmed roses, all identical, is like the convention executive who orders a dozen standardized girls to ensure the success of a banquet.

But most amateur rose-growers, certainly if they are male, are suppressed voluptuaries, and the artists among them understand that nobody should cultivate too many roses at the same time. The millionaire with his rose-garden covering half an acre is as dull as the sultan with his harem of a thousand concubines. Hired gardeners know the inhabitants of the one, eunuchs of the other, and in each case the master wearies himself with an excess of plenty. The question of how many rose-bushes a man needs for his personal happiness depends on the man himself and on the intensity of his interest in the individuality of roses. But since the law and his own vitality limit all but exceptional males to one woman at a time, or at least to one woman at a moment, there is no reason why, in his cultivation of roses, a man should not sublimate his ambition for all different kinds of women into the possession of two or three dozen different bushes. But he must be willing to give himself to them; he must cultivate them personally; he must guard them against insects, blight, rodents, ice and in our part of the world against the most dangerous hazard of all, the warm sun of a false spring, and let the author of *Lolita* carefully consider the significance of this latter point. He must also give himself time to know each one of them personally, to explore their characters, to verse himself in their endless variety of little ways.

Roses have thorns (the point is trite but must be made) and they are ruthless to the flesh of any man who handles them carelessly or who gives them a casual pinch while pretending to be doing something else. They show jealousy to each other if they are crowded and have to fight for room in the sun, and when you are bending down to care for one bush, another may claw you in the rear if you are careless. A great many roses have done this to me, but I have never blamed them, for it has been only through my own clumsiness that I have been scratched by one bush while paying attention to another.

The more thoroughbred a rose is, the more emphatic or subtle is her personality. Each bush is subject to moods, and each proved species has its own special name, which reflects (like the names of their human counterparts) much more on the donors of the names than on the roses themselves.

There is a rose called Better Times, and the professional rosier who supplied that name probably called his wife Toots. There is a splendid rose called Texas Centennial, another called after the Mojave desert, another, believe it or not, goes by the name of G.I. Joe. *Quelle bêtise!*

To my taste the worst name of them all is President Herbert Hoover, for it interposes between the rose and the voluptuary one of the best-known physiognomies of the western world, one moreover which lacks any possible association with the spirit and grace of roses. A dahlia might have been called after Mr. Hoover, a dyed chrysanthemum or even a prize tomato plant, but not a rose. Without casting any aspersions on the political rectitude of the thirtieth President of the United States, I have to report that my first Herbert Hoover spent two years in my garden without showing a single blossom, that my second went wild and my third was chewed by mice in its first winter. Stubborn as any Republican in face of the hardest evidence, I kept on trying to make a Herbert Hoover grow and finally I succeeded. In one season a bush actually bloomed, and a splendid rose it turned out to be—not supreme, not particularly subtle, not the kind a man would die for—but well turned, rather sumptuous, somewhat like an Edwardian girl in her late twenties with a strawberry curl in her hair.

I continue with this matter of names, for a bad name diminishes the essence both of a rose or a woman, while a good name may often define a character. If anyone wishes proof of this, let him consider the rose called Countess Vandal. The man who named her understood roses as Tolstoy understood women, for the Vandal with her long, cool, exquisite bud, her pale, coppery complexion like an Oriental queen's, ravishes the eye but cheats the soul. For she is almost scentless and in middle age she becomes draggled; she is *la belle dame sans merci* among the roses.

Also well named is Betty Uprichard, radiant and joyous in youth, full of girlish sparkle and excitement. On the day she is cut, Betty Uprichard is an Irish girl in love for the first time as she stands in the wind and sun with the light in her hair, and she gives out the clean fragrance of a rapture in which passion has no part. But life almost instantly becomes too much for her; she blows and fades so quickly she hurts the heart and her last hours are those of a woman whose life is over at thirty.

There are so many roses like her, and while I love them young I grieve for their destiny, which is predictable. One is Mrs. Van Rossem from Holland, who bursts out of an ample bud like a russet-cheeked, full-bosomed country girl avid for life and loving. In youth her fragrance is so intense it can fill a garden, but she spends it as fast as she spends herself on the first oaf who sees her and takes her. In no time she is blowsy, a travesty of herself when she should be at her best, her faded petals wide open as they beg for an admiration she knows she has lost and can never regain.

There are roses which resemble healthy, pretty, well-brought-up girls who simply lack the understanding to become supremely beautiful. One of these is Johanna Hill, who reminds me of someone I knew in college who all my friends agreed was a nice, nice girl. At dances she never went out into cars to neck; she was kind to lonely freshmen and every Sunday you saw her going to church with her parents. She carried an ever-so-faint suggestion of a polite perfume behind her ears—at least so I guessed, though I never knew her well enough to be sure of this—and in her second year at college she got herself engaged to a man so silent he probably had lockjaw. He studied law and, of course, he went into corporation work; he never did anything wrong and he never did anything right, and in his home, the nice, nice girl faded quickly into a neglected housewife with three children while the corporation man moved slowly upward from a Chevrolet to a Pontiac to a Buick. There he stopped.

There are roses which resemble the buxom women of Rubens—warm and dewy, lusty rather than passionate, mothers of a sturdy race who never make trouble but stay full-bodied and full-coloured to the end. The Mrs. Barraclough is one; Madame Jules Bouché is another. Full-bodied also is the rose inappropriately called The Doctor, but her bosom is Italian rather than Nordic, and if you wish to find her prototype among women, Giorgione has painted her again and again.

There are roses admired by sophisticates because they are tricked out with an unnatural novelty which makes them resemble the women you see moving slowly along Fifth Avenue at the trysting hour toward a rendezvous at the Pierre or Sherry-Netherlands with an account executive or a thrice-married broker from downtown. I cultivated one for several years and liked her reasonably well, and her presence in the garden made an agreeable compensation for the days of my ignorance when first I went to New York and saw her prototypes in the Plaza at sunset and even envied the men who could afford them. She was the Contessa de Sastago. Her basic pink was slashed with a wild, incongruous blaze of yellow in one part of her bloom, and it gave the effect of a carefully contrived platinum lock in a head of brown hair. The Contessa had also a neat figure (as you might assume), and not a little staying power, but there was too much calculation in her character. Her personality was so contrived I never was able to penetrate to its secret, and indeed I suspected it might be a disappointment if ever I found it. After she died of black spot, I never tried to grow her again.

There are roses—increasingly more of them every year—which resemble the big, sun-ripened girls who disport themselves on the beaches of southern California, drink an excess of orange juice and seem perfect until you get to know them: girls with faultless bosoms, waistlines and thighs, and only one limitation: they don't seem to mean much. Yet they are very pleasant to have around, all of them are friendly and they possess an advantage the great ones lack: a man doesn't mind giving them now and then to his friends.

Everyone knows, I suppose (and if he does not know he is doomed to frustration) that it is the power to evoke poetic emotions which renders both women and roses unforgettable. After ten years of experimenting, I can now say that most of the roses in my garden possess this power, at least to some degree. The Helen Traubel is one: a full, luscious pink, generous in her nature, she reproduces in no small degree the tones of the lady after whom she is named. Also there is the Tallyho, who cannot help her absurd name, a dark, Latin lady (or possibly Jewish), who reminds me of the cello-player painted by Augustus John when he was a young man. This is a rose you do not learn in an evening or even in a month. She is so strong in her colouring, so individual, so proud in her bearing that you fear her a little, yet she is a true woman and a very exceptional one, being at once an aristocrat and intelligent, passionate and discriminating, very complex, for despite her ardency she is one whose heart is always ruled by her head. The Eclipse has the exciting quality of a natural ash-blonde who grows old without losing either her charm or her figure. The Forty-Niner (the second-worst name I have ever known applied to a rose) has a flat, textureless sheen on her under-petals while her upper surface is a rich, satiny scarlet. She makes me think of a husky tomboy who outgrows cokes and comics and basketball games after she has know admiration and love, but somehow—somehow I am never quite certain that her maturity is permanent, or that if she were offered the choice of a coke or a Château Yquem, she might not prefer the former in her heart.

A relatively new floribunda, disastrously named Fashion, is like a bevy of laughing, delightful girls who never grow old, for the salmon pink of her small but exquisite blossoms never fades until the petals fall, and though she is only a floribunda, her fragrance is as intensely mature as that of any of the full-grown hybrid teas but one. There are also a few old-fashioned girls I cherish and would not be without: the delicate, pearl-grey, pastel-pink Madame Butterfly whom our grandfathers adored, and that nobly enduring white rose, Frau Karl Drushki. Both remind me of Tennyson: the former a young girl who never went abroad without a chaperon, the latter a great lady who rode in carriages with a coachman up front in the days before anyone had heard of Freud.

Men who love roses will differ among themselves about dozens of varieties, just as men who know music will differ in their affection for composers. But just as all men who understand music set Bach and Mozart in a special place at the very summit of their love, so do all rose-growers agree about two transcendent examples of the species. One is dark and the other fair, and (as of course you know), their names are Crimson Glory and Peace. Beside these two queens even so exquisite a flower as Charlotte Armstrong is condemned to the role of a lady-in-waiting wearing a tiara and not a crown. These two roses are so celebrated it would be an impertinence to describe them in detail, the one with its texture of deep red velvet, the other with the hue of Homer's rose-fingered dawn, and literally so, since the pure, shining-pale gold of her petals is fringed with a delicately flushing line of pink when she is dawn-young. As one is the queen of the dark ladies, the other of the fair, each complements not only the tones of the other, but also the character. Crimson Glory is the most passionate rose in the world. She does not bestow her passion lightly, nor throw it away, but she keeps both her essence and her loveliness the full length of her days. It is her supreme virtue that it is not until she has reached middle-age that her figure, her scent and her air reach a full maturity. Milton has given her mood in the lines:

> *Sometimes let gorgeous tragedy*
> *In sceptred pall come sweeping by!*

The Peace was bestowed upon us by a Frenchman descended from a line of rosiers who trace their craft all the way back to the French kings, and it was the Americans, not he, who called her Peace. Her creator's name for her was *gloria dei* and so I think of her always, for her passion, her nature and her essence are entirely spiritual. Untouchable and serene, dawn-like, she is not a queen but a goddess.

17 INTERMEZZO

Years ago in the days between the wars I went to Greece on an Italian coaster which travelled from Brindisi across the Adriatic and thence along the coast of Epirus towards the Corinthian Canal and Athens. It had to be a very small ship to fit the canal and in that season a great many people seemed to be going to Greece. When I tried to get a drink in the smoke-room I found myself wedged between a corpulent, yellow-toothed citizen of Salonika and a theatrically cadaverous character whose age was middle and whose face might well have come from anywhere. I escaped to the deck, found an unoccupied yard of railing, and soon afterwards was joined by the cadaverous man, who informed me that the Salonikan was a brothel-keeper and that he himself was in the torpedo-making business.

"I cannot think," he said in language excessively formal and with an accent indeterminate, "of any other profession more congenial to a man of my temperament. Even the word 'torpedo' charms me. It is Latin, as you doubtless know, my dear, young sir. In Latin it is 'xorpedo' and the English meaning of 'xorpedo' is 'laziness'. That is because the primitive torpedoes never moved. They were anchored mines. *Mais nous avons changé tout çela, n'est-ce pas?* Now we can fire a torpedo four—even five miles, strike a ship, and boom-bang-boom—down she goes!"

He rubbed his hands together with zest and informed me that he spoke nine languages, that his birthplace was Bucharesti, that at various times he had been a citizen of Rumania, Turkey, Greece, Tangier, France, Austria and Italy, and that at the moment he was a Jugoslav.

"I have been everywhere," he said, "except in England. I read the English classics—Shakespeare, Dickens, Trollope—and every time it is possible I give myself the opportunity to speak the English language. I love England very much. She is my ideal country."

Naturally I asked him why he had never visited England when he loved her so much, and he sighed.

"A man, even me, must retain one small illusion." He made a tiny circle with thumb and forefinger. "One small illusion is necessary for the mental health. England is my illusion. She is my *last* illusion. So you can see, my dear, young sir, it would be fatal for me ever to visit England. It would be quite impossible for me ever to do business with Englishmen. It would be mental suicide for me ever to become well acquainted with Englishmen."

He asked me if I was familiar with the poem of Goethe which begins, *Kennst du das Land, wo die Zitronen blühn*, and I said that I was.

"Then you understand me. England for me is what Italy was for Goethe. What Italy was for so many Germans. It is a thing of the mind. It is a dream which must not be permitted to receive the touch that makes a dream vanish." He quoted:

"Kennst du es wohl? Dahin! Dahin!
Möcht ich mit dir, O mein Geliebter, ziehn!

And now, so long as I never *know* England, I can continue

making my little torpedoes, and who knows?" A theatrical grin. "One of these days perhaps Mussolini will fire one of my torpedoes into an English ship."

Since that voyage to Greece I have sometimes wondered whether my younger self and the torpedo-maker did not have much in common. Growing up in Halifax when I did, reading English boys' books, meeting *émigré* Englishmen who talked of their country as Adam probably talked of the Garden after he had been thrown out of it, I confess that I swallowed a goodly dose of myth concerning that country. But unlike the torpedo-maker I went to England to study, and during the last thirty years at home have encountered a sufficient number and variety of Englishmen in my work and elsewhere to have acquired what might be called a sense of proportion. Yet I believe it true nonetheless that England is a myth-producing nation, and one of the hardest to visualize cold. She is hated extravagantly or loved extravagantly, and Englishmen seem to prefer living between these poles than living as the Scotch do, neither hated nor loved but on the whole tolerated. The beauty of the southern shires and the sheer loveliness of certain English establishments affect one like great works of art which by their power defy analysis. My student days in Oxford were by no means entirely halcyon; nobody's student days ever are. But time has crystallized many of their incidents like the twigs in Stendhal's salt-mine, with the result that only occasionally am I able to see England with realism. When I revisited England in the summer of 1958 I was very tired on my arrival and often bored while wandering about alone, and the English restaurant cooking frequently gave me indigestion. But no sooner was I back in Canada than the familiar process of crystallization began all over again.

Of the next five pieces in this book, I must admit that the first four are perhaps a little mythological.

18 OCTOBER AND SMOKE

October is the remembering month in this country and perhaps in every country north of the palms. In southern Quebec where I live from the Queen's Birthday until Thanksgiving, I spend my summers thinking ahead with eagerness to the fortnight or so before I return to town. As September falls back for the finale of October my thoughts are crowded with patterns of recall, and the memories are all good. I love October. I'm almost never angry in October, and I do my best work at that time of year and always have. Perhaps the body is like a plant that stores sunlight into the mind as the leaves of a chrysanthemum feed into the bud all the sun-filled hours of the summer months. Perhaps it is simply the beauty of the time. In eastern Canada the woods are as silent as cathedrals without priests, gothic in shape and prospect, and though their colours are Byzantine, by some miracle they avoid any suggestion of blood. Their passion is the purified emotion of the greatest music of Bach, who wooed death as a friend. As I grow older—how many other men, if honest, would say the same?—I become cold to the ordinary expressions of religion, but in October in the country I have a sense of being in church with God. And if, as happened two years ago, the weather in the first fortnight of October is grey and miserable, I feel that God has deserted me and I go into winter as though I were entering a white hell.

October in Canada atones for the poverty of our spring: Easter in Canada is nothing but a date on a calendar and a special service in church. The real spring ritual is a Mediterranean festival; in North America you must be south of Maryland before you can feel it as an Italian does. But to a Canadian, October has a meaning deeper than any Mediterranean Easter, because it is nature's supreme expression of the concept of life in death and death in life, of the fact that no matter how many individual lives and years pass away, there will be more years and lives, and that the rituals of both are eternal.

Why is it that in Canada the dying year always seems to be dying young? Why, for all the glamour and boisterous colourings, is it so unsullied, unworn and untired?

The first time such questions ever occurred to me was the first year I spent in England. I thought I knew exactly what to expect of an English spring; I had read the poets who invented the English April. But until that first English autumn it had never occurred to me to wonder why the most gifted poetic race since the Greeks had made so little of October. Some days were like Keats' season of mists and mellow fruitfulness, but most of the time October was dark russet in the day and foggy at night, and when the mists flooded the quadrangles and the moon appeared above them, it was like stepping into a cistern charged with chilly quicksilver when you left your staircase to cross the quad. October seemed a tired month that dragged into the inexpressible dreariness of an English November. Instead of feeling that life was poised on a mountain peak in clear air, I felt only fatigue and homesickness, and the weight of the generations who had lived in Oxford long before me.

Yet it is to that English October, to a night just before the end of it, that the most persistent of my memories of that month goes back.

Returning to my room one evening after eating alone in a restaurant in the town, knowing hardly anyone in the whole university and remembering how happy I had been during the last year in my college at home, I put some coal on the fire which was the only source of heat in that ancient room and went to my desk intending to work. There I found a note left by the porter while I was out. It was a filled-in form which had been printed in the last century, for the original date (18—) had been scratched out and emended to the actual date of that October day in 1928. The note was printed in Latin, but there was a blank space in which my name had been written in the Provost's pinched handwriting. The printed Latin words bade me attend the Provost in his rooms at (Arabic numerals) 9.30 that night. I gathered he had reached the Rhodes Scholar freshmen who were always on the bottom of the college list.

It was then 9.25, so I put on my gown and crossed the quadrangle to the Provost's room. I found him in his study dressed in a smoking jacket and elastic-sided boots, eighty-three years old, slim, somewhat bowed in the shoulders as a scholar should be, and looking as though he had been sitting in that same spot for at least half a century. I knew otherwise, for every Sunday he invited undergraduates to lunch and a ten-mile walk, its goal a hostel outside Oxford which he had established for tramps, pan-handlers and any itinerants who could convince the warden that they declined toil on principle. The Provost was said to judge each undergraduate by the impression he made on the tramps. He had the eccentric democracy only to be found in an old-fashioned English aristocrat, and on more than one occasion he had been heard to say to the Senior Tutor, "In this college, sir, we will take one Etonian, one Harrovian and one black man a year, and no more." The Provost's head was completely bald, but his white beard was luxuriantly bushy and long enough to cover his chest. His eyebrows, also white, were more formidable than Lord Strathcona's. Though American Rhodes Scholars insisted that he looked like General Lee, to most of us it was sufficient that he looked like himself.

On this October night the Provost invited me to tobacco and lit his pipe from a paper dip which he ignited from the fire in his hearth.

"I expect you're somewhat lonesome," he began. "I know I should be in your place."

The truth was that I had never been so lonesome in my life, but I was afraid to admit it even to myself, for Oxford had been my goal for years, and I had the feeling common to youth that homesickness is a shameful weakness.

"At this time of year," the Provost went on, "everyone from your country must be homesick. If he isn't, he should be. I was in Canada once in what you call the fall. Indeed I was taken up that singular mountain you have in Montreal. They wanted me to take a carriage—I noticed that your people dislike using their legs—but of course I walked. I have always thought how appropriate it was that Jacques Cartier climbed Mount Royal in the early autumn. I suppose Cortez' sight of the Pacific from the peak in Darien was the greater vision, but to look into the heart of America in October and fancy it was China—" the Provost's beard nodded as he shook his head. "What's your church?"

"Presbyterian, Provost."

"Ah!" he said, and shook his head once more. "Not much help there, I'm afraid. I expect it's my duty to inform you that there *is* a church of that denomination in Oxford. I understand it's a very modern, very bare building and I believe that the Senior Tutor passes the plate there every Sunday. I think he's what they call an elder. However"—the old man's face brightened—"almost directly next door to it is a tavern called the Bear." He waited a moment. "Am I right in assuming from your expression that you are familiar with it? I thought as much. Now the Bear occupies a *very* old building."

"Yes, Provost."

"But doubtless you are overcome by the oldness of everything here?"

"Yes, sir." I was too relieved to be ashamed. "I think perhaps I am."

I was afraid to add—indeed at that time I had not been able to analyse the feeling—that what really overcame me was the sense of the total insignificance of myself in an institution so ancient that half the faces of the stone sages behind the Bodleian had been eroded by time.

"At first many men from America feel as you do," the Provost said, "and I think it charming of them to admit it. And yet—" the old man had a really wonderful smile—"although our college goes back to a foundation in 1326, I believe I am safe in saying that the oldest property we possess, apart from the land, comes from America."

I tried to imagine what he was talking about. The front quad had been built in the reign of Charles I and sections of the third quad were pre-Tudor; one small section, I knew, ante-dated the Wars of the Roses.

"It so happens I can show it to you tonight." The Provost rose to his feet briskly. "It has no business being in my rooms, for its home is the Senior Common Room. But it has recently come back from the silversmith, who did something minor with it, and the porter brought it to me. I fancy he knows that the Senior Tutor considers it less interesting than a gloss in Aristotle."

The old man left the room and returned a moment later nursing in his hands what seemed to be a chafing dish of reduced size. He set it on a table under the light and I saw it was quite small, but subtly and exquisitely made, with the silver of its mounting shining as though the metal were so old, polished and soft that it did not so much reflect light as absorb it. When I looked at the dish itself I realized that it was not a chafing dish at all, for it was made of a strange dark wood in the form of two hemi-ovals so lightly balanced that the cover swung open and shut at the least pressure of a finger.

"This," said the Provost, "was the first of many American natives who have become, shall we say, members of our society. As President Eliot of Harvard pointed out when he was our guest a few years ago—was it forty years ago or only thirty-seven? I think, now, it was thirty-six—at any rate, Dr. Eliot was gracious enough to tell us that the beauty of this dish does not lie in its American origin or even in its basic American material, but in its present setting. Do you know what it was in its natural state?"

The bowl was certainly made of wood, but time and careful hands had polished it to the texture of dark satin. I shook my head.

"This dish," said the Provost, "was made of an object picked up on a south coast beach by a member of our college. Nobody in England at that time had seen anything like it. Nobody could guess where it had come from. But it was good for carving, and somebody in the college handed it over to a craftsman who fashioned it into this lovely vessel. You are still unable to imagine what it was?"

Again I shook my head.

"It has changed, of course, with time and its surroundings. And yet, only a century after it was picked up, when Columbus returned from America, men in our society were able to clear up the mystery of its origin. It is a coconut. It drifted across the Atlantic in the Gulf Stream." He looked at me from under his white eyebrows. "Sometimes I amuse myself with wondering from which of the islands it came. Of course, it may even have originated in Florida, but I fancy, somehow, that it did not. It is pleasant, don't you think, to remember that Christians in our college enjoyed it for fully two centuries before Calvin wrote the *Institutes?*"

The Provost left the dish on the table and resumed his chair.

"It is excellent to be young," he said, "but once one grows accustomed to it, I think on the whole it is better to be old."

A long silence fell in the room and I felt strangely unreal. My loneliness had disappeared, I felt remarkably comfortable, yet at the same time I had a new feeling of confidence. I was a visitor to the Provost's heritage, I was priviliged for a few years to share it, but for some unaccountable reason I was suddenly freed from its weight. I knew that in my lifetime I would do more work than the Provost had done in his. It would probably be unimportant work, but while doing it I would not always be aware that it was.

Looking across the hearth rug I saw a rhythmic movement in the Provost's beard and heard a steady note in his breathing. He was asleep. I got up and moved quietly to the silver dish and studied it under the light. I opened and closed the lid, and the simple mechanism worked soundlessly. Men in gorgeous medieval robes had sat about this dish under candlelights. Sir Walter Raleigh in his brief time in this college might have known it before he saw Virginia; men with their hair flowing in cavalier fashion had spared this ornament when they melted down the rest of the college plate for Charles I in the Civil War; gouty dons of the eighteenth century, portentous with wigs and Ciceronian periods, had drunk themselves into nightly stupors before this dish; Newman and the Oxford reformers of the last century had seen it, and a hundred years hence men would see it who crossed the Atlantic in rockets.

I moved to the window where the draperies were undrawn. The front quadrangle, the Caroline one, was filled with quicksilver and the part in shadow was darker than the darkened windows of the hall. A burst of bibulous laughter rose to me and I saw the ghostly forms of three undergraduates reel across the court from the college gate. The vast October moon, suddenly clear of a cloud-wrack, stared round over Oxford.

Turning back to the room I wondered how much longer the Provost would sleep, and whether I was expected to leave quietly or wake him or remain until the porter called to rouse him. I sat down, no longer lonely, no longer feeling small. Time passed into a cessation of time and I heard the garland of sound from St. Mary's spire which always precedes the striking of the notes for the full hour. When the eleventh note of the bell had ceased vibrating, the Provost opened his eyes.

"Ah yes, we were talking of Jacques Cartier. It was really a tremendous moment when he stood on that mountain of yours. How strange that he thought your river led to China! I've never understood why anybody wants to go to China." He got up and showed me to the door. "I wonder if you'll live long enough to see wigs in America. It occurs to me, sometimes, that within another fifty years America may be almost ripe for its eighteenth century, but I dare say things have always been different over there."

I went out into the damp, ancient chill of that October night and walked slowly back to my staircase, knowing as one does in moments of prescience that I should remember everything about that visit. Now, twenty-seven Octobers later, it seems only a few nights ago, and at moments I feel almost as young as I did then. I have yet to know, and perhaps I never will, whether the Provost was right when he said that it is better to be old than to be young.

19 MY LAST COLONEL

May with us is the cruellest month, doing most of the things that T. S. Eliot's April does for England, breeding in its last days (and then only if we are lucky) lilacs out of the dead land and mixing the memory of a seven-month winter with desire for all kinds of things, including the melting of the last remnants of snow in the hills. May with us makes me long for May in England which (if England is lucky and it does not rain every day) is one of the reasons why even her enemies love her. May in England used to be the time when Oxford undergraduates, in the days before the girls moved in to change their habits, read their Homer like young Greeks in their groves, and talked about Plato and God, if they were sober, on the tiny lane of water they called a river. May was also the month when my Celtic soul first learned to relax and enjoy the English even to the extent of drowsing in the outfield (the deep, they called it) as the eleventh man of a cricket team assembled at the eleventh hour by a college secretary who still looked misty-eyed from a twenty-first birthday party the night before. It was also the month when I met my first and last Cheltenham colonel.

The chief difference between England and this continent is that in England you can still discover things. Over here every spot which anyone has ever looked at has its charms explained to you by the tourist associations, and every local peculiarity is charted and analysed in the magazines. Wherever you go in North America south of the upper reaches of the Northwest Territories you feel as though everyone else had been there before you. In England it is not like this because the English do not bother to tell strangers about anything except places like the British Museum and the Tower which, if they are Londoners, they never visit themselves. So it was natural that my friend Henderson, in my first English May, when he suggested that we take in the Gloucestershire tennis tournament, omitted to mention that the place where it was played, Cheltenham, is the kind of place Cheltenham turned out to be. Together we set out across the Cotswold Hills in Henderson's car (cuckoos in the hedges and larks in the sky) and it was only when we entered Cheltenham that it occurred to me to ask him what the town was like.

"They've got rather good courts," was his answer.

"But what about the town itself?"

"Oh, I expect we shall see a few colonels. They go there to die, you see. But they've got jolly good courts, just the same."

Half an hour later I was on one of the jolly good courts facing a major who looked not much older than myself, but was. He lacked a chin, his hair was carroty, his face freckled and he was an extremely bad tennis player. His name, I remember, was Backhouse and when I introduced myself to him he did not shake hands. I decided I didn't like him and as soon as I found he was willing to run, I ran the hell out of him, sadistically sending the ball back and forth from corner to corner while he ran and kept hoisting it back. A first-class match was being played on another court between Bunny Austin and a visiting Austrian, and the only person watching the major and me, besides the umpire, was an elderly gentleman with a straight back, a red face, a waxed pepper-and-salt moustache and stiff white hair. Despite the heat he was dressed in tweeds. He carried a shooting stick on which he sat beside the umpire's stand and he behaved in a manner peculiar for an Englishman. Not only did he applaud whenever I won a point; he applauded whenever Backhouse made an error, and once he applauded when Backhouse slipped and fell. He was the best fan I ever had, but I thought he could not know much about tennis to be spending his time on any court I was playing on, especially when the champion of England, the purest stylist I ever saw in my life, was in action fifty yards away. But the old man continued to sit on his shooting stick and to applaud whenever I won a point and whenever Backhouse missed, and when Backhouse skidded and fell a second time he shouted "Bravo!"

When the match was over he rose from his stick and put out his hand: "Thank you," he said, "thank you very much. By the way, I'm Hemsley-Bullock."

I was bewildered, for I had never been thanked for winning a tennis match before. So I looked at Colonel Hemsley-Bullock and noted that his face was extremely red, and did not seem red from the sun.

"But surely you know!" he said. "D'you mean nobody told you?"

"Know what, sir?"

"That fellow you beat. That fellow Backhouse. Didn't anybody tell you he's a bounder? In Simla he was not received, so why should they let him in here? I told them not to let him in but they let him in. Now you have removed him, shall I say, handily, and for that, my dear boy, for that we shall have a drink together."

We passed the court where Austin was picking up after beating his Austrian, and the colonel—he could be nothing else but a colonel—led the way to the marquee, found a table and chair, summoned a waiter, presumed I would have a gin and tonic, and informed me that all Irishmen were delightful.

"Charming voices you people all have, charming, but I do wonder, I must say, why you bother coming over here. That Black and Tan affair was—well, what can one expect an affair to be with a bounder like Lloyd George for a P.M. and a cad like Wilson in the forces? That fellow Backhouse was a Tan for a bit. In Simla he was not received. That Black and Tan affair was the most disgraceful episode in the history of the British Army. It was worse than the war, which says something. From October, 1914, to November, 1918, I wasn't once astride a horse!"

I told him I was not from Ireland but from Canada, and then he surprised me. I have since noticed that the kind of English colonel associated with the Lowe cartoon has more potentialities of surprise than any other occupational type in the world. Suddenly this particular colonel broke into fluent French, and seemed astonished when I told him I was hopelessly bad at the language.

"I adore the French," he resumed in English, "and the French Canadians must be the finest of the lot. Never been in Canada, of course, but they stayed loyal, and that's more than they did in France. The French all adore a king, of course. What are you doing over here?"

I told him I was at Oxford and, of course, he asked what college I was in and when I said Oriel, he called for the waiter once more.

"Definitely another drink," he said. "When our King was in danger my college did not behave badly, but yours was superb. I was the House. We didn't do badly but you—I say, d'you have any plate left at all?"

It was then that I realized that the king to which he referred was Charles I. During the English Civil War, Charles moved his court to Oxford, whence Oxford obtained the reputation of being the home of lost causes. When the King's treasury was more broke than usual, in fact when it was entirely empty, my college had melted down its silver plate. Even in those days it couldn't have been worth more than a day's pay for the troops, and I doubt if the troops got even that much out of it.

"Yes," said the colonel reflectively, "yes. I was sent down from the House."

I asked him what for and again he became reflective.

"A badger," he said finally. "I had a badger, and I released him one day in the chapel. He was a splendid badger. He bit the Dean and a minor canon. D'you intend going into the army?"

"No, sir," I said.

"I don't blame you. The army's no life for a gentleman any more. Gunners seem to be in charge of it now. They say we Cav officers messed things up last time and I suppose we did, rather, but next time the gunners'll be driven out of France. Mark my words, the gunners'll go."

This was in 1930 when another war seemed inconceivable and I said so.

"My dear fellow, a Hun's a Hun, is he not? I'm very much afraid he'll do us in next time, for he's a soldier, whatever else he isn't. Matter of fact, I met a Hun in town only last week and sure enough, he began talking about the next war. 'What good'll it do if you do win the bloody war?' I said to him. 'You still won't be a gentleman. Your women will not be desired.' Are Canadian girls gay, by the way?"

I was confused by the change of pace but this did not seem to matter.

"English girls are *not* gay. Their teeth have a deplorable tendency towards protuberance, they've too much chest or none at all, and let me warn you—they're apt to be damnably mercenary. French girls? Well, yes. But in recent years I've discovered Italy. You must come with me some time to Italy and I guarantee you'll find it rewarding. Italian girls —ah, yes, yes, yes!"

I know nothing more satisfying than to sip gin and tonic on a summer afternoon after exercise, and this I did with the colonel until five-thirty, when he suddenly woke out of a long, glassy-eyed trance and informed me that English food was a barbarity.

"However, there *is* a pub in Burford which does one rather well with roast duck. So we shall dine in Burford, eh?"

I had forgotten Henderson, but now I remembered him and told the colonel I had come with a friend and must seek him out. I found Henderson tired and sweaty in the changing room and he told me to go along with my colonel. So I rejoined the colonel, who had a Bentley with a chauffeur, and back we went into the Cotswolds. We stopped at two pubs along the way, one of them called *The Merry Mouth*, and though the recollection is hazy, it is my impression that we consumed at least two more gins apiece before we arrived in Burford, where we were told there was no duck on the menu that night.

"I'm afraid this means Oxford and the Clarendon," I heard the colonel say as he ordered another gin in the public bar.

Twilight was soft over Oxford when we drove into the Cornmarket and stopped in front of the hotel, and as soon as we were ensconced at a table, the colonel demanded champagne cocktails.

What we ate I cannot remember, for I was beyond tasting it; what we drank is also a mystery, but I do recall the colonel asking me many questions about myself, repeating that Canada must be a splendid country and inviting me to his country place which was somewhere in Shropshire. I also remember seeing a pair of waiters walking towards us as closely linked as Siamese twins holding two separate trays which seemed to overlap, each tray containing four bottles and four glasses, and my fingers closing on empty air when I reached for the nearest one. Afterwards I remember myself in the doorway of the hotel with a waiter's hand under my elbow and a waiter's voice in my ear murmuring: "One must be careful, sir, what one drinks with the colonel." My next recollection after that is of myself sitting up fully clothed in bed in my room in college and feeling so terrible I nearly fell down when I rose to undress. The next morning was not a halcyon one, and when Henderson came around at noon to drive me back to Cheltenham I almost told him I couldn't make it. However, I did manage to get into his car, and if larks and cuckoos were busy on this trip I did not hear them. We reached Cheltenham, we changed, and we went on to a court to meet our opponents in the first round of the men's doubles.

One of them was the same Major Backhouse I had beaten the day before. He was playing with a military captain whose name I forget, and who played a little better than Backhouse, but still not very well. I was atrocious, but thanks to Henderson we won in straight sets and when it was over we offered them drinks and went to the marquee. This time the liquor was ginger beer, which we sipped in silence. However, I had a feeling that the major was appraising me, and after a while I discovered that the feeling was correct.

He coughed discreetly and said: "I'm afraid I should have warned you against that man who picked you up after our game yesterday. That man who calls himself Hemsley-Bullock."

I started: "You mean that isn't his name?"

"In Rangoon," said the major, "it was plain Bullock. In Rangoon he was not received."

20 OXFORD REVISITED

I have always believed that the kind of efficiency which expresses itself in external organization is lethal to serious education. Mark Hopkins at the end of a log and a student at the end of the other, a wine party where undergraduates get partially drunk and chatter in French, German and even in Latin and Greek—there were such places once and I was at one of them. An excess of efficiency in higher education breeds communists, Republicans, eager-beavers and consumer-slaves. The worst university I ever attended was by all odds the most efficient I ever saw; the best would have horrified a freshman at the Harvard School of Business Administration. The worst college chieftain I ever knew was by profession a Wall Street banker, and so humourless he rusticated the editor of the university newspaper for printing the word "navel" in a poem. The best college chieftain I knew in my student days was a clergyman of eighty-plus who walked ten miles every second day of his life, rode his bicycle on the days when he did not walk, and took his baths in a tin tub into which his servant poured some dozen buckets of lukewarm water every morning at seven o'clock. I had been hearing for years that Oxford had changed out of recognition, that the girls had altered the essential masculinity of its character and that post-war English organization had made the ancient establishment indistinguishable from an American Ivy League college. So it was with some dread that I decided to revisit Oxford after twenty-six years, and I confess to a queer feeling in the pit of my stomach when I boarded the familiar train in Paddington for the hour's run out of Town into Oxfordshire.

With me that morning was an old Oxford friend whom I had not seen for a generation. We had kept in touch over the years by reason of a curious accident: he had been one year my junior and I had lent him a commentary on Juvenal just before I went down. He had forgotten he had it until five years later, when he got married, and his wife had found it among his books and he had mailed it to me in Canada. From this had arisen a desultory correspondence, about a letter a year, until my return to the Old Country that spring. Now he was the father of five children and the husband of a warmly happy wife; he was also a prominent undersecretary with rooms in Admiralty Arch, and his second boy was in his second year in our old college.

We travelled together on that fine June morning with the unspoken affection of two old friends who had been intimate before their careers had begun, whose careers had been far apart and in different lands, and who each had wondered, on meeting again, whether any of the old feelings remained. All of them did. This man was the best kind of man his island can produce: quietly humorous, rooted in the country's ancient history, very able, cultivated, musical; free of the edges and the self-startling aggressions which afflict so many of us to whom life has been a transition. He knew I had loved Oxford and he wished to prepare me against disillusionment, and as the train pulled out into the green countryside he spoke:

"Oxford has changed a very great deal, you know. In many ways it's almost a state university now. Most of the old goings-on have disappeared, and frankly I think it a good thing they have. One can't afford to be lax in organization any more, as we all found out in the war."

I listened to this with a sinking heart and wondered if the old place had been sold a batch of IBM machines. In my day nothing had seemed so admirable, considering the purpose of the institution which tolerated it, than the manner in which Oxford had kept its books and awarded its degrees. All the books were kept in longhand by treasurers and bursars who, most of them, were devoid of any formal business training whatever. It was a chore they undertook, and reflecting on this, it did not seem at all curious that my friend was known in the Civil Service as an expert on currency although at Oxford he had studied Latin, Greek, History and Philosophy. I wondered if he had ever received his degree formally. I hadn't. I never owned a parchment to prove that I graduated from Oxford, and so far as I know, baccalaureate parchments are not even printed there. They graduate you, of course, but it is not necessary to attend encænia in order to obtain a degree, nor is it necessary to take extra examinations if you want "M.A. Oxon" after your name. All you had to do, at least in my time, was to leave five guineas with the college treasurer and ask him to "keep your name on the books". If your name was kept on the books for the proper number of terms (I had long ago forgotten how many were required) you became M.A. Oxon in the same way as you became twenty-five years old.

"What about the Oxford eccentrics?" I asked my old friend. "Are there any left?"

He shook his head: "Not in harness, I'm afraid. These days the dons usually retire at sixty-five just as they do in America."

"Something has been lost."

"Yes, but more has been gained."

"What about the undergraduates?"

He laid down his paper: "We've had a pretty rough time in England, and the competition to get into a college is very stern indeed. My boy feels it and I'm rather worried he may even miss a Second. There's a lot of competition merely to *stay* in. Those evenings when the Bullingdon rioted—there's no more of that, you know. Some of those extraordinary things—the chaps Evelyn Waugh wrote about—there are none of them any more, and a good thing too, if you ask me."

"Do you remember," I asked, "that man in Magdalen I think it was, that man who took the regular furniture out of his rooms and lived on silk cushions and ate dates and figs for his breakfast and wore slippers with toes like a Turk's?"

"I seem to recall that he was sent down." He looked at me with a smile. "By the way, why do you men from the other side think it so necessary to emphasize oddities over here? It's not we who are odd, it's you who are odd."

"Do you remember," I persisted, "those two men who duelled with rapiers in New College gardens?"

"They were sent down, too. As a matter of fact, one of them has done quite well since."

I had bought *The News of the World* in the mean hope that my friend might disapprove. He glanced at it with a slight grimace after he had folded his own copy of *The Times*, and now we both opened our papers and began to read.

After a moment he said from behind *The Times*: "Must you really read that thing? After all, we're in a public place."

"Listen to this," I said, and read him a headline: "NOW HER PARENTS WILL HAVE TO KNOW."

He sighed: "You know, Hugh, over here one grows rather accustomed to *The News of the World*."

He returned to *The Times* but about five minutes later I found what, vaguely, I had hoped I might find. There was the headline: LORD ENCOMBE SENT DOWN, and just beneath it in slightly smaller letters: COLLEGE DEER SHOT.

"Ah!" I said.

"What squalid item have you discovered now?"

"Something that may turn out to be very, very wonderful. As soon as I've finished it, I'll let you read it yourself."

It appeared that a certain young nobleman called Lord Encombe, who sported a beard and kept a pet Spanish snake which he wore like a collar around his neck, had shot a fallow deer in the park of Magdalen College, a felony punishable by two years in the penitentiary if the college should be sticky enough to press charges. The dead beast had been hung in a college room for several days in the hope that the meat might become tender enough to eat, but as term was nearing its end it was barbecued while still pretty tough and one night on the bank of the Cher a party assembled to consume it. The Proctors had got wind of the affair and paid the party a surprise visit, with the result that His Lordship was informed the next day by the President of Trinity that he must depart from the University before midnight. Lord Encombe had then entertained at a champagne party which had terminated in what the newspaper described as "a disturbance in the quadrangle which later spread into the streets of the town". A further consequence had followed from this: three undergraduates were arraigned before a magistrate together with another young man whose identity was uncertain but who had described himself to the court as a poet. When questioned by the press, Lord Encombe's friends said:

"Both his grandfather and uncle shot deer while they

were in Oxford. They were not sent down. It's only in this socialist age that people are sent down for that sort of thing."

I passed the paper over to my friend, who read the account and looked up with a smile much less reluctant than he had intended to make it appear.

"As that wretched paper is always right, I must presume this happened. But it's absolutely unusual these days, you know, and I very much doubt if many people thought it funny. Oxford is much more serious than it used to be, and so far as I can tell, it's as modern as any university in America. The traffic in The High is frightful now. It was bad enough in our day, but the High has become worse than Tottenham Court Road. Some of the colleges are in danger of being shaken down by it."

The spires came into view and seemed as they had always been. We went to college, where we had guest rooms, and in no time it was as though I had never left Oxford. The same undergraduates were lounging on the grass with their books in the same June sunshine; the same bells struck the hour. The beauty of Oxford, so overwhelming that when first I encountered it I was lonely and unhappy for months, shaken as a man is when he encounters something almost too much for him—it was still there, and in this, the loveliest week in the loveliest of all her terms, Oxford was forever and ever herself. We walked for miles, and after dark that night, sitting on a bench in the quad, both of us were astonished by what we had experienced. Generally when you return to a place where you were happy in boyhood it seems smaller, different and it hurts. But Oxford on this warm Sunday seemed just the same. Like God Himself, there the amazing place was, seemingly indifferent to all her thousands of lovers, yet endlessly capable of evoking a love which had changed their lives.

"Lester Pearson once said, it was Oxford which had saved the Commonwealth. So many Indians, Pakistani, Ceylonese and others—no matter how much they might have hated the British politicians, when it came to severing the links with Oxford, they just couldn't bring themselves to do it."

St. Mary's chime prefaced its tolling of midnight with a perfect garland of sound. Then, one after the other—for of course the clocks were not synchronized—the bells of Oxford rang. It was seven minutes before the last of them had announced that so far as it was concerned, another day had begun.

My friend got to his feet: "Well, I must turn in now. I wish I could stay longer, but I have to be in my office at ten tomorrow morning and that means an early train." As we went up the dark staircase between the Caroline and eighteenth-century quads, he said: "All the same, I think if you stay here a little longer, you'll find great differences. For one thing I hear the treasurer's quarters—remember they were buried somewhere so that nobody could find them—have been enlarged. They simply *had* to improve their accounting system, and I understand they have machines now."

I slept dreamlessly for eight hours, woke to find my friend departed, put on a dressing gown and crossed the quad to the communal baths. I looked at the basin in the left-hand corner to see if the cobweb was still there and it was, it was larger now, it had weathered a little, it was so solid that no spider could fight his way out of it but it was the same cobweb that was there twenty-six years ago. I bathed, shaved and had breakfast, and then I remembered that I had promised to get in touch with the Master of Balliol.

Now I don't think it necessary even to mention that telephones are not installed in the rooms of undergraduates in Oxford, nor on their staircases, nor in the rooms of the tutors. The Provost has a private phone, I believe, but to the best of my knowledge his is the only one, and the Provost in my first year had the bell removed from it so that he would be unable to hear it when it rang. The telephone was, and still is, an antique switchboard in the lodge, presided over by one of the most antique of the college servants.

In the lodge I found that the servant in charge of the telephone remembered me, as well he should have done, for once he had been my scout. I remembered him with affection and the sense of poignancy one associates with lost opportunities. The year Blenheim won the Derby one of the buttery boys had been brother to one of the boys who worked in the Aga Khan's stables. The Aga had two horses in the Derby that year, and Blenheim was not the favourite. Indeed at the time Constable (that was my scout's name) gave me the tip that in the Aga's stables Blenheim was the horse they talked about, you could have got odds at thirty-six to one. My father had told me never to take tips from stockbrokers or racing men, so I had to let a small fortune glide past my hands untouched.

Now Constable was ending his days on the college telephone system, and I asked him to put me through to the Master of Balliol. He boggled.

"Is there anything the matter with the phone?" I asked him.

"Oh no, sir, it's the same old phone. But you see, sir, only gentlemen in college or who are M.A.s can have calls put through on it. Except for taxis, of course. If you wish a taxi, I may call."

"I don't wish a taxi now, I wish the Master of Balliol. I'm a M.A., so put the call through."

He gave me a troubled look : "I'm rather afraid you're not an M.A., sir. You see, we had to look you up when we heard you were returning. Your name didn't appear to be on the books."

"Oh!" I said. "Well, perhaps I might see the treasurer? What's his name now?"

He told me and I was mildly surprised.

"Do you mean we have a real general for treasurer now? Not a don?"

"Yes, sir. Retired general, sir."

"So the general tells me whether I can use the phone or not?"

Constable laughed uneasily: "That would be about the size of it, sir."

I left him and walked through two quadrangles to the region where the old treasurer had lurked, found the door, knocked, entered and was greeted by a fairly young-looking man too old to be an undergraduate but lacking that *je ne sais quoi* one associates with a don. He wished to know what he could do for me and I told him he might find out whether or not I was an M.A.

"You'll have to consult the treasurer on the point," he said, and indicated a chair.

It looked like a don's room; in fact I believe it once was a don's room. It looked like anything on earth but an office, though I did hear a typewriter tapping and was a little disturbed by its sound. In my day I don't think there was a typewriter in the entire college. A wisteria vine trailed past a corner of the window and outside there was a sort of hum of summer, which was not really connected with the lovely day but was probably a reverberation from the traffic in The High.

A door opened and an elderly gentleman looking exactly like any retired don came padding in, shook hands, regarded me with a gentle smile and asked what he could do for me.

"I'd just like to know if I'm an M.A.," I asked him.

"Oh dear, what for?"

"Constable in the lodge tells me I can't use the telephone if I'm not."

"Did he really? Well, I expect he's right." Another gentle smile. "Were you up, by the way?"

"Yes, I was up all right."

"I rather fancy that if a man thinks he was up, he was up." He chuckled. "When *were* you up?"

"I went down in 1932. I read Mods and Greats."

"Ah, that means you were in the period of my predecessor. He was the most meticulous of calligraphists."

"He was also the most meticulous of accountants. They said he never made a slip in his whole time here."

"Things are different now. Ah yes, since the war so many things are. Let me see now—when did you say you were up? Oh yes, you've already told me. I'm afraid it may be something of a trial to find that particular book. Did you take steps to assure yourself of an M.A.? Did you recall the necessities as regards keeping one's name on the books?"

I assured him I had, and also that I had left five guineas for that purpose.

"Dear me, I fancy if a man leaves five guineas, that's a thing he remembers. Just a moment, please."

He left me alone for several minutes and returned bearing a ledger. Looking at me over his half-moon glasses he smiled again.

"The book exists." Then he pored over it, turned pages and stopped with his finger at a place. "Here you are! Just as you said. You were up in my predecessor's time."

"Good!" I said.

"But I'm afraid your record terminates with your last term. Your name—ah, this is a pity, really. You said you left five guineas? Your name ceases with your last term."

"In other words I'm not an M.A.?"

He sighed and shook his head. "It appears not."

"I'm sure I left those five quineas."

He was quietly reflective. "Would you care for us to trace them?"

The thought of this kindly man hunting back through all those years to find what had become of the five guineas I had mailed to a treasurer now with God was too horrifying to contemplate. Perhaps I had not sent them at all? Embezzlement was unheard of—I mention the word only because on this side of the water it might be inferred that this was a possible explanation—but twenty-six years is a long time and I *had* taken my degree *in absentia* and perhaps—

"Something has just occurred to me," I said. "There's just an off chance I didn't leave those five guineas."

"Oh, I rather expect you did."

"Don't try to search the record, though. It's all right. It doesn't matter at all."

"You require an M.A. for any particular purpose?"

"Only to telephone.'

"Quite so!" He drew a pad toward him, made a series of slow, careful calculations in a meticulous hand, and when he was finished he looked up. "According to my reckoning, you may have an M.A. for forty-one pounds, two shillings, farthing."

"That seems rather steep for a phone call—even to the Master of Balliol."

He smiled, nodded and for five minutes we chatted about sundry matters. Then it occurred to me that despite his leisurely manner this was the end of term and that he would be getting out the battels for a college twice the size of the one I had known years ago. In other words, he was just as busy as any North American treasurer ever is.

I apologized for taking up his time, thanked him, and went out. I walked up to Carfax where Constable had told me there was a call box, but there were seven people waiting to use it, so I continued to walk down Cornmarket to the Broad, turned into Balliol and was about to ask the porter if the Master was in residence when the spirit of the place overcame me. Was it really necessary to waste the time of the Master on such a lovely morning towards the end of term? I walked out again, down St. Giles to St. John's, entered and walked through the quadrangles to the gardens in the back. In a nook I came upon one of those little memorials in which Oxford really speaks from the heart. This nook was a rock garden, and in the centre of it was a bronze plaque:

TO THE MEMORY OF
HENRY JARDINE BIDDER
1847–1923
FELLOW TUTOR BURSAR
VICAR OF ST. GILES
KEEPER OF THE GROVES
THIS ROCK GARDEN WHICH HE MADE AND
LOVED IS HIS MONUMENT

I sat watching the sunlight wash the back of St. John's, that back which Andrew Lang described as "possibly the most lovely thing in all Oxford". It had been copied so far as the proportions were concerned (just as everything else lovely in Oxford and Cambridge had been copied so far as the proportions were concerned) in that extremely efficient university to which I referred a while ago. Now I thought of the gentle old clergyman pottering about in his rock garden, teaching Divinity for nearly half a century, sipping his port in the common room. I thought of him with an especial contentment as bursar of this college where our own former Secretary of State for External Affairs, according to his own words, spent the happiest time of his life.

21 HAVE YOU HAD MANY WIMBLEDONS?

Had it not been for English cooking I would have missed Wimbledon that year. I would have failed to see the tiny patch of blue in the grey sky which introduced that succession of happy little accidents which terminated, after three days of watching tennis, in a dinner in Soho with one of the most charming ladies I ever met.

It was 12.35 on the Third of July and I was sitting in a pub off the Strand reading my mail, sipping bitter and wondering what to do with myself for the rest of the afternoon. I had no ticket for Wimbledon, and as everyone knows who knows anything about this queen of tournaments, if you have failed to obtain a seat for the last days by the previous January, your only sure chance of getting one is to be a competitor or to become a member of the Royal Family. There is always room, not much but some, in the royal box above Centre Court.

Looking out the window of the pub I saw a river of glistening black umbrellas meandering past in the drizzle which had been falling for the last two days. Inside the pub was a scene I would have given much, in the early summer of 1940, to know I would be able to see eighteen years later.

There they were, the English, and to anyone with vivid memories of 1940 their living presence was still slightly incredible. There they were drinking the same beer and preparing to eat the same food. In fact these were the same men I had seen in this same place before I had even heard of Hitler. They were the same men Dickens knew: faces beefy or lean, waistcoats checked or black, some jovial and some melancholy, but all as sure of themselves as they had always been, satisfied men, absolutely convinced that even if they, personally, indulged in such hobbies as canary training or collecting match boxes they were normal while others were not. They were at home in their habits as nobody else seems able to be, and the thought occurred that of all the blunders Hitler ever made, his worst was to spoil an English June. You may rob an Englishman of his property and he won't care for you; you may go off with his wife and he will accustom himself to her absence. But if you interrupt his habits he will ruin you as he ruined Louis Quatorze, Napoleon and Hitler. If Hitler had marched to the Channel in September the English might not have minded so much, but he did it in June. No colours were trooped, no retreats were beaten, no Derby was run, Ascot and Wimbledon had to be cancelled for six years and beaches were infested with barbed wire. The evacuation of thousands of London children even made it possible for some cranks to tamper with the English diet, and to suggest that English food should be cooked as other people's food is cooked.

They had failed, all of them, and though the Alsop brothers warned Americans that England was on her last legs, and *Time* marvelled at the recovery of West Germany, the facts were that the English were on the same legs on which they have always stood and that they had made the only recovery most of them had ever wanted to make, which was the resumption of their habits. The food on the counter of this pub was the same food I saw here first in 1930. Behind it was the same man. He was six feet five and thin; his chef's cap was a yard high, and his voice had a timbre to be found only in the permanent purlieus of London. When he used it, his words forced themselves up through a long throat in which the mechanisms were almost visible, past a rampart of adenoids his parents had seen no reason to have disturbed, and out the nostrils of a long nose down which a pair of popping eyes surveyed the world with an expression of perpetual astonishment that the world had the bad sense to exist.

He caught my eye and came over with the bill of fare, which contained the inevitable items: veal and ham pie, pork pie, rump steak and veg, cold beef and veg, plaice and chips, potato salad. Spoiled by a quarter of a century of good cooking, including a year of my own, I winced.

"You gets no bread," I murmured, "with one fish ball."

"Might I recommend the veal an' 'am, sir?" said the man with reproving cheerfulness, "P'raps you might relish a potyto salad, sir?"

"Thanks, I'll just have another half-pint."

His long nose lifted ever so slightly. "You must ask the wyter for that, sir," and he left me.

The waiter came and the warm bitter was delicious. But surely, I thought, somewhere in London, somewhere near, it must be possible to eat an English fish, the best fish in the world, which has not been dropped in boiling fat? Even if it costs me a guinea, I thought, after five weeks of restaurant boiled veg and veal and ham pie,—what I ate in private homes was of course different—of boiled rump steak and French fries, I'm going to taste a genuine Dover sole. A pork pie was served to the man beside me and I saw the tendons of his wrists go tense as he sawed through it, then an expression of perfect content emerge on his face as he munched the morsel. I drained my beer and left, and ten minutes later, walking up the Haymarket towards Piccadilly with the Ritz in my mind, I saw that blink of blue in the western sky and all thought of lunch vanished.

"It may clear up," I said to myself. "Yes, it just possibly may clear up and just possibly this drizzle will keep a handful of people away."

I knew of course that this was the wildest wishful-thinking, for rain never keeps an Englishman away from anything. The last time I had played tennis in England, against Cambridge in 1932 when I was the secretary of the O.U.L.T.C., it had begun to rain about bedtime the night before the matches. It rained all night and it was still drizzling at breakfast. The Cambridge secretary came to me as I was drinking my coffee and said: "Well, it doesn't look very good for the grass." I agreed that it did not, and added that it might be a good idea to cancel the whole affair and play it a fortnight later in London at Queen's, when we would be finished with our final schools and the cricketers would be playing each other at Lord's. "We can't do that, I'm afraid," said the Cambridge man. "After all, we've never done that before." So, for two days, we played on en-tout-cas courts with puddles of water on them, we slipped and fell, we ruined forty-one rackets and every time a ball was hit a big splash of mud exploded into our faces. *The Times*, in reporting the matches, described the weather as "unfavourable"; *The Telegraph* conceded that "conditions for tennis were difficult, which possibly accounted for the disappointing nature of the play". The vulgar English press published pictures of us with our flannels covered with mud and informed its readers that we were playing tennis and not anticipating the rugger season. But I remember that some two thousand Englishmen sat or stood in the rain to watch this dismal spectacle, and with this thought in mind I bought a ticket in the underground and stepped into a crowded train heading for the All England Tennis and Croquet Club.

"Well," I said to myself, "at least I can buy a general admission and listen to the applause. At least I'll be able to see the greenest grass in the world and maybe one or two consolation matches on the outside courts. And in the enclosure perhaps I can even eat something."

Anyway, I was going to Wimbledon, and it did not even hurt to recall that more than a quarter of a century had passed since I had gone there for the first time. *Happy Days Are Here Again* was the tune of that season, and never have I been happier than on the happy day when I poured down from Oxford on a motor cycle to Wimbledon. The sun shone, the air over the green shires was honey-coloured and from every hedge in southern England the cuckoos mocked married men.

Who won at Wimbledon that year? A proof of Wimbledon's beauty can be found in the fact that I, who can tell you who won dozens of heavyweight fights I have never seen, can't remember whether my first Wimbledon was won by Tilden, Sidney Wood or one of the great Frenchmen. The player I best remember from my first Wimbledon was not the winner, but a blond Dutchman, long since lost to the record books, called Hans Timmer, who carried Cochet to five sets in the first round. The crowd knew he could not win, but they loved him because, in his grave Dutch way, he contrived to reveal how much he valued the game he played. Most illuminating is Wimbledon's attitude to the champions, for to be a mere winner means nothing to the Wimbledon crowd or to the genius of the place. Wimbledon crowds knew perfectly well that Ellsworth Vines, at the height of his powers, was the most formidable player in the world, but they found him neither interesting nor—there is only one word for it—important. For one thing he didn't like the game; for another he was enslaved by an American coach, the first of the long line of efficiency experts whose dully competent minds think that a sport can remain a sport after it has been reduced to a problem in geometry and tested by percentages. The Wimbledon crowds of a generation ago regarded Mercer Beasley, watching Vines with his notebook in hand, with the enthusiasm a householder shows when he discovers a termite in his walls. But they venerated Tilden, they opened their arms to Von Cramm and Budge, and Borotra they adored. They knew perfectly well—no tennis crowd can be compared to them in knowledge—that the Basque's ground game was faulty and that time and again he threw away his chances by squandering his strength in the early sets. But he was an amateur, one of the last of the great simon pures, and when he flashed he looked like the spirit of the game itself.

At Southfields station the train stopped and we got out into taxis, four strangers to each car, and were driven to the courts. Opposite me from where I sat on a jump seat were three women, one looking like every English games mistress I ever saw, another applecheeked and elderly, the third thirty-ish with gorgeous shoulders, a skin that looked like the petal of a white rose dipped in cream, but an expression which should have made, and probably had made, many a man pause before he tried to cultivate her acquaintance.

Suddenly this almost-beautiful creature spoke in a clipped voice: "Shall we have to see Gibson this afternoon?"

"She plays the Haydon child, doesn't she?" said the elderly lady.

"I expect she does. Last year when Gibson came over one

was told one should like her because she couldn't help her colour. One tried. But of course it was impossible. Didn't you find her ghastly?"

"I thought she had great dignity," said the lady mildly.

"Did you really?" said the woman with the gorgeous skin. "How very odd!"

Then with a charming smile the lady said: "Have you had *many* Wimbledons?"

The woman with the gorgeous skin fell silent, the lady with the apple cheeks leaned back twinkling, definitely one up.

A moment later, after fumbling in her bag, she produced a sheaf of those thin little papers which are Wimbledon tickets.

"Oh dear," she said as though talking to herself, "here I am with extra tickets for the last three days. I got them in Worcestershire last winter from our club, expecting my sister to come, but my poor sister took ill, and now with this wretched weather it's been most frightfully difficult to know what to do with them."

Not believing that this was real, I leaned forward.

"Ma'am," I said, "if that's your problem, I'd just love to help you solve it."

"You mean you've come all the way out here without a ticket? How extraordinarily hopeful of you!"

I opened my wallet and produced a five pound note.

"Oh, but they're worth nothing like that much."

The girl with the gorgeous skin said to me: "You seem to be in the most remarkable luck, I must say. But then, you Americans so often are."

"What an extraordinary thing for you to say!" said the elderly lady. "Really, I'd have thought that by this time *everyone* in England would know the difference." She twinkled at me charmingly: "I had quite a few Canadian boys with me during the war. They were very naughty with the girls, I'm afraid, but I did adore them, and a woman can't really mind if a man's naughty, can she?"

But I had noticed that she had made no offer to sell me her tickets, and I knew why. I could almost hear her thoughts. It would be such a bore, she was thinking, to have a mere tourist beside one for three days of Wimbledon. Much better an empty seat than that.

"Have you ever played at Wimbledon yourself?" I asked her.

"Oh yes. Very badly of course, but I played several times."

"I nearly played once," I said, and shamelessly I went on: "I was Oxford tennis secretary in a very lean year, and I could have got in on that."

"Then I expect we have quite a few friends in common?"

I mentioned a few well-known players of yesteryear, and she knew all of them, and as we got out of the taxi I understood that the unhoped-for had happened.

"No nonsense now about paying for these tickets," she said. "They've been paid for long ago and I won't hear of any nonsense about five pound notes."

"We'll see about that later," I suggested.

"Well, we certainly shan't see about it now." We found our seats among the fifteen thousand spectators at Centre Court, and saw Ashley Cooper serve an ace against Mervin Rose. "Oh dear, these mechanical Australians! Why do they bother to play at all when one always knows what they're going to do? Ah well, perhaps the doubles will save the tournament."

"Why the doubles?" I asked her.

"Well, of course in men's doubles tactics and imagination can still make a difference, don't you think?"

She was right about this, as she was right about so many

things. When the tournament was over, I was not the only one who concluded that the men's doubles not only saved the 1958 Wimbledon tennis from being the only dismal tennis the tournament has ever seen; it is the sole department of the game which may save the game itself from what Kramer and Hopman have done to it. There was only one match in the men's singles—I didn't see it because it was a quarter-final—which had any interest at all. That was the one in which the young Englishman Wilson, an amateur just down from Oxford, came within two points of beating the actual winner. The semi-final between Cooper and Rose, above all the final between Cooper and Fraser, made people long for the time when human beings like Tilden, Cochet, Crawford, Von Cramm, Perry and Budge leaped or glided over those wonderful oblongs of green grass. It even made a few very ancient spectators long for H. L. Doherty.

The final between Cooper and Fraser—about this there was universal agreement—could well be taken as the ultimate proof that Kramer and Hopman with their tennis factories have all but ruined the game. Two perfected products of the Australian assembly line, so identical you could not tell them apart except by their hair cuts, for four sets slammed identical services at each other and followed them up with identical volleys which settled the point about nine times out of ten. The final had only one interesting moment, and that was when Cooper in the last game faced Fraser on his own service at forty-love. Suddenly the machine became human. He served a double fault, he swung at a sitter and missed entirely and at forty-thirty, pivoting under a pop lob three feet from the net, he belted his smash into the stands three tiers above the royal box. For a moment it looked too good to be true. Such an exhibition almost made a human being out of his opponent, but the machine reasserted itself immediately. Cooper served two perfectly placed balls,

Fraser dutifully returned them to Cooper's advancing racket, two routine volleys put the balls away and won Cooper the championship. The applause for the winner was correct and perfunctory, but he was almost forgotten before he left the court. *"Cooper est un jouer,"* wrote the veteran commentator of *Le Figaro* in Paris next morning, *"parfait mais sans âme."*

But the men's doubles game still defies the science of the factory managers, and this year the three best teams in the doubles were amateurs. The defending champions, the ancient pair of Mulloy and Patty, were beaten in the best match of all in the quarter-finals by Krishnan and Kumar of India. The Indians, well made but too short for a power service, had wrists like cobras and imaginations that sparkled. They gave all they had, they changed the pattern of their game at least half a dozen times in beating Mulloy and Patty, who were astute themselves, and they won in the fifth set. They were tired the next day, and the Swedish pair of Davidson and Schmidt beat them after another brilliant match to enter the finals against the finalists of the men's singles, Fraser and Cooper.

The mens' doubles final was not as interesting as the previous two rounds, but for anyone who loves the game of tennis it was immensely satisfying. The two Swedes have tremendous services and massive overheads, but their ground game is weak and often they make errors the machines never commit. In singles neither of them would have a hope against Cooper and Fraser. But in doubles they proved that two amateurs, if inspired and in good condition, can upset the best-laid plans of the planners. Within ten minutes it occurred to the Swedes—you could see it on Davidson's face when he went over to speak to Schmidt—that although their opponents were perfect they were absolutely mindless. Everything the Australians did was flawless; it was also predictable. Serve, cross court volley, down-the-centre volley, smash—the same strokes, the same positioning, the assumption that errorless power is all you need. But by the middle of the first set it became apparent that something was happening to them, that although they appeared to have the initiative they really lacked it, because the Swedes were thinking faster than ever. Davidson often flubbed a backhand, and Schmidt's backhand, by championship standards, was hardly a stroke at all. Yet the Swedes were winning. They were winning because they were in places where they should not be even though they often played strokes which would warrant a man's expulsion from an Australian or Californian tennis factory. The Australians continued to play with mechanical perfection, disliking the game as most of them appear to do, and the Swedes became steadily more inventive. They took the first set easily, the second more easily still, and in the third Davidson, who is also an expert soccer player, was so relaxed he often trapped a loose ball with his toes, juggled it, and with careless exuberance back-heeled it across the net to Cooper or Fraser when the Australians needed another ball for the service. In the third set they handled the Australians as a pair of matadors handles a pair of bulls, and when it was over the crowd went home happy.

So did I, for as long as Wimbledon can produce tennis like this, as long as two amateurs can still win an event in the greatest of the tournaments, the game has a small chance of survival. But best of all, as usual, was the atmosphere of the place. The old lady and I sitting side by side for successive afternoons became fast friends even though we knew we would never see each other again after the tournament was over. "I've enjoyed my Wimbledon very much this year," she said, and never did I feel I had been paid a nicer compliment.

But we did see each other again, if only for a few more hours. Going back to town in the underground, it suddenly occurred to me to ask what she was doing that night. She twinkled and said "nothing", and when I asked her to dinner she twinkled again and said "yes". While she tidied up in her club I strolled down to the public house at the end of the street and relaxed at the bar with a pint and an old copy of *The News of the World*. At the appointed time I sallied back to the club, and together the elderly lady and I set out for Soho. In Greek Street we found a French restaurant and for the first night in weeks in a restaurant I actually tasted the food I ate. We drank a bottle of Beaune, and after the coffee she even consented to a glass of Remy Martin.

"This has been *very* nice," she decided as the taxi took us back to her club. "I thought it was charming of you to take me to that place. French cooking can be quite refreshing—for a change."

22 THE CURTAIN FALLS ON THE GRAND STYLE

(Epitaph on the Suez Crisis, 1956)

Since that autumn day in 1956 when Sir Anthony Eden's government gave up on Suez, the English people have suffered nothing in the concrete sense. Their health is better than the health of any English population in the past; their business men have been piling up dividends; their working men have never felt so secure; their sovereign is the most popular in their history. It is curious: since that day of apparent defeat the British Island seems able to offer a better life to its people than ever before.

Yet, and this is not curious at all, something quintessentially English is gone forever since that autumn day, something as unique to the southern portion of the British Isles as the lawns, the dreaming spires or even the far, storm-beaten ships which became as much a part of the world's consciousness as the legions of Rome, and to millions of Englishmen its passing was a real agony.

I remember as though it were yesterday the day it went, which was the day Eden threw in the towel. Walking along Sherbrooke Street that morning I encountered an Englishman who had been living in Montreal for years, and we fell into step. Though he was certainly an Old School Tie man, he had seemed to like it with us; almost, he had become a citizen of Canada. Yet on that day it was obvious that there was only one country on earth he could ever regard as home, even though he had admitted a few years previously that after living on this side of the water he could no longer live in England.

"All that's necessary now is for Winston Churchill to die," he said bitterly. "I can almost see his funeral. And what a mockery it will be when it happens."

I glanced at his profile and thought: "How curious, how utterly curious the English are!" For this man was not even a Tory; had he been a member of parliament he would have voted against Eden's government, and only a few days earlier he had spoken against Eden with anger. Had his feelings changed because the humiliation had been so public, because the image had fallen in the face of every Philistine in every modern Gath and Askelon?

"You know," he said quietly, "I rather wish Churchill had not lived to see this."

I knew then what he meant; suddenly I knew the meaning of his pain, for Churchill was the last exemplar of what perished on that autumn day. History could never take away from him his title of *restitutor orbis* in the sense that he had saved our civilization, but not even his will had availed to save the British Empire or the spirit which once had animated it. No wonder Englishmen all over the world —and non-Englishmen too—were hanging up their harps beside the waters of various Babylons. Nobody can save an organism from the final consequences of having been itself. The Empire which had warred down every foreign foe from Philip of Spain to Hitler, which had spread its language into a *lingua franca* employed even by its enemies, had been powerless against the final enemy, because the final enemy had been conjured up by its own peculiar genius, which had to die in order that the genius of others might live.

"It was bound to end, of course," said the Englishman as we waited for a light to change. "But to peter out like this! To be treated like a shoplifter by a trio like Nasser, Dulles and Eisenhower—somehow I had expected the end of it all to be a little more dignified."

The light changed and we went on: "Was it Hemingway who said that no lion outside a zoo ever dies a natural death? In that case it seems we stopped being lions some time ago."

"Don't you think England might turn herself into a Swedish lamb?"

"But then she'd not be England, would she?"

"Anyway, she won't die over this," I said. "This is only a matter of power."

"Oh, I suppose she can exist. She can become a part of a European union with Germany at the head of it. She'll live somehow, I suppose. But she won't be England."

Yes, England would live and Englishmen would still inhabit the famous places. There would still be Oxford and Cambridge and Canterbury, children would cross the stripling Thames at Bablock Hythe and the blossoms along the Cher and the Cam would be as fragrant as ever in English Junes. Cuckoos would cry from hedges on golden afternoons and the plok of cricket balls would echo from elms that were ancient when Malbrouck marched to war. There would be beer and darts and shove ha'penny in the pubs, there would be crumpets and tea and *The Daily Mail*, and even the odd clergyman pinching the odd nursemaid on Clapham Common. There would be coronation ceremonies in the Abbey, retreats would be beaten in the Horse Guards and somehow enough money would be found to keep a good pack baying across Leicestershire. The England of Chaucer, Shakespeare and Donne, of Milton, Dryden and

Wordsworth, of Dickens, Tennyson and Thackeray would be as alive as it ever was, along with the living language and laws. All of this would last, and probably the New Men with their science and committees would enable the English people to live more comfortably than English people had ever lived. But would that be England?

For what died that fall, and visibly, was neither a people nor a government but a style; a style and the world's attitude towards it. With the death of that style England was bound to become like Athens without her fleet. As the Athenian hierophant donned his ceremonial robes to receive visiting dignitaries from Macedonia and Rome, so in the future will vice-chancellors receive visiting Americans, Asians and Africans. But the vice-chancellors will no longer be the chiefs of universities educating the blue-eyed masters of the world, and at least some of the visitors will feel as Cicero and various Cæsars felt towards the Athenian hierophant when they made the grand tour to the beloved Greek province. Is it a tragedy that this should come to pass? And if so, a tragedy for whom?

This England which has passed away has surely been one of history's rarest wonders. Athens, no larger in proportion to her own world than England has been to hers, held power for less than a century, but England was a power for more than four hundred years. Nor was it the power that really mattered; it was the by-products of it, the stream of genius, the stream of talent which mere style, at least for the moment, could turn into a counterfeit of genius. Even more than France, England valued in her heart nothing but excellence, and hers was the kind a champion fencer must have, for she depended on little else for her life. She was the wildest of gamblers: from the day William the Conqueror burned his boats on the Channel shore, she staked her life again and again, century after century, on one calculated risk after another. Nothing is more deliciously English than the customary claim to moderation and common sense. The Whig peer who reasoned that if one were careful one could manage to jog along on half a million pounds a year thought himself the most moderate of men; so did Lord Chesterfield, when he wrote that appalling series of letters to his son. So, probably, did Clive when he saw no reason why he might not conquer India with a regiment. So did the cavalry officers who remarked after Balaclava that after all it was not as bad as Chillianwallah. The quintessence of moderation, so the English thought, were the Victorian statesmen who repealed the Corn Laws, knowing as they did so that forever afterwards England would have to depend for her food on her capacity to impose her will on alien producers situated thousands of miles away. No wonder they believed there was nobody else like themselves: nobody else ever lived like they did and got away with it.

The world called them arrogant and they never understood why, for they did not feel themselves to be arrogant: it seemed a mere recognition of realities that wherever there was a stage its centre should be reserved for themselves. Even the Scotch and the Welsh, to the end regarded by the English in a good-humoured way as provincials, even as admirable provincials essential to the well-being of England, agreed in their hearts that there was a difference between the English and everyone else on earth, and understood how absurd *they* would look if they talked like the English, felt like the English or even—as some of them tried to do—acted like the English.

The essence of style—and the fencer has it above all other athletes—is that it makes extremely difficult actions appear easy, while at the same time it can, on occasion, elevate the most commonplace ideas to a position of prime importance in the world's eyes. In this art even the French, one of the few nations not overly impressed by the English, were willing to admit that the islanders surpassed them. Of course, there was a good deal of ham in the style—does not every good play-actor know that he dispenses with ham at the peril of losing his audience? Drake and his mythical game of bowls when the news came that the Armada was beating up out of the Western Approaches; the Oxford students pretending that their ability to write Greek verse came to them from nights of drinking with their friends; the cavalry soldiers who went hunting through Massena's *vedettes* in the Peninsula; the various English admirals who insisted on shaving the moment a lookout descried an enemy fleet on the horizon; the superb professionals who never failed to pretend they were amateurs at heart—what was the fun in winning the world if you could not win it in just that way? This style was at one with the perennial necessity of staking the entire bank account on a single calculation. Unlike a herd nation like Russia or the United States, England simply could not afford to lose many pieces on the board. Least of all the great powers could she afford to live with the dash of a spendthrift. But to *appear* to live like one while in reality the pennies were pinched—with what skill did the management of the Hudson's Bay Company learn how to do *that*! Yet there were times when nothing could serve but the total gamble, and when those times came, and the entire nation was staked on the board, how could the croupier be sure that the stake was total when he found himself confronted by a blandly casual face? Nelson steering without charts in the twilight into Aboukir Bay knew that if his line went aground the Empire was doomed, but when Troubridge's ship actually did hit a shoal, it was remarked with cheerful nonchalance what a pity it was that poor Troubridge should miss the fun, but how convenient, just the same, that the shoal should be so conspicuously marked. Jellicoe at Jutland was a poor imitation of Nelson anywhere, but on that day he knew, he really did, that he was the only man alive who could lose the war in an afternoon.

The Scotch and the Welsh, if not the Irish, gave up with the English centuries ago when they learned by bitter experience that the English cared no more for common sense than the French cared for logic. What was the use in objecting to English arrogance when in the moments of crisis to which it constantly exposed the nation, this arrogance was often the only weapon between the nation's throat and the enemy's point? It has always seemed folly to me to argue whether Wellington or Napoleon was the better general. The only thing that matters is that Wellington beat Napoleon because it never occurred to him that Napoleon was in his class: "Bonaparte's mind is, in its details, low and ungentlemanlike. I never believed in him. I always called him Jonathan Wild the Great."

In the end, of course, the world became too large, and so did the English population. By the close of the nineteenth century there were millions of Englishmen to whom life was pretty drab at home, but by that time—and how eagerly they discovered it—there were also many colonies, and the too sad truth was that too many wrong people went out to them, and that too many excellent people lost something when they left their native island. A Scot or an Irishman can grow a new skin abroad, but an Englishman seldom can, and this was a tragedy for which England has paid an awful price. The Grand Style as practised by a Chatham or a Salisbury was not at all the same in the hands of a remittance man or of any of the thousands of Lord Jims who saw no reason why they should not behave like Elgins and Curzons in African kraals or in stilt-villages along the banks of the Irrawaddy. It was an exquisite example of Gresham's

Law when the bluffs were called and the cheques turned out to be stumers. The style was finished for good, at least in the eyes of outlanders, when the Kitcheners and Haigs of the First World War presided over the slaughter of the last English generation which had been trained to wield it. And in any case it was doomed in the end, for its fatal weakness was that it could not be shared.

England had been schoolmaster to the civilized world and to much of it that was uncivilized; no nation had ever been more eager to teach to others the arts whereby she herself had thrived. But pupils who love and admire a master, when finally they have learned their lessons truly and in their own place have done work and built states of comparable excellence, crave and even demand the right to be acknowledged as equal guests within the parthenon, and this the masters of the Grand Style seldom if ever conceded in the one region where concession was required—their own hearts. A Durham could come out to Canada and help our statesmen lay the groundwork of a new kind of nation, but it never once occurred to him that independence need be a synonym for the final equality. On a lower level Gunga Din was a splendid fellow in his way, but he was expected to remain Gunga Din, and it could only be admitted that he was a better man after he was dead. Indian students could return from Oxford with the athletic blazer, they could run up double centuries at the wicket, but it was not quite enough; no, never *quite* enough. An American millionaire might buy his suits in Savile Row and even be known as a good man over Leicestershire, but inevitably he became aware, if he were at all sensitive, that though the last gap might be invisible, it was probably as wide as ever. "Dear Henry!" remarks a character in an English novel when two people are discussing Henry James, "Dear Henry, he was always just a *little* too far away, wasn't he, to hear precisely what is was the Duchess actually said." And in Canada not so long ago: "Of course I think Canadians are perfectly charming, so long as they're *Canadians.*" And one understood exactly what this would imply in the case of any Montreal matron who presumed that her daughter's presentation at court was—well, one understood exactly, did one not? Red carpets could be rolled out for Eisenhower, but when Eisenhower said in his Guildhall Speech that Abilene and London were sisters under the skin, inevitably an Englishman was heard to murmur that this might well be true providing the skin were thick enough, but that it was his impression, though, of course, his ignorance was vast because he had never looked into it really, that Abilene was a town somewhere in America with one of those odd names that Americans seemed to like.

It had to go, of course. The vast congregation of England's foreign admirers (even Hitler and Mussolini, even Lord Haw Haw had been among them for a time) had waited so long for the recognition that never came that they finally gave up and did their own recognizing of themselves. Too many of England's lovers had discovered with embarrassment that the love they so freely offered was not really desired, since the total acceptance of love commits an honourable man to grant a total equality in every unspoken sense of that word. And, of course, there were the others, the many others who had somehow passed unnoticed as human beings in the great, careless days. So many of them had been cheerfully labelled as Gyppies, Wogs, Wallahs and Blackfellows (how much less insulting those terms would have been had malice evoked them!) that now they could not refrain from the vulgar pleasure of making the most of their belated opportunities when the light-hearted master began making noises like a very tired old lion. In the autumn of Suez not even Gunga Din seemed to care any more whether the Sahib would admit him a better man than himself. So many people, Sir Anthony's Tories discovered that fall, no longer cared, and I really believe that what shook them hardest was that a man as banal as Dwight D. Eisenhower should have presumed to give *them* a lecture on good behaviour. That the United States should have voted against them they had discounted in advance, but that a man like Eisenhower should have talked to *them* in the exasperatingly forbearing tones of a school captain catching a group of boys from the Lower Fourth out of bounds—as my friend remarked that day on Sherbrooke Street, somehow they had thought the end of the Grand Style would be more dignified. But the solid gold Cadillac, its chauffeur up front wearing his best public relations smile, rolled on indifferent and within a week had entirely forgotten about them.

Yet, when more years have passed, I wonder how the world is going to seem without that fantastic, reckless and infuriating arrogance. It was the elemental fire that forged the English diamonds. Without it there could have been no Elizabethan Age, no Eighteenth Century, nor the amazing morality called forth to redress the appalling crimes. Without it the world has in *Time* magazine a strange substitute for the old arbiter of excellence. Now a good many of us are left to wonder how we shall fare in the job of handling that colossal responsibility the English shouldered so lightly because they had never troubled to take the precaution of weighing it. It is a real question whether New York is going to do any better than Alexandria did after the decline of Athens, or whether Montreal or Melbourne are likely to make themselves any more precious to humanity than were two comparable provincial capitals of the late Roman Empire.

23 EDUCATION AND MONTAIGNE'S LAW

"Human society," said Montaigne, "goes very incompetently about healing its ills. It is so impatient of whatever happens to be pressing it at any particular instant that it thinks only of getting rid of this, reckless of the cost. But good does not necessarily ensue upon the removal of a particular evil. Another evil may ensue upon it, and a worse one."

This kind of idea is bound to be compelling to a man raised in the Calvinist persuasion, but as I grow older I realize with a sort of grim acceptance that although Calvinists may be impossible people to live with, it is pretty hard to argue against their general view of existence. Nor was Montaigne himself a Calvinist even by temperament; he was one of the best-balanced thinkers who ever lived. And if human society in his day, which was leisurely and not in the least hyperthyroid, displayed this fatal tendency, how much more does it do so now? What Montaigne says here, if applied to the behaviour of politicians, nations and public groups in the twentieth century, is so true that it comes close to having the validity of a general law, and that is why I feel like talking about it at some length.

When we stop to think back on the catastrophes of our time, nothing is more frustrating than our hindsight knowledge that most of them could have been averted if intelligent people had acted in even a moderately intelligent way. Montaigne explains why they did not. That fatal compulsion on the part of human groups to rid themselves of the irritation of pressure of some particular problem has been the largest single cause of the troubles of nearly every bad historic decision taken in our time, and a quick glance through the record of a most unfortunate century shows this with ghastly clarity.

In 1914 the leaders of the Austro-Hungarian Empire were exasperated by the pressure of southern Slavic nationalism (a minor worry to the rest of mankind) and determined to get rid of it once and for all by resort to military action. The result was the First World War, in which the Austrians succeeded in ridding themselves of their own Empire and a million and a half of their young men, while in the world at large some thirty million other human beings died also, though most of them had never heard of the quarrel between Belgrade and Vienna before they were conscripted into the army or persuaded to enlist.

In 1917 the German Government, pressed by a war on two fronts and determined to rid themselves of it at any cost, sent Lenin through the Fatherland in a sealed train, their idea being that Lenin would take Russia out of the war by means of revolution. As a result of that revolution the Soviet Union, a generation later, was powerful enough to do to Germany what it did.

After the armistice of 1918 it was the turn of the western democracies to come under the sway of Montaigne's Law, and they soon proved that the Law is no respecter of ideologies or good intentions. Punch-drunk from four years of trench warfare, believing their own propaganda, they recklessly assumed that if a second war should ever threaten them it would be caused by the same suppressed nationalisms which had begun the first. So they "liberated" nearly every European ethnic group they could think of, an operation which in many cases amounted to nothing more than handing over the control of tiny racial groups to camerillas of amateur politicians who otherwise would have been useful as civil servants or college professors. Naturally the balkanized continent was unable to function economically, and the Americans thereupon compounded their initial folly by withdrawing from the League of Nations because the Republicans would stop at nothing to get the Democrats out of Washington, and the American people as a whole were determined once and for all to rid themselves of the pressure of having to worry about European affairs. The result was—but why go into it further?

All around the world during this century the operations of Montaigne's Law kept grinding out the same kind of result. In 1931 the British Tories came to the conclusion that anything was better than the success of socialism in Britain, so they sold British credit short, they created a monetary crisis which drove England off the gold standard, they got the Labour Party out and replaced it with the most incompetent and vacillating administration in British history. Soon afterwards Hitler came to power, and the French Tories went their British colleagues one better by announcing the slogan "Better Hitler than Blum". Once again it is unnecessary to repeat what resulted from these policies.

While the second war was in full course and the allies at last were sure of winning it, the American Government determined to knock out Germany reckless of any other consideration. They deliberately closed their eyes to the manifest ambitions of Soviet Russia and to the meaning of Stalin's obdurate refusal to offer the slightest excuse for a *quid pro quo* in those famous conferences where the vodka was drunk and the caviar devoured, with the result that Russia in no time became a greater menace to the West than Germany had ever been. To cap the performance the American authorities then split the atom over two cities of an already defeated Japan because they were too impatient to contemplate another month or two of conventional warfare. The full price of this last decision has yet to be paid.

This record is so impressive that the Calvinist in me is tempted to hang his hat on it. However, there must be some important exceptions to Montaigne's Law or the human race would long ago have become extinct, so let's consider a few of them.

There are no exceptions, I should say, to the law as a general principle, but there do seem to be instances where public men and governments have contrived to short-circuit its effects. One of these was the British decision to withdraw from India before they were overwhelmed by a violent national revolution. Another was America's saving of Europe by the Marshall Plan. A third was the manner in which the Canadian government, immediately after the Hitler War, changed the nature of our national economy from a basis of agriculture to one of industry. In this latter case it must be admitted that they soon got dizzy from success and let the country in for an inflation which may make some of us yearn for the simplicities of the farm, but the decision itself was not recklessly taken and it was implemented with sober skill.

There must be quite a few other exceptions to the rule which I have not noted here, and if so, then I would guess that all of them shared the same common denominator that can be discovered in the three examples I have cited. That common denominator was merely the willingness, or the ability, to study the full implications of a problem before jumping into the middle of it.

The British had examined the Indian situation for years

before they got out, and they had given themselves time to train an Indian civil service capable of taking over the management of the nation. The Marshall Plan was the kind of operation in which the American genius always excels, and it was debated in the United States for almost two years before it was put into effect. The Canadian decision to change the nation from an agricultural to an industrial base was taken in an atmosphere of calm reflection which few democratic administrations can ever hope to enjoy. Thanks to the feebleness of the opposition in those post-war years, the Liberal government could afford to act intelligently without jeopardizing its chances at the polls.

All of this proves that the law has an obvious corollary: when people have time to think, they have a reasonable chance of acting wisely. When they act wisely, they act with a vision of the entire field in which their remedies are to be applied, and not out of an impatient longing to rid themselves of a passing vexation. So it follows that Montaigne's Law is a law only under certain conditions, and is not a law under others.

My reason for this not entirely pessimistic assessment of the human predicament is the present debate about the most important of all human collective adventures, education. The easy-going public of this continent has at last been forced to admit that while the educational system has done a splendid job in producing a race of consumers, and almost as good a job at producing a class of producers, it is falling down in the other great purpose of modern materialism: the moving of large objects through space at record-breaking velocities. This realization has compelled the democratic public of the United States, only nineteen percent of whom buy a single book in a lifetime,* to devote a few of

---

*According to Robert Kenyon, President of the American Magazine Publishers' Association, who bases this figure on data compiled by Gallup Poll Researchers.

their wandering ideas to their educational system. What they learned about it was an old story. For years their experts had assured them that American popular education enjoyed the lowest standards of any comparable system in any civilized country in the world. But what difference did this make? American prestige was unchallenged, it was self-evident that the United States was the greatest nation in human history, egg-heads are always knockers, so who cares? But now it was an intolerable idea for Babbitt that Russia could move larger and bigger objects farther and faster than Americans could, and he was determined to change this situation, and fast. This made it necessary for him to read a few digested reports from the experts, which informed him that the American system for years had been geared to the lowest common denominator of lazy mediocrity; in brief, it had been geared to himself.

People who live in glass houses should not throw stones, and quite a few Canadians in recent years have also been reading reports from school authorities in our own country. Their tenor is very similar, for the best the champions of our system can say is that it is not yet (note that word "yet") quite as bad as the American. Great improvements have been made in education since the war in Canada. The drab brick schoolhouse which often was mistaken for the town jail has been transformed into a bright, new, homogenized structure of glass, brick and plastic so full of sunlight that pupils with tender eyes have to wear dark glasses. Salaries have been raised all over the nation, and in one or two provinces the financial remuneration of an experienced teacher approximates to that of an inexperienced engineer. But the curriculum and the standards—well, how much more resistant are we to the ache in the little heart of a youngster who doesn't want to do his homework?

It is a common human failing of which I myself am constantly guilty to imagine that we knew more at eighteen than we actually did. When I look at my neighbour's son and compare him to myself at the age of eighteen, my neighbour's son naturally seems more ignorant than I was when I was his age. In these cases memory is a poor guide. I know that at McGill the best students are better than the best in my time, but in recent years I have also noticed that the average does not seem as good as it was even six years ago. There is no concrete test which works in this kind of comparison in subjects like literature, history and the like, but in elementary mathematics you can easily make comparisons which are accurate. Mathematics is a subject in which the student advances step by step; it is a subject in which standards are fixed. You can do your sums or you can't.

With this idea in mind I made a point of asking school teachers whenever I met them whether there were any tests to check the standards of now and yesteryear, and a short while ago I found a principal who had made one. He was the chief of a Montreal school with a reasonably old tradition, and he had given to his best senior pupils the same school-leaving exam which had been offered in the year he himself had matriculated, which was 1928. In that year the proportion of firsts, seconds, passes and failures was the same as it is now, but the papers the pupils wrote were different. The principal found that nobody in his present crop could even pass the exam which had been passed thirty years ago by sixty-five percent of the students who sat for it. This was not because the present ones were less intelligent; it was because they had not advanced far enough to cope with the problems set. On the average they were a year and a half behind, and when I heard this, the Calvinist in me muttered *mene, mene, tekel upharsin*.

But the people who really wrote *mene, mene, tekel upharsin* on the blackboards of North America were the Russians when they began shooting into space those miraculous little pieces of hardware. It was only then that the blast of propaganda quieted down sufficiently for us to hear, through one or two moments of silence, that in Russia the calculus is being taught in the equivalent of our tenth grade, that Russian high-school students are expected to master (note the word "master") at least one foreign language, and that in Russia the university population now exceeds a quarter of a million students. Shortly afterwards we discovered something even more embarrassing. Apparently the Soviet authorities are so confident in the success of their scientific forcing houses that they permit fifty-five percent of their university students to elect courses in the humanities. While it may be assumed that the history they are taught is even more mythological than ours, figures like these in the present state of international society have the unpleasant sound of boots crunching over a graveyard. The Russians are not only surpassing us in science; they are also training their youth in general thought.

About the same time this news penetrated the propaganda curtain our advertisers have built, President Eisenhower himself expressed alarm at the physical condition of the youth of his country. It appears that sixty-seven percent of American males can now be relied upon to fail some elementary physical fitness tests which were passed by ninety-two percent of the Europeans in the same age-group. The reason given for this failure, though not for the failure of the young North American brain, was the physical softness produced by the habits of a consumer society. However, this did not deter the President's chief economic adviser from stating in the next election year that the chief purpose of the Republican administration is to "maximize" consumption in the United States of America.

The trance induced by television and advertising, the mental paralysis resulting from the pressure on men compelled to work and worry in order to meet rising prices, rising taxes and a constant flood of new needs bred by the propaganda machine, has so far made it impossible for North Americans to do much practical thinking about the reform of their educational system. The drift continues; the drift in the trance. But at any time in the near future there is bound to be another shock, and no palliative will be found to numb its effects. North America when backed against the wall may eventually lie down and die, but it is not going to do so without at least attempting something to avert it. Sooner or later this continent is sure to make some changes in its educational system, and what scares me is the state of mind of the changers.

For the question they will ask—the question some of them have already asked—is the wrong one: how can the system provide the consumers with an army of scientists numerous enough and competent enough to compete with the Russians today and the Chinese tomorrow? Because both public and politicians are determined to continue "maximizing" consumption, the prospects are not very promising for education. If change comes it will come through political decision. Education will therefore be dragged into the political arena, and in a democracy there is no other place where Montaigne's Law, together with the better recognized law first enunciated by Sir Thomas Gresham, operates with an efficiency more fatal.

For the politicians, even less than the general public, are not concerned with the real purposes of education, and not many of them understand what education is. At the moment they desire its improvement only because they want to rid themselves and the electorate of the feeling of inferiority given them by Russian success. I have yet to hear a responsible American politician (Mr. Stevenson, not being in power, cannot be called politically responsible) express the hope that the colleges will turn out another Socrates, another Milton, another Freud, another Schweitzer. Most of the politicians who have spoken on this matter, including President Eisenhower himself, are so obsessed by the counterpoint of production and consumption that they seem to believe it possible to produce scientists in the same way the Ford Company produces automobiles. The former Nazis they hired for their rocket programme insist that if they are given more money they can beat the Russians, but this is a most dubious proposition. There is only one way for the United States to keep pace with Russia, and that is by changing its attitude towards education as a whole. The methods must be changed and the aims must be changed. But there is not the slightest indication that the politicians realize this, or would dare advocate a total educational revolution even if they did. A politician out of office is a politician without the shadow of power. If the consumers do not wish a basic change in the system, no basic change is likely to come within the system as a whole.

What has made a nonsense of most modern education in North America is simply the misapplication of Jefferson's axiom that all men are created equal. Nobody believes this in anything that matters to the famous Common Man: the Common Man does not for an instant believe that an untrained fighter is the equal of a trained one, or that a boy with slow reflexes can play ball like Babe Ruth or Ted Williams. But in education it is convenient to believe that all men are created equal, and this has been the nub of the whole difficulty ever since any of us now alive can remember. In order to be true to the democratic ideology, our schools for years have supported a system in which excellence has been penalized. The lowest common denominator literally controls the curriculum, and able pupils are compelled to languish at the dullard's pace. This was how it was when I went to school, but since then a flood of new theories has invaded the system with results which would have horrified even the schoolboards of my day. In some educational philosophies it is argued that it is virtually a form of sadism to expose a dull or lazy child to the competition of excellence, so grading is abolished. Failure, it is claimed, will turn the dull boy into a neurotic. It never occurs to people who think like this that frustration will do the same for the excellent boy.

There is only one cure for this betrayal of excellence in favour of democratic conformity, and that is segregation: not segregation as it is understood in the State of Arkansas, but according to ability. The reason why foreign students produce better results—beyond the fact that they work harder and waste less time in frills—is that the excellent are separated from the herd in the high schools and in some cases on lower levels still. They are given the special treatment they deserve and are able to make progress according to their talents and not at the pace of a boy who will never make progress at all. Older countries long ago accepted the bitter truth that only a handful of the human race is capable of advanced thinking. Older countries understand that civilization was not and cannot be created by the masses, but comes to the masses as a gift from a small élite of talented men who have this high privilege, and who go sour and bad unless they are allowed to serve as best they can.

These elementary principles cannot escape the notice of the many fact-finding committees established to investigate the problems of North American education. And that is another thing that scares me.

For the politicians are not interested in improving education as a whole, nor at the moment is the general public which elects them. Faced with the necessity of segregating according to ability, it is all too probable that a decision will be taken to segregate potential mathematicians and scientists for special treatment, while the remainder are left to sink or swim in the old system of easy credits and a smattering of this and that. And there you have an ideal situation for Montaigne's Law to turn up another double-zero on the board.

The basis of all education (not of training but of education) is still the humanities, and when I say "basis" I mean that word literally. Science is the flower, not the basis or root, of the educational system. C. P. Snow is absolutely right when he insists that humanists should know more about science in a general way than most of them do, but science overdeveloped in a society of ignorant consumers is not a blessing but a menace, as the scientists themselves have been the first to know.

"Crafty men condemn studies; simple men admire them; and wise men use them"—the famous line is as good and true as it ever was. Babbitt despises studies unless he sees their results on a quiz show, and in that case he was simple enough to admire them before he learned that he had again been tricked by an advertising agency. But the idea that the humanities can be *used*—how can Babbitt be expected to understand this when he knows nothing about them? How can he know, never having read or been taught, that geometrical principles are not confined to mathematics, but that there is a human geometry also, and that in history there is a geometry sufficiently accurate to cause one of the most profound minds of our century to say, in the most famous line he ever wrote, that those who refuse to remember the past are condemned to repeat it? That segregation according to ability will be introduced into North American education is certain, though when the first steps are taken remains to be seen. But if it is applied only to students of science and not to the system as a whole, it is safe to say that at some time in the not too distant future Montaigne's Law will be adduced to explain the worst collective disaster the free world has suffered since the fall of Rome.

24 SUNSET AND EVENING STAR

After a day of grey clouds the evening broke glorious. The zenith was dark as doom, but the whole west cracked open into a lake of orange, lemon and lime-green in which individual clouds lay as still as that eroded sword of Mycenae in which the old bronze glows like rusty fire. Through a stretch of ten miles the sentinel elms on the rim of the hills stood outlined in perfect clarity. A flock of birds, mosquito-small in the distance, swirled across that celestial lake of colour before flying south into the dark.

I came down the road and found some young people I knew. They were boys and girls in their late teens, one or two of them with a year of college behind them, and I thought how wonderful to be a boy with a girl on such a night as this. But after talking with them a few minutes I discovered that this was not the case.

They were bored. It was too cold for the motor boat and their various Dads were using the family cars and there was nothing to do because there was no place to go. They couldn't water-ski on the ridges of the hills facing the rise of the moon and they couldn't drive their fathers' cars over the downs. They couldn't get there without walking so they stayed in the dark of the street near the Neon sign. I left them with the feeling I used to have in the depression when I passed the unemployed on park benches.

For without poetry these youths were poor. Poetry had been stillborn in them, or they had never been exposed to it. They had many advantages unknown twenty-five years ago and they were thoroughly nice young people, but their education had produced in each one of them a fear of being alone and an incapacity to be happy unless there was something to do. It occurred to none of them that "the gang" has always been an infallible symptom of poverty.

Not when I was a boy nor at any time in the past were all young people poets or even consciously fond of poetry. But if they had received any education at all, they were at least aware of it. Ever since the Greeks, poetry had been basic to the education of civilized people. Not all of them may have liked it, but it affected most of them to greater or less degree. It taught them to find a country landscape more interesting than a city alley; it improved their vocabulary; it made it easier for the sensitive among them to sublimate their sexual drives into creative channels; it made them richer.

As the colour died, the evening star appeared and a little later the moon broke the cloud-wrack and the night opened up. I thought how Homer had made Helen the loveliest woman there ever was not by describing her, but by telling how the elders of Troy fell silent when she passed them on a moonlit night along the city walls. I thought of that greater story in Homer which Freud considered so profound: Ulysses stopping the ears of his seamen with wax and having himself bound to what Freud called "the mast of sublimation" while his ship sailed past the Sirens' isle.

About the feet of the Sirens lay the bones of the men who had touched them, killed by literality. I thought also of the manner in which beautiful girls are described in popular American literature since the war. Each is set forth like a prize bitch in a dog show, all her points specified and described as though she were a pleasure-machine, so that the reader can be absolutely sure that the writer has not cheated him by leaving anything to his imagination. A beri-beri has come into literature with the desiccation of poetry.

For this condition several circumstances are responsible, but the chief criminal is the educational system. Poetry has been almost excluded from it. In few schools are children any longer required to learn verses by heart; the old choral recitation of verse has been thrown out as "uncreative" because it is unoriginal, and for quite a while there has been an idea abroad that making toy houses and cutting out paper patterns on the floor provide the best possible training for creative personalities. Of course, poetry is on the list of required reading for all English exams, including those set by college entrance boards, and if the pupil is lucky in his teacher the results can be as they always are when poetry and youth encounter each other. But it is in college that the shades of the prison house really close down, for there the unhappy student is almost certain to encounter professors who have been trained to murder poetry as efficiently as the German-trained philologists of fifty years ago murdered the ancient classics. Ground out by the Ph.D. system, they use almost any kind of literature as the raw material of what is called critical scholarship, and the very necessities of their trade compel them to concentrate on poets whose writing is dense, or full of obscure symbols and broken lines, or loaded with cross-references and *double-*

entendres. Poetry like this gives them material to teach. But

> *When shepherds pipe on oaten straws*
> *And merry larks are ploughmen's clocks,*
> *And turtles tread, and rooks, and daws,*
> *And maidens bleach their summer frocks . . .*

what can a critic do but tell a youth to read it?

Whenever there is something to sell, there is bound to be a racket somewhere. The vested interest of the power-élite in the poetry world is two-fold: they seek a corner in prestige, and they also seek the economic perquisites which go along with this new species of expertise. Valuable college posts are the rewards of the critic-poet in a society where nobody but other poets and the captive-audiences in English courses read modern verse. The origin of this new power-élite, as almost everyone must know by this time, is the artistic revolution fired in the 1920s by T. S. Eliot, Ezra Pound, James Joyce and a constantly growing army of camp-followers who have copied their mannerisms, and in addition have elevated their choice of subject-matter to a new kind of cliché. At the end of the nineteenth century it was a cliché that sunsets and roses were poetical, and their presence in a line of verse made that verse look like a poem. Since the success of Eliot—the greatest worldly success, surely, of any poet in the last two centuries—objects usually associated with fear, squalor and ugliness have replaced the old subject-matter, and God help a young poet who fails to understand this.

> *Let us go then, you and I,*
> *While the evening is spread out against the sky*
> *Like a patient etherized upon a table . . .*

This celebrated line once struck the traditionalists like a deliberate slap in the face. Here was a new vision, and at the time a great one; here was the shock of truth in a world which Rupert Brooke had lamented had grown old and cold and dreary, its roses no more vital than *pot-pourri*, its sunsets described so often that hardly anyone who had read the poetry of the time could any longer see what a real sunset looked like. Well do I remember the time when it was pointed out to me that this line of T. S. Eliot was the most important single line ever written by an English poet. I also remember the character of the man who introduced me to it.

He was an Englishman in his late twenties, and I thought —probably with truth—that up to then he was the most brilliant man I had ever met. He seemed to know everything. He spoke with fascinating familiarity of "Tom" and "Ezra" and "Wystan", and in his little spare time between his scholarship and long evenings of rabid discussion about art, he himself wrote verse which we understood "Tom" had seen and found promising. Trained in Cambridge by the new school of literary critics (shortly afterwards *émigrés* from this group came to Harvard, Yale and other Ph.D.-giving universities in America, saw them and conquered them in a decade) this Englishman's attitude towards traditional poetry was that of a communist towards traditional statesmen and economists. He was in on the new ground floor and he knew it. When he mentioned Shelley and Wordsworth it was not because he enjoyed what they had written; it was because they were "important" to their time in the sense that Oliver Cromwell, in the Marxists' book, was important to his. The Romantics had revolted and established a new literary power-élite around the year 1800; now it was their turn to be ousted by still another power-élite led by Eliot, Pound and Joyce. This Englishman was as alert to heresy as any communist I ever met in the Thirties. For a while even Pound fell under a cloud, not even Auden was really safe, and Yeats redeemed himself only at the end, much like a Menshevik joining the C.P. at the last hour before that wonderful day in October, 1917. But the Lenin of the movement was T. S. Eliot, and the lovesong of Prufrock the speech at literature's Finland Station.

Under the influence of this Englishman, whom I genuinely liked (for in himself he was a fascinating and vivid personality) I began studying the high priests of the new Dialectic. I became acquainted with the critical writings of F. R. Leavis, Cyril Connolly and a host of authors, including, of course, the Master himself, who quickly found his niche as a critic when his poetical vein ran out. Dutifully I turned my back on the poets I had loved (Shakespeare, for some reason, was exempt) and joined the column that trudged off into the wasteland.

I was young, and if it were not bliss to be alive in that new dawn, it certainly wasn't dull. The depression was making us so angry that the modern youth who call themselves Angry Young Men seem by comparison like comfortable bourgeois. No wonder we worshipped Eliot in those days. Though he seemed to have no real interest in politics outside of literature, in which he was proving himself a master politician, indirectly his influence on practical outlooks was immense. A whole generation of young men and women felt rejected by the social and economic system of the time. Very well. Did not Eliot describe with unparalleled power precisely how hideous that system was, how ugly it had become, how little worth it was?

The winter evening settles down
With the smell of steaks in passageways . . .

or, *The morning came to consciousness*
Of faint stale smells of beer
From the sawdust of trampled streets . . .

or, *Remark the cat which flattens itself in the gutter*
Slips out its tongue
And devours a morsel of rancid butter . . .

No question about the power here; no argument about the genius; no doubt about the truth of this vision for the poet who saw it. But in retrospect what is really amazing has been the rapidity with which this new subject-matter became clichéd by the army of Eliot's imitators, and how, in a sense, it is unnatural that the revolution he started should have held its power without a Khrushchev coming along to modify it.

For Eliot's vision—humourless, passionate and intense—is utterly devoid of love of any kind, and even devoid of hate. Despair is in it, but dislike much more so: a critical dislike of life itself most of the time, the unrelieved weariness of a middle-aged man passing through his climacteric. A poetry of the menopause it really is, and the Master himself has described it perfectly as "thoughts of a brain in a dry season".

So the revolution conquered, and in almost no time poetry was reduced from a living force to a museum study among the young, and the evil day drew nigh, quicker than any young man could have guessed who rejoiced in this youth in the 1930s.

Nearly all observers who have revisited countries they once knew, and which since have been captured by a totalitarian revolution, have noted a universal phenomenon: people have become so accustomed to an arid life of thought-control, to the cueing up and the shoddy goods in the stores, that they seem to have forgotten what it was like in the same land only a dozen years before. The world of modern poetry to a large extent has become like that now, with the successful poets ensconced in universities giving courses in literary criticism, and writing at odd moments brief little word-groups which seem like critical cryptograms in broken lines, the thought so subtle or so obscure, that nobody really understands what it signifies. One of the most curious aspects of the revolution in literature has been the discarding of the age-old axiom that unless a book or a poem is a communication, it does not really exist. This new verse, much of it, deliberately avoids communication, which apparently belongs to the dead past which the revolution overthrew. Even more curious—or is it, really?—has been the durability of the revolutionary subject-matter: the Freudian symbols, the cats in the alleys, the frustrated and frustrating half-dreams, half-thoughts, half-lines. Most curious of all is the fact that this subject-matter is often chosen by quite lusty youths who romp with their girls and enjoy the woods and lakes and rivers of the land, and then return to their desks to write cryptograms about how bad it all is. Big Brother is certainly watching.

Now as the moon mounted the sky I heard the hoot of an owl in the gully and recalled that Englishman with his detective's mind who declared that it was the duty of the critic "to liberate poetry from the tyranny of the past". I also recalled the moment when I understood how parochial he was. It was in Russia just before the war, when I used to spend hours looking at the glum faces of the proletariat liberated from the past by the Bolsheviks.

25 YOUTH AND THE MODERN LITERATURE

The idea of writing this piece came to me after seeing a play by William Gibson called *Two For The Seesaw*, which struck me as another of those beyond-this-nothings until I realized that most of the young people I know admire it extravagantly. They champion this play as they do *The Catcher In The Rye*, and one young television producer told me he would like to pin back the ears of anyone who criticized it. *Two For The Seesaw*, he insisted, is a great work of modern art. If so, it is more than a mere play; it is another notation on literature's social seismograph.

In the 1930s it was a commonplace that the arts reflect the condition of the societies that produce them, and many learned articles were written in those days pointing out that the broken images of Braque and Picasso, the discords of Schoenberg's music, the weird emptiness in the core of Kafka's novels were cryptic messages from the subconscious of post-war Europe. As is usual with a new artistic vision, these messages passed unnoticed for years. The famous Armouries Show of *les Fauves*, which barely antedated the outbreak of the First World War, was greeted with derision or incredulity by the critics of that day. But half a dozen years later *les Fauves* were hailed by the *avant-garde* as the true prophets of Europe's disintegration, and now, of course, their style has become a *cliché*.

In America in the early decades of the century there were no paintings as archetypal as Picasso's, nor was the American literature of violence much more than an expression of American youth in revolt against puritanism. Compared with Europeans like Céline, Kafka, Malraux, Malaparte and Koestler, even Ernest Hemingway was only a new version of that familiar character, the American innocent abroad delighted with his situation in being a spectator of struggles and agonies essentially alien to himself and the world that made him. Even Jack Reed was a tourist on the scene of revolution, not an integral part of it. Nor again were the books written by young Americans after the Second World War comparable to the war literature of Europe in the Twenties and Thirties. Mailer's *The Naked And The Dead* and Irvin Shaw's *The Young Lions* certainly tried to evoke horror, but for most of their readers these books tried too hard. *The Young Lions* was theatrical and *The Naked And The Dead* seemed to owe more to its author's desire to belong to the Russian psychological school than to his observation of the actual men and officers of the American Army who won the Pacific War. Even Dos Passos' trilogy of social novels called *The U.S.A.* was an external book, more the product of the author's mind than of his feelings, and after the Spanish Civil War, Dos Passos himself repudiated the Marxist thesis which gave the novel its form.

No, the tragedy recorded in English and American literature in our century has been of a different sort from the one reported from the European continent. Politics and war have had relatively little to do with it. To find its true expression you must go to authors less brilliant than

Hemingway, less intellectual than Dos Passos, less sensational than Mailer, less self-conscious than the young people who write for the "little" magazines. Ever since the death of Queen Victoria, the social tragedy which has haunted the imagination of the broad middle group of British and American writers has been the wearing away of the importance of the family. Much of our truest (though little of our best-written) literature has reflected this, and the pattern is easily traced.

John Galsworthy is no longer popular with the critics and I suppose he is unfamiliar to most readers under forty. Yet I have never been able to believe that any Englishman in the past twenty years has written a novel as true and important as *The Forsyte Saga*. It may be old hat now, but it was a good hat in its time, and if it is not valuable as a work of art, it is indispensable for anyone who wants to know what England was like at the end of the nineteenth century.

At the beginning of the *Saga* we see the Victorian British family of the upper middle class at the height of its power and self-confidence. Solidly established in massively tasteless houses in Bayswater and Nottinghill Gate—how appropriate that those houses should now take in boarders!—the Forsytes ruled London unchallenged. They invested in consuls, real estate and the Empire; they were a primitive economic unit translated into modern terms by the Industrial Revolution, finance capital and the Royal Navy; they were more provincially minded than any ruling class the English ever had. It is Galsworthy's distinction to have written the classic text-book on the Forsytes' decline and fall.

They failed, according to Galsworthy, because no such family could withstand the shocks of emotional demands. Not revolution, but marriage for love undid them. The young Forsytes who insisted that love should govern their lives were the pallidest of revolutionaries; when young Jolyon was invited back into the fold by his father he came running. But by the turn of the century the crack had appeared in the edifice, and what marriage for love had started, the 1914 war finished. The book ends with the last true Forsyte an old, defeated man with no heir bearing his name. His father and uncles had sired many sons, but Soames had only a daughter, and the daughter had allied herself with a way of life the Forsyte Family had loathed and distrusted.

For the next step in literature's record of the collapse of the family system we must cross the Atlantic to the United States. At the beginning of the 1914 war the American family seemed as entrenched as the Forsytes had been at the time of Victoria's Jubilee. You encountered it week after week in the pages of *The Saturday Evening Post*, and its ideal son was Booth Tarkington's Penrod. You saw it travelling *en masse* all over the nation in the beginning of the automobile age. It was a much nicer family than any of the Forsytes, and it was also much more naïve. It was neighbourly, democratic, optimistic and fond of family fun-parties. But apparently the termites were at work at its foundations, and the detective's instinct of America's writers soon discovered them.

The literary attack on the American family struck with sudden violence in the early Twenties in the writings of Mencken, Nathan, Dreiser, Lewis and at least a dozen lesser men. Sinclair Lewis held up Babbitt as the typical American middle-class *pater familias*, and the whole world rejoiced in the discovery that this all-American symbol was a boob. In Lewis's book the family never disintegrates; after a feeble revolt, Babbitt creeps back into the familiar setting with the motor car, the sun porch, the new gadgets, the Rotary and Boosters' clubs, the Saturday nights of bridge and platitudes.

But the message Lewis proclaimed did not go unheeded by the generation of Americans who were the age of Babbitt's son. "Better be dead than live in Main Street or Zenith!" In the 1920s, millions of young Americans fled from the small towns to the big cities, and by the end of that decade the traditional American family of *The Saturday Evening Post* was on its way out.

In the depression, the American family was assaulted by something much more formidable than ridicule. The economic bottom was knocked out of it, and in the next decade the revolt against family life became strident. In almost all the literature of the Thirties and early Forties the family was depicted as the source of most of the miseries of the authors' characters. The attack was sharpest in the very area where the old institution was strongest, in Boston and New England generally.

The novels of John Marquand—*The Late George Apley, H. M. Pulham, Esquire, Point Of No Return*—are full of sad anger beneath the suave commercial surface Marquand imposes on all his work. In the first two of the stories the characters are crushed by Boston's matriarchy and the family wins a Pyrrhic victory. But in the final story the hero escapes. Driven to New York by his father's financial failure, John Gray in *Point Of No Return* weathers the depression and the war and becomes a successful banker. He marries a girl from the Middle West (herself a fugitive from the family), and between them they create one of those brittle, two-child compromises. They live in the suburbs and conform to the artificial *mores* of other two-child parents as uprooted as themselves. The wife is more of a status-seeker than the husband, but he must make a good pretence at going through the motions of status-seeking lest his political and economic soundness be discredited. The most important material possession in the Gray family is the station wagon which takes the bread-winner to the commuter's train and the children to the progressive school. Their chief driving force is anxiety.

With Marquand, who cut his literary teeth between the wars and who comes from conservative New England, the American family has not quite collapsed. To quote his own best title, it has merely passed its point of no return.

But things change very fast these days, and in the work of the most famous young post-1945 American playwrights and novelists, the American family disintegrates completely.

Arthur Miller and Tennessee Williams are so near to each other in age that they are almost contemporaries, but the few more years Miller has under his belt, combined, possibly, with his Jewish ancestry, have made a considerable difference in his attitudes. Miller describes himself as a depression product, and to the best of our knowledge he has never relinquished his Jewish faith. So he cannot help having an acute sense of social institutions, together with a conviction that justice and a sound political and economic system are essential to human well-being. Miller's plays are all set within a frame.

Miller's best play, *Death Of A Salesman*, depicts the final ruin of a *Saturday Evening Post* American family. Willie Loman is more than a mere salesman; he is a commercial attitude and a philosophy of life. All his days he has tried to live up to the commonest of American ideals: he was a good mixer, an optimist, a lover of football who would sooner have his boys on the team than at the top of their classes. Popularity was his god, his ambition was to be known as a Great Guy; so he went through life on a shine and a haircut glad-handing everyone he met. He had hundreds of acquaintances and no friends, and at the end of his life, broke and sick, he realizes too late that even his sons have turned against him as they have come to understand that the training he gave them has made them helpless to meet the competition in a world utterly different from the one depicted in the pages of *The Saturday Evening Post*. In many ways *Death Of A Salesman* is not even a tragedy: Willie Loman is too stupid, too much victimized by the legend of his consumer society to qualify for that high dignity. He is crushed like a worm under a wheel. But his wife's epitaph on him, spoken after he has committed suicide in a futile attempt to give his ruined family the benefit of his insurance policy, has an eloquence which will live. "Attention must be paid!" she says. And so it must.

Tennessee Williams picks up the American family where Miller has left it. In almost every one of his plays the family is in ruins *before the curtain rises*. His heroes are weaklings, homosexuals or ambivalents; his women are nagging, self-deluding vampires; his only men of force are barbarians like Kowalski in *A Streetcar Named Desire* and Big Daddy in *Cat On A Hot Tin Roof*. Sex, fear, greed and despair are the bonds in Williams' plays, and there is a kind of inspired innocence, a provincialism quite new, in the author's apparent obliviousness of any other pattern of life save the one he sees. Hardly anyone in a Williams play ever tries to understand himself in reference to society, or society in reference to any historical pattern deriving from the past. Albert Camus in *La Chute* has his hero say: "I fornicate and I read the newspapers." But Camus' man at least understands why he has come to this. He has been through a Hitler occupation in which he saved his own life by betraying his friends; he knows that his fall is due to more than his own weakness. But Williams' people exist in a present which is a meaningless limbo. The vast external world which once fascinated writers has no interest whatever for him. All his action is within the tiny group of *déracinés* he shows us on the stage. Here, one might say, is Disintegration Personified.

But lately the personification of disintegration has gone even farther; lately it has reached the place where the process of disintegration has anæsthetized all feelings save the pangs of loneliness. And this idea brings me back to the place where I came in.

In William Gibson's *Two For The Seesaw*—a marvellous title, really—there are just two characters on the stage, a man and a woman who are total strangers when the play began. There are no families, no friends, no callers; there is nothing but this pair acting in one or the other of two small rooms above which towers the impersonal skyline of Manhattan. The hero has been abandoned by his wife (we learn in Act Three that she has divorced him *in absentia*) but long before that event he has fled his home town of Omaha for the big city where he has no job and no prospects. The heroine is a Jewish girl of natural vitality and kindliness who was born in the Bronx. Her husband, we soon discover, has casually walked out on her two years before the play opens, and she has lived up to the masochistic chivalry of her generation by paying for the rail ticket which conveyed him to his next girl-of-call in Florida.

The action of the play is almost all dialogue. The girl and the man (we discover he is a lawyer!) talk to each other over the telephone, they argue, they make jokes and wisecracks, they share meals and of course they are soon making love. So they pass the Manhattan winter. The man studies for his New York bar exam and the girl encourages him. The girl falls ill and the man nurses her. But none of these shared activities leads to anything. The moment the bar exam is passed, the moment he is free to earn a living in New York, back the man goes to Nebraska for no good reason save an unconscious desire to escape from any possible permanent ties. At the beginning he could not endure a life of total solitude; at the end he cannot face the effort of working with a woman to produce a home. He is not a bad man; he is kind, gentle and wistful. He is not a stupid man; he has some competent insights. But this is how he acts. And the curtain falls with the girl standing alone in her room at the end of an affair she has known all along would end just like this. In the future she sees nothing concrete, but she knows the affair will be repeated with some other man because that is how life goes, and as she leaves us, we hear her wondering what the next man in her life will be like.

Beyond *Two For The Seesaw*, it seemed to me, the story of social disintegration cannot go. But this does not mean I am right, for half a dozen years ago I came away from *Death Of A Salesman* with the same feeling. Who knows? Perhaps in this consumers' paradise some playwright will have the insight and technical skill to create a believable *pièce de théatre* out of a lonely woman and the images that come and go on the television screen which has become her sole link with society.

I know it is risky to make too much out of these subconscious prophecies which come from literature. Nature rebuilds as she destroys, and life always manages to go on. Yet it means something pretty important when we hear almost all young people interested in literature asserting that plays like *Two For The Seesaw* and novels like *The Catcher In The Rye* tell the world exactly how their generation thinks and feels.

The Catcher is still the most significant of the lot, and it is certainly the tenderest. It is without doubt the most terrible indictment of an older generation ever written by an American. Young Caulfield's parents are not brutal, they do not seem to be indifferent to him, indeed they appear to have been determined to give him everything his heart desires except the one thing all young people desire most of all from their parents—a lead in life and an anvil on which their young hammers can strike sparks. Moreover, as Caulfield and his millions of youthful reader-friends see it, the whole society to which this permissive generation of parents belongs is phony from top to bottom. Merely to detect the phony becomes young Caulfield's goal; he is the catcher in the rye. But at the end of the book he sees no possible prospect of himself ever succeeding as a human being. A discontented youth in my time could fight against fascism, but nobody can fight against a feather bed.

Now the most curious thing about the young generation of today seems to me to be this. On the one hand their favourite literature depicts solitary individuals or solitary couples going their own sexual ways as best they can without responsibility to anything save the obligation to be tender. On the other hand the only reasonable goal many of them recognize is marriage. That may be why they pair off so young and make a separate peace with a society they shrug their shoulders at. The creation of a family of their own is what millions of them look forward to, but as they see it, the family exists in a kind of limbo; it is something they construct as a fort to keep society out. "We will create a world for two"—for dozens of young college couples I know, this line from *Lili Marlene* has the compulsion of a slogan.

But no world for two, not even with children, is enough even for one, and for a reason stated twenty-three-hundred years ago. Man is a social animal, and he cannot escape the consequences of being one. The last time in history when a social organization was confined to two people and their immediate progeny was the Stone Age of the Cave Man. If property was not enough for the Forsytes sixty years ago, love, sex and tenderness are not enough for anyone now. My God, I feel sorry for some of them who do not understand this.

26 FOOTSTEPS OF GENIUS

Ah, did you once see Shelley plain
And did he stop and speak to you
And did you speak to him again?
How strange it seems and new!

When I was a boy these lines of Browning thrilled me, for I was raised in the belief that everything we value, from Christianity to the pasteurization of milk, had come to us from a handful of men who had been singled out by the Divine Spirit and whom we described as geniuses. Merely to see a living genius was considered a privilege, and we agreed with Emerson that the search after great men should be a legitimate dream of youth. Certainly it was my dream when I grew up in Nova Scotia to meet and speak with a truly great man before I died.

The most undeniable genius of our century is Albert Einstein, and when I first left home for Europe the idea that I might see him in some public place was an exciting one. I was therefore thrilled, during the winter of my last year in

Oxford, when Einstein came over from the Continent to deliver a series of lectures setting forth his latest theory of the nature of the universe. In those days there was much discussion about whether we lived in a finite or infinite universe, and it was expected that the results of Einstein's latest researches would tell us at least in general terms, where we were.

Few lectures Einstein ever gave can have been more frustrating to him than this Oxford series. His courtesy and modesty were legendary, but the press pestered him wherever he went, and university gossip had it that he was pained when he discovered that hardly anyone understood what he was talking about. The reporters who flooded the town had lean pickings. They had not expected to understand the equations, but they had hoped to find at least one or two scientists attending the lectures who would tell them in simple English whether the universe was curved or rectangular, expanding or static, finite or infinite. So far as I could discover from reading the press—as an undergraduate I was not admitted to the lectures nor would I have learned anything if I had been—all they found out was that Einstein's hair was turning grey and that he liked to take long walks by himself.

It was his walking habit that brought us together for the first, though not for the last time. One day during Einstein's stay in Oxford I woke up at noon feeling as a young man does when he has helped celebrate a friend's twenty-first birthday the night before. After getting something to eat, I decided that only Spartan measures would rid me of my malaise, so I put on running shorts and shoes, two sweaters and a scarf and set out for a run around the three-mile path that circles the Christ Church meadows. In the narrow section where the path winds along the Cherwell between trees and shrubs I rounded a corner and all but ran into a strange and wonderful man.

"Please," Einstein said in a strong German accent, "can you tell me where I am?"

While I struggled for breath, he smiled: "I am entirely lost in the trees."

Two years later when I was at Princeton, Einstein left Europe with a price on his head and was spirited off his steamer at the mouth of New York harbour lest some of Fritz Kuehn's hoodlums make an attempt on his life. After a few days he arrived in Princeton to begin his long sojourn there. His arrival sent a flutter through the little town, which was not so accustomed to celebrities as Oxford was, and his walking habits soon made him a familiar figure. Princeton thinks extremely well of itself, but with the exception of the barbers, who were sure they could make an improvement in his appearance, neither town nor gown was too sophisticated not to feel flattered by his presence among them.

In those days some of my best friends were ex-bootleggers who had survived from the days of prohibition, a much respected body of men in Princeton because of their service to the community during the previous Republican administrations. They loved their town dearly. They regarded foreigners with contempt, and foreign country to them began on the other side of the Delaware River about a dozen miles away.

Late one night I was munching a hamburger in a diner, while my vocabulary was being enlarged by three bootleggers who leaned on the counter and told me things about the United States that are not recorded in either the press or the history books. Suddenly their gravel voices ceased, and looking over my shoulder I joined them in a long stare at an apparition in the doorway. He had vast brown eyes open in child-like enquiry, he had a wild mop of hair and he was wearing a baggy suit of clothes. When he saw us looking at him his face broke into a wonderful smile, his hands made the apologetic gesture of a man discovering himself an intruder in the wrong place, and while we stared he turned out of the shaft of light and disappeared into the dark.

Before the monosyllabic conversation within the diner could be resumed, a burly character wearing a truck-driver's cap came swaggering in, plunked himself down at the counter, demanded coffee, looked around at the rest of us and said, "Whaddya call this dump?"

Now it was apparent that this man was a genuine foreigner, for even if his base of operations had been as distant as Pennsylvania he must have known what Princeton was. He may have been new on the run, or he may have come east with a load from across the mountains, and as he slurped up his coffee I saw one of the bootleggers contemplating him with the professional expression of a butcher sizing up a carcass to estimate how much it weighs. This bootlegger was a simple man but a passionate one; insanely loyal to his friends, he was subject to dark movements in his soul which more than once I had heard emerge in a kind of poetry. Once in his speakeasy the lights had gone out and the moon, striking through the window, had illuminated his face in a manner utterly uncanny; his eyes had rolled white in the moon and he had broken into a stream of profanity which had no connection with the failure of his lighting system. When I asked him what the matter was, he had answered in what Evelyn Waugh would call a lapidary phrase: "That God damn moon reminds me of jail," he said. So now as I saw him contemplating this truck-driver who had entered the place just after Einstein had left it, I was glad I was not in the truck-driver's shoes. Two years ago the bootlegger had served what he called a nine-spot for slugging an out-of-state revenue officer with a baseball bat.

"What goes on in this town," he said in a gravel voice while fixing the truck-driver with a slow stare, "is something a guy like you would not understand."

"Yeah?" and the word was not a question but a challenge.

"Did you see that old guy with the hair?"

"What old guy with what hair?"

"That old guy that was in here before you."

"I never saw any old guy." The truck-driver shrugged. "What goes on in this place nights?"

The bootlegger's stare remained in sullen fixation, and the truck-driver gave a look over his shoulders at the other men, who were silent in the way Americans of that type know how to be on certain occasions.

"Okay," he said, "so what's so special about this guy?"

The bootlegger shifted his weight and eased his shoulders under his suit: "You wouldn't know, but that old man is working on the next war. He's making photoelectric cells in this town, and when the war comes he's gonna let them loose, and when he lets them loose nuthin's gonna stand against them."

The truck-driver finished his coffee and rose: "That a fact?"

The bootlegger turned his thumb in slow motion in the direction of the door. "Okay, you can get going now. And next time you drive that load of junk through this town, you can keep right on going all the way through. In this town we're used to big shots."

A few nights later I happened to be walking through the campus with a young English physical chemist on the way to a Schoenberg recital at the McCarter Theatre. It was a windy night and under the elms it was very dark with only a few lights flickering where paths intersected and a few windows illuminated with graduate students behind them poring over drab details which would be compiled after a year or two in Ph.D. theses which nobody but the examiners would ever read. Near the Classics Seminary we came upon Einstein standing still and apparently waiting for us to overtake him.

"Please," he said, "I go to the concert but I am new here and now I do not know where I am."

The Englishman's voice quivered with delight as he remarked that we also were going to the concert and that perhaps Dr. Einstein would permit us to show him the way.

"But how," said Einstein in a genuine wonder, "do you know who I am?"

"Oh, sir!" said the Englishman.

"You are too kind," the genius said as he fell into step with us. "You two young men go together and you have things to talk about."

We assured him that what we had been talking about could wait for another occasion, and the three of us continued side by side through the windy darkness.

"Do you like Schoenberg?" Einstein asked us.

One of us murmured that we did not know, and the other of us added that this would be the first time we had ever heard his music.

"I have been told, sir," said the Englishman, "that one must be an exceptionally good mathematician to be able to understand Schoenberg's scale."

As though he had heard this for the first time, Einstein nodded with great emphasis and said: "But that is so true!" And then he said: "Unfortunately I am such a poor mathematician I do not understand him at all."

A great gust of wind went shrieking through the trees,

a pattern of light tossed wildly in the shadows of waving branches, and rain began to fall.

> *Ah, did you once see Shelley plain*
> *And did he stop and speak to you*
> *And did you speak to him again?*
> *How strange it seems and new!*

27 PORTRAIT OF A YEAR

The year 1955 was surely one of the loveliest years any living person can remember. Like a woman of perfect tact, she let her moods follow her natural growth in harmonious sequence from beginning to end. Through January and February she was bright, flashing and thoughtless, in March she turned teen-ager and dumped four feet of snow on our sidewalks just in time to tie up the traffic on April Fool's. Then, with one of those mysterious shifts of mood and feature you often see in a growing girl, she became shy and reticent, and in mid-April we had no idea what kind of woman she was going to turn out to be. She gave us the answer in May, which she entered like a supple girl of perfect deportment, yet one who knew what she wanted and how to get it, and the most delicate shades of green became her well. In June she married the countryside and at once began to produce a family the like of which hardly anyone could recall. Peonies and roses overflowed the gardens, and in the fields the wildflowers were so dense they hid the hay. All through July and August she was a richly passionate woman in the prime of her lust, full of light and power and radiance, and she gave herself so profusely there were times when her lovers lay gasping and praying for relief from her presence. Relief came in September when her beauty cooled, and the bones of her face showed fine and aristocratic. By October she was a great lady knowing her life had been so full she could afford to be serene, wise, thoughtful and remembering. Not even in November did any unsightly violence mar her decline. Her blood cooled almost imperceptibly and her approach to death was never vulgar or loud. One day we woke up to find her white and cold, as tactful in death as she had been seemly in life. "Come live with me," she had said in various accents as long as the breath was in her, "Come live with me and be my love and we will all the pleasures prove."

28 CAME THE REVOLUTION

Prophets usually get what they deserve, for they are a cantankerous lot as a rule, and since the time of Malachi the fate of most of them has been oblivion or derision. If they prophesy correctly, and they seldom do, everyone forgets them. If they prophesy inaccurately—but why continue with generalities when once more I am using the essay form to creep back into an affair I should never have entered in the first place.

I first took to prophecy in the late summer of 1956 when I was asked to write an editorial for the *Montrealer* magazine and looked around for something to write about. Seeing the Liberals as serene as the moon, I predicted that they would soon be on the park benches, and with the mixture of metaphor in which all prophets indulge, I added that "the Liberal glacier is sliding over the edge of the cliff".

When the Tories made this bet good eight months later, my prediction that they would do so was, of course, forgotten. What was not forgotten was another prophecy I had written six weeks before that famous June Election. In the interval the Tories had chosen Mr. John Diefenbaker to lead them, and at *that* time it was obvious to anyone who knew the Province of Quebec that if Mr. Diefenbaker won a single French-Canadian seat he would be doing better than anyone in Quebec expected. I accordingly had recourse to still another metaphor. "Do the Tories really want to win?" I asked, and answered the question for them with the statement that at the very moment when their ship had sighted harbour, they had fired a torpedo into it. It never occurred to me, nor to anyone else I knew, that a Canadian political party could win a federal election without a single Quebec seat. Just after my little effort reached print, Mr. Diefenbaker proved that it could. I have since been told that this editorial of mine now hangs, suitably framed, in Conservative Party Headquarters. I hope it does. I have always wanted to write at least one piece of prose which had a chance of becoming immortal.

Mr. Diefenbaker encouraged me to continue my prophetic career a little longer, and on the eve of the 1958 election I prophesied that he would win forty Quebec seats, and was called a fool by all my friends for going over the prescribed number of twenty-two. When the ballots were counted he had won fifty Quebec seats, so there was nothing left save to prove my impartiality by quoting Sophocles for the benefit of both our senior political parties.

"Call no man happy until he has lived his final day," says the chorus after Oedipus blinds himself. With equal truth this sentiment (so I reminded the politicians) could easily be reversed: "Until he has lived his final day, call no man unfortunate." I wish the Conservatives would hang up this last sentence of mine, which was written as an accolade for them, but I suppose that is expecting too much. In the present state of affairs it might be construed as Liberal propaganda.

Hindsight is not only safer than prophecy; it is much more interesting. By hindsight we can not only recognize that Mr. Diefenbaker has led a revolution in Canadian politics, but also how he has been able to do it without any of the usual revolutionary fanfare.

To anyone who has followed the politics of North America through the last century, it seems pretty clear that the successful leader, at least most of the time, is in tune with the subconscious of the public whether he knows it or not. A man may go on for years saying and believing the same thing, and the thing he says and believes may be true, but it will not help him unless the public listens, and the public will never listen until it is good and ready. The successful democratic leader does not even have to be popular, though it helps, and possibly is necessary, if at election time he is less unpopular than his opponent. Nor need the public understand what it is doing when it elects him; all it has to do is mark the ballot right.

Mackenzie King has been the supreme beneficiary of the workings of the subconscious of a modern electorate; at least he was up to a few years ago. I don't suppose anyone would quarrel with me for calling King the most astute politician (I said politician) produced in North America in the twentieth century. He was able enough to have had a substantial career in almost any normal profession except motion pictures, vaudeville and literature, but only in Canada—only in the Canada of his own epoch—could a man like King have become head of state. This he could do, despite being the most consistently unpopular individual in Canadian history, because he had the knack of making his opponents appear more unpopular than himself at election time. But there was much more to it than that. His genius for compromise, his massive public hypocrisy balanced by his uncanny personal acumen, his humourlessly drab style, his capacity to turn his incapacity for leadership into a political asset, the psychological conjuring act which enabled him to live in two worlds at once (Ottawa and the hereafter)—in the days of the Liberal glory, Mackenzie King could almost have been called the outward and visible expression of the nation's subconscious mind.

For what were we in the days of Mackenzie King? The new generation is too young to remember, the older one has almost forgotten.

We were, and yet we were not, a nation. Inheriting from an extremely complex history (of which most of us were ignorant) a peculiar and intricate set of political reflexes, we had grown up more loyal to our regions than to the nation as a whole. And Canadian regionalism had aspects comical and bewildering to the outsider. People living in Cape Breton used to speak of "going to Nova Scotia" when they crossed the Strait of Canso, just as Newfoundlanders still speak of "going to Canada" whenever they leave their island in a westerly direction. Maritimers lumped the general hinterland together in two broad categories—Upper Canada and the West. By Upper Canada they meant *both* Quebec and Ontario, and by the West nearly everything between Hamilton and Japan. The fulcrum of the nation's politics, it was generally agreed, was the ancient fortress of Quebec Province, whose extreme nationalists pretended that the British North America Act was not a constitution but a mere treaty of alliance. Moving farther west into Ontario, the enquiring politician in those days was forced to recognize that if Quebec was determined to remain the French Fact in America, Ontario was equally determined to disagree with everything Quebec wanted, and to insist upon its own image as the British Fact in Canada. No matter how many visiting Englishmen told him that Toronto and Cleveland were indistinguishable in English eyes, the Ontario voter knew himself for what he was: British, Protestant and Conservative.

Here, in the old eastern regions of British North America, were formed the habits which every Canadian political party had to deal with from the time of Sir John Macdonald to 1957. Our history being what it was, the only reason the diverse provinces had agreed to confederate had been their mutual determination not to become American states. So who could blame the Liberals for balancing the lever of their policy fair and square on the fulcrum of Quebec? So long as Quebec held fast, they couldn't lose. If the divisions in the rest of the country did not frustrate the Tories, the Tory conventions could usually be relied upon to appoint a leader who would defeat himself even before the voters had a chance to get to work on him.

It was Mackenzie King who developed the perfect formula to fit these conditions and this state of the national mind. Compromise—compromise in everything—became the rule of the Old Master. Conscription if necessary, but not necessarily conscription; a national flag, but not necessarily an official national flag; a bilingual country, but not necessarily bilingualism. So automatic was his technique that when the Drys began pressing for prohibition during the war, and the Wets were beginning to feel alarmed, he came up with the formula we still follow: a bottle of whisky with its alcoholic content diluted by one third, a figure which probably corresponded exactly to the percentage of teetotallers in the nation in that particular year.

You could compile a list of these logical illogicalities as long as your arm, and why blame King for them? He had to govern us as we were. He knew, if we did not, that the last thing Canadians of his day would tolerate was a leader who led, because nobody could lead one section of the country without enfuriating the other. So it went year after year, and if the Liberals are now on the park benches —if most of them don't even have that much of a luxury

—it is because they assumed it would go on forever.

Yet even in King's heyday there were portents that it would not. To my continuing amazement, I was a minor one myself. Born in Cape Breton and raised in Halifax, a provincial of provincials who visited every European capital before I crossed what I used to call the New Brunswick frontier, I published at the height of the King era a book called *Two Solitudes* which sold more copies in Canada than any Canadian novel since *Maria Chapdelaine*. Literary merit had no connection with this sale; the book merely happened to put into words what hundreds of thousands of Canadians felt and knew. It contained a passage which dozens of strangers mentioned when they wrote to me about the book. Athanase Tallard, the old French-Canadian *seigneur*, spoke for hundreds of thousands when he said the following to an English-speaking friend:

"The trouble with this whole country is that it's divided up into little puddles with big fish in each one of them. I tell you something. Ten years ago I went across the whole of Canada. I saw a lot of things. This country is so new that when you see it for the first time, all of it, and particularly the west, you feel like Columbus and you say to yourself, 'My God, is all this ours!' Then you make the trip back. You come across Ontario and you encounter the mind of the maiden aunt. You see the Methodists in Toronto and the Presbyterians in the best streets of Montreal and the Catholics all over Quebec, and nobody understands one damn thing except that he's better than everyone else. The French are Frencher than France and the English are more British than England ever dared to be. And then you go to Ottawa and you see the Prime Minister with his ear on the ground and his backside hoisted in the air. And Captain Yardley, you say God damn it!"

Now here is a curious thing, and more curious still is the

fact that no political leader seemed to see it in the days when he might have used it for his own advantage. The West, inarticulately but loudly, had been saying "God damn it!" ever since the end of the First World War. For the West is new: so new that there are thousands of people still alive in Saskatchewan who remember living in sod huts on the open plains. Only to a limited extent did the western homesteaders and the settlers of British Columbia feel or retain the throb of the old emotions which had made Canada such an unwilling federal state in the middle of the nineteenth century. As time passed the first settlers were joined by hundreds of thousands of immigrants from Europe to whom Canada's early history meant nothing. The real cause of the Westerner's impatience with Quebec (which is far more vehement than anything you can find in Ontario today) is not, as Quebec nationalists believe, a dislike of Roman Catholicism. It is not even dislike of the French language unless somebody compels him to learn it. It is the assumption, often brashly expressed, that Quebec opposes the western notion of pan-Canadianism. A Nova Scotian can still feel at home in his local county, a French Canadian in a parish along the river, an Ontario man in a small town beside the lake. But counties and localities mean little on the ocean-like plain between St. Boniface and the Rockies, and out there people think in larger geographical horizons if not in larger human terms. Canada herself—that was the Westerner's notion of home! And during the last thirty years this western attitude has been growing to the proportions of a new force in Canadian politics.

The old parties never seemed able to recognize this force —which is simply the spirit of pan-Canadianism—because of the strange manner in which the Westerners expressed it. Politically they expressed it in splinter parties which had no real connection with western needs and attitudes. The old Farmer Progressive Party was "western"enough, but its aims were too local to give it a chance outside the prairies, and it soon disappeared. But its disappearance did not mean that western protest was over. Immediately afterwards the C.C.F. began to gain ground, and then Social Credit, both of them parties which had their theoretical origins in British urban conditions and had no indigenous roots in western Canada. Yet year after year one of them got into power in Saskatchewan, the other in Alberta, and finally Social Credit made inroads into British Columbia as well. No socialism, no social credit, followed these victories at the polls. It should, therefore, have been obvious to everyone that these splinter parties were protest parties elected by people who had lost all patience with the formulas followed by the Liberals and Tories, formulas which were based on conditions quite alien to the western experience.

Meanwhile still another change was occurring in Canada: the population was growing at an unprecedented rate. In 1914 Canada entered the First World War with a population under eight million souls. In the Twenties, with the bones of 66,000 potential Canadian farmers mouldering in French and Flemish earth, the drain of emigration to the United States all but cancelled out the population increase brought about by the birth-rate and by immigration from Europe: as late as 1942 the figure still stood below a dozen million. But in the thirteen years since the war, the population of Canada has jumped to more than eighteen million, and it rises by geometrical proportions.

Out of this came another new force, and in spirit it was allied to the West. Now there are millions of voters in Canada too young to remember Mackenzie King, and too little formed by the eastern Canadian experience to recall the regional emotions of our ancestors. This new generation—prosperous, self-confident and politically naïve—has produced a vast psychological change in Canada. Without anybody consciously planning it, this new force encountered Mr. John Diefenbaker and Mr. Diefenbaker encountered it, and they married each other. For Mr. Diefenbaker met his political bride armed with a mighty weapon: his sincere, lifelong and obsessional devotion to the pan-Canadian ideal.

At the beginning of the 1958 election campaign, as part of a panel for a national magazine, I had the privilege of interviewing the new Prime Minister on the eve of the greatest election victory in Canadian history. I never met a Canadian public figure with such messianic passion, and this struck me as interesting, because on the two occasions when I had met him before his elevation, Mr. Diefenbaker had suggested little of this volcanic force. Something must have unlocked it, and it was my guess that it was the sense of vindication which comes to a man advanced in years who at last discovers a public willing to accept what he has been offering all his life. I left him with the thought: "Nature abhors a vacuum, and even the placid Canadian people abhorred the vacuum in leadership created by their own traditional habit of mind." Whatever else he may not be, the Prime Minister is certainly a man who is willing to lead. Events showed that a country starved of leadership for nearly half a century had reached the point where it craved leadership more than anything else.

Most significant of all was the Prime Minister's absolute confidence in the success of his mission. In answer to the question of why he had decided to become a lawyer at the age of nine, he said, and Hansard wrote it down:

"It was a set course, and it was never deviated from, never changed. The course was determined for me as a youngster, undeviating and unchanging. It was all determined for me. I determined myself that that was the thing

I was going to do—and I determined it because of my mixed racial origin. I am the first prime minister of this country of neither altogether English nor French origin. So I determined that that was the thing I was going to do. I never deviated from this course, and I determined to bring about a Canadian citizenship that knew no hyphenated consideration . . . It's the reason I went into public life. I'm very happy to be able to say that in the House of Commons today in my party we have members of Italian, Dutch, German, Scandinavian, Chinese and Ukrainian origin—and they are all Canadians!"

Here speaks the authentic voice of a new force in Canadian public life, and it is the same force which the West has for years been stammeringly expressing through the splinter parties which Mr. Diefenbaker's victory destroyed as a federal power. It is the force which wrecked the Liberals not because they were opposed to it in principle—far from it—but because they recognized its existence too late. After the death of Mackenzie King, the dominant force in the Liberal Party was Mr. C. D. Howe, a man who served the country well in a technical sense, but also a man born and raised in the United States, and naturally deaf to the strange complex of emotions in the growing country of Canada. Equally deaf were the business men of East and West alike who failed to recognize the vitality of this new national feeling, and turned over, or sold out, a third of the nation's future to American interests. Whether it was necessary for them to have done this, or whether it was necessary for them to have done it to such an extent, is for experts to decide. But of this there can be no doubt whatever: the saving of Canada from the maw of American corporations is going to be the largest central issue in Canadian politics for a long time to come. When the full implications of this colossal sell-out are brought home to the Canadian people, as brought home they are bound to be, there will be some ugly scenes, and the time may come, and sooner than we think, when men who consider themselves respectable, and even patriotic, will be appalled to hear themselves called quislings. Too many people have endured too much—too many people have hoped too much—for this strange, illogical, Canadian adventure to perish, or for this out-broken spirit to be processed into something with no more soul than a business corporation. After nearly two centuries of blind groping, the image of a Canadian identity has finally emerged out of the shell, and it is too late to push it back again. This force which Mr. Diefenbaker has tapped may be intangible, but it is a very real one indeed, and its political assertion is revolutionary in the most exact sense of the word. How odd that our first real political upheaval since 1867 should have been ushered in by a man whom the Tories chose to lead them!

29 FIFTY GRAND

After years of half-hearted trying, I made it at last; I became half a century old.

This traumatic date fell on a Wednesday, one of the days when I lecture at McGill. Looking at the class assembled in rows in front of my desk, I began thinking about the difference between their ages and mine, adding and subtracting and multiplying while I felt myself growing older and older by the second. Then I remembered how much better adjusted they are to the twentieth century than I am, and this made me feel young and immature. Then I looked down at my notes, which began with an historical reference, and felt old again.

Directly in front of me was a cheerful youth sitting beside a golden girl.

"If I were as much older than myself as I am older than you two," I thought, "I would have been born the year of the Battle of Eylau."

No, that would not do; they had never heard of the Battle of Eylau. So I thought of something else.

"If I were one and three quarter times as much older than myself as I am older than you, and a citizen of Montreal, I would at one time have been a subject of Louis XV. If I were twice as much older than myself as I am older than you, I would have been alive during the War of the Spanish Succession."

But in front of a generation like this there was no point in such reflections. The War of the Spanish Succession? To them, battles like Ypres, Gallipoli and the Somme are as remote as Blenheim is to me. Even the last war has become hazy to them. A few days ago, mentioning some of the writers connected with the last war, I had discovered that none of them had ever heard of Ernie Pyle, and this seemed all the more astonishing because two members of the class were Americans.

If you are fifty years old today and work with ordinary survivals of the *ancien régime*—in other words, with people over the age of twenty-eight—you feel young, vigorous and grateful to the medical profession. But if you are fifty and work with people of college age, even for three hours a week, there is only one word that fits your own conception of yourself. You are immortal. Not like Lazarus or Rip Van Winkle, but immortal like a Greek god who stayed pretty much the same from the fall of Troy to the fall of Athens.

I'm not being fanciful about this: try talking to the modern young about events which seem recent to you but are no longer part of your ordinary conversation. Talk to them about Chamberlain's flight to Munich or *Mein Kampf* or the breadlines or any of the famous men of the Thirties. Even if you aren't a parent, you will be startled.

Nor will you be right if you pretend that you were just as oblivious to the past when you were their age. You weren't. Twenty-five years ago, more or less, the First World War (*the* war) was not considered remote by college students, neither did what had happened before that war seem unimportant to them. In those days, in those last days of history's continuum, we lived in the shadow of the past and we knew it whether we read history or not.

But this new generation lives in the shadow of no past older than 1945. From 1945 all the way back, history to most of them seems much of a muchness, interesting to those who find it so, packed with delightful characters but of no special significance. "We really ought to know more about it," a girl said to me the other day, and she sounded exactly like the polite Americans who tell us they really ought to know something about Canada.

I keep harping on Santayana's remark that those who cannot remember the past are condemned to repeat it. Does it still hold good? I'm damned if I know. Certainly an obsession with the past makes a good many nationalist politicians repeat some of the past's worst examples, much as the sons of neurotic fathers repeat their fathers' compulsions. But if you are ignorant of what the neurotic can do to you, what is the final use of your own capacity to adjust to others like yourself?

Fiftieth birthdays are traditionally occasions when writers make a pretence of being philosophical as an excuse for talking about themselves, and the note sounded is usually one of guarded optimism. After saying with an insincere laugh that everyone over fifty expects to die at any moment, we set about explaining how advantageous it is to be fifty. Clifton Fadiman, on his fiftieth birthday, told us that he could now afford the luxury of being honest, and in proof of how luxuriously honest he had become, he said he no longer cared how many people knew that he got no pleasure out of the novels of William Faulkner, and that he preferred Thornton Wilder to Hemingway.

But the pleasures of honesty impress me little. For what is the use of honesty (or is candour the *mot juste?*) if you lack the intelligence to understand what you should be honest about? At fifty I know little of honesty. All I know for sure is that I am the prisoner of my own life, which in turn has been the prisoner of the most prolonged and violent transition human society has suffered since the fall of the Roman Empire. People who have survived transitions see some things with the clarity of an X-ray machine, but there is no evidence that they see the general picture as accurately as they believe they do.

What I understand clearly—or think I understand clearly—is that I am tired of this transition which has nullified the value of so many fine things I have learned. It gives me no feeling of security to think back on any aspect of it, no nostalgia, no desire to return to the cradle or the school. I wish the engineers would take a twenty-year vacation and leave us in peace. I wish things would settle down so that a day would come when I could cease feeling like a twenty-year-old with his way to make. For that is exactly how I do feel, and with reason, in my fiftieth year.

I became a classical scholar just at the moment when the classics were dropped from the educational system. I began to enjoy silent movies (being in a place where I could be discriminating about them) the year Hollywood switched to sound and condemned itself to one more decade of adolescence. I worked hard to become a Rhodes Scholar, and having become one, graduated from Oxford in 1932 when only one Rhodes man in ten got a job of any kind. The only thing I learned through acquiring a Ph.D. degree was that such a degree is worthless even in the rat-race of academic job-hunting. I learned to play a lovely game called rugger, which once was the autumn sport of the Maritimes and the Pacific coast; I have lived to see it abandoned because the equipment costs too little and advertising pressures have taught Canadians to become a nation of spectators, with the result that the football they watch is played by imported gladiators. In the nineteen-thirties I had a dramatic sense and wanted to write plays, but there was no market for them in the society of that era. So I wrote six novels, four of which were published, and when the last was finished I believed I had finally mastered a difficult and complex art. The spring that novel appeared the bottom dropped out of the fiction market and is still out. Now television dominates my trade and has made the play popular again—but only the kind of play which suits the I.Q. of the average thirteen-year-old. Must I go back and learn the mastery of still another craft in order to live and communicate? And if I do, won't the same pattern repeat itself? The moment television verges on maturity, won't some new technical improvement hurl it back to the childishness which all new technical developments impose on an art form?

This is a truth I can state honestly at fifty—that I am tired of seeing one worthy activity after another outmoded by new gadgets and fads. But it is also true that I don't regret having learned these prehistoric crafts, and that only twice or three times in these last fifty years, and then not for long, have I ever wished I were dead. I can't pretend to be joyful at the knowledge I am fifty, but with candour and honesty I can say I am thankful to have done with my forties.

One day three men are going to found a society called Forty-Year-Olds Anonymous for the benefit of that unhappy age group thrust by fashionable morality and their own decency into life's isolation ward. These days there is a perpetual open season on the forty-year-old man. The young want to do him down because he is their most formidable competitor, and the old want to keep him in his place lest he discover his power and knock them out of theirs. Psychiatrists, psychologists, medical men, clergymen, newspaper moralists and magazine writers gang up on the forty-year-old with the ferocious self-righteousness of a covey of Afro-Asians moving in on an American technical assistance expert who keeps mumbling that all he wants is for everyone to be happy. They tell him he has passed his point of no return and make him feel guilty for having done so. They assure him that sex is at this very moment putting the big bite on him, that his wife is unhappy on account of him, that he is turning his children into neurotics, that he is drinking, smoking and working too much. Barbiturates claim him for their own, but instead of profiting by them. he hammers his bed with his heels and wishes he were a little boy again. Whenever he gets tired he remembers that *Reader's Digest* article and feels for his heart. Whenever he is worried he remembers those pictures he saw in *Life* of a representative forty-year-old stomach. Furtively he slinks out of bookstores carrying *Peace of Soul* and *The Mature Mind*, and at the breakfast table he sneaks a quick glance at Mary Hayworth to see what the latest forty-year-old wife has to say about the outrages of the latest forty-year-old husband. He desires what he doesn't want in order to prove to himself that he is still capable of desiring it. He learns the bitter truth—that people are seldom sorry for one another, they are only sorry for themselves. And through all this decade, he will see his fiftieth birthday taking a bead on him like a firing squad.

That must be why so many of us say we are glad to be fifty. We are so sick of dreading the thought of it, of being blamed for everything just because we are in our forties, that when we finally reach the big birthday we become as young and irresponsible as English clerics pinching nursemaids in public parks. Almost immediately there comes to us a *savoir vivre* we were too proud to practise the day before.

One of the best things in my fifty years of life has been

the game of tennis, chiefly because on the tennis court experience atones for a lot of lost youth, so long as you confine yourself to playing with erratic youngsters who make you a present of two points a game, or to other men as old as yourself. At fifty I know my limitations in tennis and live in accordance with them. But at forty I was proud, and on my fortieth birthday I nearly got a coronary trying to prove myself young enough to beat a twenty-eight-year-old retriever I could barely have nudged out even when I was his age. I crawled off that court a beaten man, feeling older than I will feel when I am dead.

On my fiftieth birthday things were different. I played my tennis the day before, slept well as a result of it and rose about nine o'clock on a sunny morning. I loafed around till eleven, then strolled down to the liquor commission and took a bus home with my arms full. I ate a hamburger for lunch and walked slowly eastward along Sherbrooke Street to the university, feeling pretty good.

That afternoon as I sauntered through the campus, the students swarming and buzzing in the sun, a proud thought came to me. My transition generation is a beaten-up crowd, they tell us—neurotic, alcoholic, sexually maladjusted, politically unreliable, ulceric—all the things the newspaper moralists have grown rich telling us we are. The candles that once burned at both ends have gone out long ago, and a new generation of critics assure us that at no time did they give a lovely light. But if anyone that afternoon had asked me what I had to show for my fifty years, I would have answered in the name of all of us and said, *Si monumentum requiris, circumspice*. And remembering that Latin has finally been ousted from the school curriculum in favour of a course aimed at training people to become better televiewers, I would have mistranslated that proud phrase from Wren's tomb: *If you really want to know, look around.*

All around me at that moment were specimens of the new generation, those un-neurotic ignorants, those lazy competents, those spoiled responsibles I had become so fond of, who knew damned well it is better to have love on a credit rating than love on a dime. Only a month ago they put on a delicious musical called *My Fur Lady* in which they had made delicious fun of every aspect of the state of mind which had produced a country in which they could walk into jobs the moment they graduated and become fathers and mothers at the age of twenty-three without entirely ruining their economic futures. For a passing moment I felt proud of us. Whatever else we might have failed to do, at least we had not been aggressive to the young. We had spoiled them outrageously; some of us in an effort to provide them with everything an advertising agency could dream of had even assisted in selling out a third of the nation to the Americans in order to make the money that much more quickly. But aggressive towards them we had not been, and I truly believe that ours is the first generation in history that forgave its children for being younger than itself. A *soupçon* of comfort on a brisk March birthday, a *soupçon* at least.

The next day I went to the Faculty Club for lunch and two older friends looked up from pre-luncheon Pilsners and smiled as I entered the lounge. I had almost forgotten the hurdle I had cleared, but they had seen a mention of it in the paper, and one of them smiled.

"Welcome!" he said, as I sat down and relaxed.

814
M164s
MacLennan, Hugh, 1907-
Scotchman's return.

60 7815 I H MAIN